CREATING MARKET SOCIALISM

CREATING MARKET SOCIALISM

How Ordinary People

Are Shaping Class and

Status in China

Carolyn L. Hsu

Duke University Press   Durham and London   2007

100723 6063

Duke University Press gratefully acknowledges the support of Colgate University
Research Council, which provided funds toward the production of this book.

To my friends in Harbin

CONTENTS

ACKNOWLEDGMENTS

Academics spend so much time working alone that we sometimes forget that all of our writings are profoundly collaborative projects. My name may be the only one on the front cover, but this book would not exist without the contribution of many wonderful people. I am especially grateful to Nancy Ries for reading the entire manuscript several times and giving me insightful and detailed comments at every round. I would also like to thank the following for reading selections or previous iterations of the book and offering valuable feedback: Richard Madsen, Akos Rona-tas, Christena Turner, Joseph Esherick, Paul Pickowicz, Wendy Wall, Christopher Henke, Jessica Allina-Pisano, Eric Allina-Pisano, and Michele Chang. Many thanks to Alan Smart for our conversations about *guanxi*, and to Alena Ledeneva and Nancy Ries for helping me see the connections between guanxi and *blat*—and kindly answering all of my ignorant questions about Russia. And I owe Andrew Kipnis a debt for inspiring me to realize that *suzhi* was a key concept for making sense of my findings. Of course the errors and flaws which remain are all my own, but there would be many more without the probing questions, accurate criticisms, enlightening suggestions, and kindly encouragement that these people provided for me.

I need to thank Deborah Davis, my first professor of sociology, who fostered my interest in Chinese society and gave me the confidence and desire to become an academic. She continues to be my role model for uncompromised excellence in teaching and scholarship. In doing my best to follow Professor Davis's example of enthusiasm and rigor in the classroom, I have discovered the rich rewards of teaching. I thank my students here at Colgate University for their questions, insights, and energy, which have pushed me to think more deeply and work harder on my own research.

I would also like to acknowledge my gratitude to the Sociology and Anthropology Department and to Colgate University for their truly generous support (financial and otherwise) for junior faculty members. My 1997–98 research was funded by the National Science Foundation, while resources for my 2001 and 2004 data-gathering trips were provided by Colgate University through internal grants.

To turn closer to home, I owe my thanks to my family, especially to my father for always believing that I was smart enough to do this. I am grateful to Lara Scott, my sister-in-all-but-blood, for many reasons: for her unstinting encouragement; for our endless conversations working out the relationship between our faith and our work and our teaching; and for always reminding me of the presence of the merciful God who led to me this place. I thank God for my beautiful and brilliant daughter, Lin, who thinks it's cool that Mommy wrote a book but will no doubt be disappointed that it doesn't have more pictures. Last, but most of all, I thank my husband, Christopher Henke, who had the bad luck of being the most accessible copyeditor, informed sociologist, writing critic, and emotional coach available to me through the long and sometimes tedious process of taking this project from its initial conception to its final incarnation as a bound volume. Chris was and continues to be my best editor, critic, encourager, and friend, and he loves me far more than I deserve.

Chapter 1

HOW NARRATIVES SHAPE INSTITUTIONAL CHANGE

The most dramatic story of the end of the twentieth century was the decline of socialism. From a social science perspective, it can be seen as a tale of massive de-institutionalization. Socialist states were probably the most intrusive in the history of the world, creating and controlling institutions that penetrated every aspect of life. They also constructed a huge cultural apparatus to disseminate a belief system designed to support those institutions. The story of post-socialism is the story of the wholesale retreat of the state from that active role and the concomitant dismantling of the structural institutions and moral underpinnings of society. This situation has given social scientists the unprecedented opportunity to study how new institutions and belief systems are formed.

In the USSR and east central Europe, it was the collapse of the socialist regimes which precipitated the collapse of institutions. In the People's Republic of China, it was the party-state itself which initiated the destruction of socialist institutions and undermined its own cultural apparatus. The discrepancy between these two paths has led to two divergent conceptualizations of the post-socialist transition. In Europe, formerly communist states were interpreted by researchers and bureaucrats alike through the lens of "transition culture," which assumed that Marxist regimes were defective and destined for collapse, and that their damaged citizens and flawed institutions would be cured to normalcy (i.e., democracy and capitalism) by the intervention of Western experts. By contrast, in China, the cathartic collapse never happened, which meant that the dysfunctional party-state was leading the transition, rejecting the rightful place of Western expertise. Consequently, the scholarship on China focused on evidence that the Chinese state would fail in its effort to develop adequate institutions for successful marketization and finally yield to the revolution which should have succeeded at Tiananmen Square in 1989.

The weight of that evidence against the Chinese party-state certainly seemed formidable, at least according to Western scholarship. Researchers pointed out that, by the mid-1990s, state-owned enterprises were operating at a loss, yet they still employed 65 percent of the urban workforce (Weston 2000:247–48). Capitalist reforms had disemboweled workers' rights, replacing the famed "iron rice bowl" with "plastic cups" (Rosemont 2000). The decollectivization of the countryside led to a "floating population" of up to 100 million peasants flooding into the cities. Academics claimed that, confronted with what seemed to be the worst of socialism combined with the worst of capitalism, the Chinese party-state was incapable of effective action. It had relinquished the socialist mechanisms of controlling its cadres and citizens, but failed to find alternative methods (Walder 1994). It was fending off accusations of systemic cadre corruption (Lu 2000).

Within China, intellectuals had once been the reform movement's most ardent supporters, but by the late 1980s they also expressed their own bitter disappointment with the regime. In the 1980s, the Sinologist Perry Link was taken aback by the depth of their despair, as they listed China's major problems: "entrenched, pandemic corruption; a state led by doddering men still trapped in the ways of the 1930s–1950s, their formative period, and opposed to basic freedoms and any shifts towards democracy; an economy stalled halfway through a critical reform program; an educational system crippled by a serious lack of funds and flawed even in its basic conception, producing a populace that was ever more mercenary, illiterate, and uncivil . . ." (Link 1992:5–6).

China scholars and Chinese intellectuals debated what would be the tipping point to the collapse of the entire system—would disgruntled workers ally with intellectuals in a protest movement which would dwarf the massive demonstrations of 1989? Or would corruption and infighting tear the Party apart from the inside?

As I arrived in China in 1997 to embark upon the research for this book, I expected to chronicle a crisis of institutional disintegration and cultural demoralization resulting from the collision of an incompetent state with an amoral market. I chose the Rust Belt northern city of Harbin for my case study, to avoid being blinded by the atypical wealth of China's coastal boom-towns. In some ways, I did find evidence to back up my initial expectations. The "iron rice bowl" institutions of the socialist workplace were being weak-ened and undermined, but they were not being adequately replaced. Workers at state organizations found themselves losing their pensions and access to medical care as the state phased out its responsibility for these services. Yet no one seemed to know how private firms could (or should) provide these services, nor were personal retirement accounts or private medical insurance widely available from trustworthy sources. State sector layoffs forced people out into the market, but the state failed to institute sufficient regulations to protect workers from exploitation at private firms. Nor was it possible for most urbanites to obtain bank loans to start their own businesses. More and more goods and services were available on the market, but the lack of regulatory agencies meant that falsified products and other scams were ubiquitous.

Yet there was no crisis (except for the 1997 Asian Financial Crisis, which China weathered surprisingly well). Instead, as we know now, the PRC's tran-sition to post-socialism can arguably be seen as a success — if success is defined as an 8 to 10 percent annual economic growth rate and unexpected politi-cal stability. Harbiners complained about the government with enthusiasm, but they neither expected nor desired the regime to fall. Although they could provide astute critical analyses of social problems in urban China, they were generally optimistic about their futures. Far from being demoralized, atom-ized individuals struggling with uncertainty, the people I studied were build-ing moral, meaningful lives within vibrant networks of friends and acquain-tances.

Neither neoliberal nor neo-institutional theories offered a satisfying expla-nation for China's relative success. Scholars who operated on neoliberal as-sumptions insisted any economic problem was due to insufficient marketiza-tion. If post-communist Russia or Bulgaria or Slovakia were in crisis, it must be because they were being held back by state intervention, either in the form of rent-seeking state elites or incentive-dampening state institutions (Aslund 2002). Yet China, with its interventionist state and lingering socialist institu-tions, demonstrated higher rates of growth than any other post-communist country, year after year.

Neo-institutionalists, in contrast, point out that post-communist states are not blank slates, but instead are forced to use the detritus of their former institutions to construct new ones. David Stark and Laszlo Bruszt illustrate this with a wonderful image of Hungarian children attempting to play a capitalist game (Monopoly) from memory, using the pieces from a game designed to teach socialist values (Stark and Bruszt 2001). However, if we look at China's socialist institutions or at the reform-era institutions cobbled from their spare parts, neither appear to be any more conducive for marketization than, say, Russia's. For example, scholars have argued that entrepreneurs were impeded in Russia by inadequate institutions, unfriendly policies, irrational regulations, hostile (and exploitative) local officials, and unavailable capital (Barkhatova 2000; Barkhatova et al. 2001; Radaev 2002). Yet similar conditions also plagued China in the 1990s (Wu 2001; Tsai 2002). Even so, entrepreneurship flourished in China, growing year by year until 8.7 percent of those in the labor force (10.9 percent in urban areas) were running their own businesses in 1998 (State Statistical Bureau 1999). Meanwhile, in Russia, self-employment hovered under 2 percent and actually declined between 1991 and 1996 (Gerber and Hout 1998:15).

Neo-institutionalists are correct in their view that the post-socialist transition should not be viewed as a liminal state between two stable systems, but that instead social actors are constantly constructing and reconstructing institutions with available resources. Yet neo-institutionalists are hobbled by their tendency to focus on elite actors, as though they were the only players taking part in this process. In Harbin, neither market forces nor state elites were able to create adequate institutions and the moral underpinnings for the local inhabitants, so who was doing it? The answer, to a surprising extent, was that Harbiners were doing it themselves. The ordinary people of the city, in dialogue with the state and market forces, were collectively shaping the economic institutions of market socialism as well as a moral discourse to support it. They were doing this through their practice of everyday life, specifically by constructing collective narratives which made sense of the economic opportunities brought about by the market reforms. These shared stories determined the collective moral criteria used to frame and judge them. This is not to elide the contestation and conflict involved in the process, which will be evident throughout the following chapters. However, I argue that contestation and conflict result in a shared repertoire of dominant, even hegemonic, stories. These collective narratives shape the strategies of social actors, thereby affecting patterns of participation in various practices, which in turn influences which practices will become institutionalized.

We cannot understand the shape of post-socialist institutions without empirical research on people's words and actions—because their stories and participation help to shape the content of those institutions. The project of this book is to describe how that empirical research can be done. To this end, I use the techniques of narrative analysis and ethnographic observation to reveal the process by which ordinary people actively shape the institutions of stratification in market socialist Harbin.

The Institutions of Social Stratification

This book analyzes one set of institutions—those which make up the system of social stratification—and the ordinary people who helped to shape them. Institutions are social patterns or sets of social practices which are "chronically reproduced" (Jepperson 1991:145). In other words, institutions are the scripts social actors follow; they are "the way we do things," and the constituent rules of society. The institutions of stratification are the sets of social practices which produce and reproduce inequality in a given society. These would include, for example, the institutions which make up a system of education, such as the practice of rewarding symbolic credentials (degrees, grades, awards) to social actors who successfully follow certain rules and scripts.

I chose to focus on stratification institutions because they involve everyone and affect their daily lives, and yet they carry enormous implications for society. After all, stratification systems (by definition) shape the class structure, if not in Marx's sense of the term, at least in Pierre Bourdieu's. Stratification systems determine which social actors have access to power and resources. Ethnographic methods are very useful for examining the institutions of stratification; people think about them, talk about them, negotiate them, and act upon them in daily life, not just when a social scientist shows up with her list of interview questions. Last, but not least, I needed a non-sensitive, non-risky topic which people felt comfortable talking about in public, both with each other and with a foreign researcher armed with a tape recorder.

A social stratification system is comprised of three types of institutions (Grusky 2001a:3):

1) The institutions that determine the worth of various forms of capital: *economic capital* (money), *social capital* (connections), *human capi-*

tal (educational credentials and formal knowledge), and so on. In Marxist societies, social actors also strived for *political capital*, manifested in Communist Party membership and rank in the party-state bureaucracy. Bourdieu argues that different forms of capital can be exchanged, but that the "exchange rates" differ from society to society, so that a college degree (human capital) could be cashed into differing amounts of income (economic capital) depending on the local institutions (Bourdieu and Wacquant 1992:99).

2) The institutions that determine how those valued forms of capital are allocated across occupations and positions: the rules of the game. These institutions shape the hierarchy of occupations, defining the levels of capital adhering to the position of businessperson, government official, priest, "housewife," and so on. For example, high status occupations tend to require high levels of capital for entry, including impressive educational degrees (human capital), good connections (social capital), and money (economic capital) for tuition, handsome interview suits, and/or bribes. In socialist societies, Communist Party membership (political capital) was often necessary. But in these prestigious positions, social actors gain high levels of economic capital (generous compensation), social capital (connections), and more.

3) Those mechanisms that link individuals to different positions, thus generating unequal access to valued forms of capital. Sexist or racist practices at schools, for instance, may keep women and racial minorities out of desirable positions. Elite firms may judge job applicants as much by their tastes, fashion sense, and skill at small talk (cultural capital) as by their formal skills and educational credentials (human capital), a practice which favors the children of the upper class over their less well-born competitors (Bourdieu and Passeron 1979).

Stratification systems also must contain a moral logic or ideology which undergirds and justifies these institutions (Friedland and Alford 1991:248–53). Forms of capital are valued when they are associated with moral virtues. For example, in the United States, economic capital is highly valued and associated with the admired virtues of hard work, discipline, intelligence, and innovation. In contrast, in imperial China, economic capital was regarded as a by-product of random luck rather than virtue, and was therefore considered less valuable than other forms of capital, such as human capital (Kuhn 1984:27).

In order to be legitimate, a stratification system must also contain convincing moral arguments that some occupations and positions deserve greater compensation or status than others. When socialist states deliberately instituted new stratification systems in their societies, they were well aware that they needed to establish a new morality to accompany those institutions. They invested a great deal of energy into the institutions of propaganda and political education in order to convince people that political capital was valuable, and that cadres[1] should be ranked highly on the occupational hierarchy while landlords deserved to be demoted to the bottom. Post-socialism, then, involves not only the dismantling of social stratification institutions, but the concomitant disintegration of the ideological underpinnings which supported them.

Of course I am not the first scholar interested in the institutions of social stratification in post-socialist societies. Almost immediately upon the fall of communism, scholars began to argue about which groups would eventually gain power in these countries. On one side, scholars argue that post-socialist stratification systems will eventually converge with capitalist ones as market-based institutions replace socialist ones (Nee 1996; Nee and Matthews 1996; Domanski 2000). Contrary evidence is explained away as lingering effects of incomplete marketization. On the other side, the power conversion hypothesis insists that the primary beneficiaries of marketization have been state elites (Rona-Tas 1994; Walder 1996). In studies of rural China, this has led to the theory of "local state corporatism"(Walder 1995; Oi 1999), which argues that local governments have gained most of the power lost by the central state and that local political elites manage many of the successful firms propelling China's economic growth. Yet, as Nan Lin points out, different localities within China have created different economic institutions in response to the reforms, and neither market transition theory nor local state corporatism theory can account for all the variation (Lin 1995).

This debate between convergence theorists and those asserting power conversion or local state corporatism inspired a plethora of empirical studies which analyze different forms of capital (political, academic, economic) and their relative value in post-socialist societies. Such research reveals that, in terms of gaining income, human capital seems to be rising in utility compared to political capital (Logan et al. 1999; Bian and Zhang 2002; Wu 2002; Zang 2002; Wu and Xie 2003). On the contrary, in terms of gaining power, political capital seems to be persisting in importance (Walder 1995b; Li and Walder 2001).

What is striking about these studies is how constrained they are by the assumptions underlying the sociological study of stratification in the West. One glaring example is the presumption that economic capital — or more simplistically, income — is a valid measure of other forms of capital. The socialist state deliberately sought to devalue economic capital, especially in the form of cash income, and it was quite successful in this endeavor. These scholars offer no justification for why economic capital should be considered the dominant form of capital in post-socialist societies, except for the unspoken belief that since money is so central in industrialized capitalist nations, this must be the "normal" state of things when the state is not meddling unnaturally in society. They hold onto this assumption despite substantial evidence to the contrary. Even though economic returns to private sector occupations increased enormously in the first fifteen years of the reform era, Chinese urbanites were no more willing to leave their state sector jobs for the market than they had been under Maoist socialism (Zhou et al. 1997). Clearly, these social actors believed that a higher income was less valuable than other types of rewards.

The focus on economic capital is only one symptom of a larger problem. Stratification systems in industrialized capitalist societies are generally stable. The institutions which define the value of various forms of capital and the rules of allocation across occupations have become so well established that they are generally taken for granted. (For example, people may complain about unequal access to college, but they rarely if ever question whether tertiary education is a legitimate mechanism for sorting people into different occupations.) These institutions are unlikely to change in dramatic or unexpected ways. As a result, scholars who study stratification in the stable capitalist societies tend to focus on the mechanisms of inequality, seeking to explain those characteristics (such as educational level, family background, gender, or race) which affect an individual's chances to achieve a position or obtain economic or human capital. Post-socialist systems of stratification are far from stable, and it is not clear what forms of capital will eventually be valued, or what the rules of allocation will be. Consequently, it is not even clear which occupations are the most or least prestigious; the occupational hierarchy itself is in flux (Jankowiak 1993; Jankowiak 2004b). Yet post-socialist scholars mimic their colleagues working on established capitalist societies, confining themselves to queries about which characteristics help individuals gain the most economic capital or the highest positions (with occupational prestige determined by nothing more rigorous than scholarly assumption).

These projects fail to take advantage of the unprecedented opportunity presented by the fall of communism. The socialist stratification system (and its supporting ideology) has been severely undermined, and new stratification systems (based on other moral rationales) are emerging to take its place. This opens up the possibility of asking the kinds of research questions which cannot be asked by scholars studying stable societies. Researchers in the West ask: Who gets into college? But researchers in post-socialist societies can ask: Which social actors will determine the value of a college education vis-à-vis other forms of capital—and how? Not only can we ask which occupations are rising in prestige and which are on the wane, but we can analyze how social actors shape the rules of allocation and affect the criteria which determine the status of various occupations in the occupational hierarchy. Scholars have tried to rank occupational status in both China and in east central Europe (Jankowiak 1993; Bian 1994; Domanski 2000; Jankowiak 2004b), but without bothering to figure out whether their occupational categories are relevant, much less how these categories have been constructed.

The current research on post-socialist stratification systems also neglects to examine the moral aspect of stratification. Once again, this is a reflection of stratification research in industrialized capitalist societies. In more stable societies, the moral arguments behind stratification institutions are not areas of contestation; instead they are taken for granted and unquestioned. Furthermore, the very *content* of the ideology of Western industrial capitalism masks its moral nature. This moral logic argues that human beings are independent, rational individuals who compete with one another to maximize economic gains; it is a moral vision which claims that morality is not particularly important. However, in the socialist system of stratification, the moral logic was extremely visible (through state propaganda), explicitly moralistic, and often highly contested. Indeed, Susan Shirk describes the Chinese socialist system of stratification as a "virtuocracy" (Shirk 1984). We should not be surprised that people in post-socialist societies would be more consciously concerned about the moral aspects of stratification—and much more skilled at negotiating and contesting that moral content—than their counterparts in the United States or other Western societies.

How Ordinary People Co-create the System of Stratification: The Role of Narratives

If ordinary people play a role in shaping the institutions and moral logic of stratification in post-socialist societies, how do they do it? By constructing collective narratives—shared stories about different aspects of stratification which include causes and consequences, and meaning. These collective narratives will make implicit moral judgments about the value and exchangeability of various forms of capital. They will also make moral assessments about the status of various occupations and the rewards they deserve. Because these narratives shape the strategies of social actors, they will affect patterns of participation in various stratification practices, which in turn influences which practices will become institutionalized.

All of this will make more sense if I begin with the institutions and work my way backward through the process. Institutions are patterns of practices that do not require action or intervention to be reproduced. In other words, they are established procedures that are so ingrained that people find it much easier to follow them than to deviate from them (Jepperson 1991). A common analogy is a road, or a system of roads. Just as travelers find it easier to follow existing roads than to bushwhack their own path, social actors find it easier to participate in their society's institutions rather than inventing their own practices. They enter into educational institutions, for example, rather than invent a whole new set of practices to educate themselves (and then try to convince other social actors to view their knowledge as valid). Because institutions are practices, institutions must be embodied. When people stop participating in a practice, it no longer functions as an institution. For example, arranged marriage and apprenticeship are practices which have been largely de-institutionalized in most Western societies.

To stretch the analogy further, we can see the dismantling of socialist institutions as a situation in which many roads were destroyed, but few were replaced. Although the state and market forces created significant constraints, in the resulting rubble there was still a plethora of potential paths which could become new roads. Essentially, my argument is that the paths which attract the most travelers will become roads, and the practices which attract the most participants will become institutions. Naturally, the state or market can interfere in the process. If I get swept up in the analogy, my imagination envisions the state controlling a fleet of bulldozers, while the market intervenes through natural and environmental disasters. Even so, social actors still have a great deal of leeway in their choices.

If roads are missing, how do people decide which paths to take? If the existing set of institutionalized options is inadequate, how do social actors decide which un-institutionalized practices to utilize? How do they make sense of the information about their potential options and determine what is the best course of action? To answer these questions, I turn to the narrative theory of social action. In recent years, a growing scholarship in sociology (Abbott 1992; Steinmetz 1992; Maines 1993; Somers and Gibson 1994) and anthropology (Briggs 1996; Ochs et al. 1996; Ries 1997) has argued that narratives are the cognitive tools used by social actors to organize information and construct strategies of social action. Following the philosophy of Paul Ricoeur, narrative scholars argue that people are storytellers by nature, and it is the process of telling stories which makes us human. Psychological experiments have shown that people construct narrative plots even when confronted with non-narrative information, such as still pictures or images of small colored rectangles in motion (Polkinghorne 1988:19).

In post-socialist societies, because of the insufficiency of established institutions, people were confronted with too many possibilities. Yet according to the narrative theory of social action, all social actors are constantly bombarded by too much information about their circumstances and are confronted with too many options to effectively comprehend. In order to make sense of this input, they organize it into narratives, through a process called "emplotment." In other words, our capacity to create narratives is what gives us the capacity for complex social action.

> Our very capacity for attention, and for following more or less long-term and complex endeavors, *is* our capacity for selection. Extraneous details are not left out, but they are pushed into the background, saved for later, ranked in importance. And whose narrative voice is accomplishing all this? None but our own. In planning our days and our lives we are composing the stories of the dramas we will act out and which will determine the focus of our attention and our endeavors, which will provide the principles for distinguishing foreground from background. This, moreover, is not only story-planning or plotting, but also storytelling (Carr 1984:368).

What differentiates narratives from other forms of discourse is that narratives are stories. By definition, stories have characters and plots with causal events unfolding through time. Narratives are also moral: they tell about actions and consequences, explain the results of virtues and vices, and make judgments about what is valuable and worthwhile rather than cheap and false. By their nature, stories exclude a great deal of information from consideration and organize the rest unequally—highlighting some pieces as vitally important, while relegating the rest to secondary interest. This organizes the input in such a way that a certain course of action becomes obvious, while other options become unthinkable. Because a given set of circumstances can be emplotted with different plots and characters, the choice of narrative has implications for social action.

Social actors have repertoires of narratives and narrative components which they can mobilize as they confront different situations during their daily lives. Like Bourdieu's concept of habitus, narrative repertoires are cultural forms which structurally constrain and shape social action. Yet while social actors (and their actions and beliefs) are passively and subconsciously shaped by habitus, people actively and creatively utilize the contents of their narrative repertoires, which should be understood as cultural "tool kits" (Swidler 1986).

In sociology, this narrative-based view directly confronts the dominant conceptualization of social action—in which individuals calculate the course of action which will best maximize their interests. Interest-based theories assume that social actors seek as much information as possible in order to make the most accurate calculations to know how to act. In contrast, narrative theory argues that people must limit the amount of input they deal with in order to organize it in such a way so that they know what to do. People may tell themselves a story which claims that they are making rational decisions, based on an assessment of their interests, but in reality it is only social scientists who construct elaborate mathematical formulae which calculate the relative weight of every possible variable (and we only do it when we write scholarly papers, not when we need to make decisions about which job to take or which conference to attend).

An Example

To compare these two approaches, we can examine the case of a Harbin factory worker in 1998, Mr. Gong. He was fifty years old, a Communist Party member with a middle-school education, who worked at an unprofitable state-owned factory that made agricultural machinery and had recently laid off many of its workers. According to the interest-based model, Mr. Gong should have made a list of all his career options (stay at the factory, start his own business, find a job in a private firm, retire early, etc.), and then calculated his best course of action by gathering all the pieces of information available to him. These variables would include: his low salary, the recent layoffs at his factory, the likelihood of more layoffs, the probability that he would get laid off, the slim chances of getting his pension after he retires, the potential earnings he could have if he started his own business (most peddlers earned more than he did), the difficulties of raising start-up capital, the supply–demand situation of the market, the effect of the Asian Financial Crisis or Russian-Chinese border disputes on potential suppliers and customers, and so on. The fact that even this partial list, which fails to take his family members and all their variables into consideration, requires this middle-school graduate to analyze complex economic indicators and predict international politics reveals the weakness of this theory. If we focus only on the information that Mr. Gong should have known well (his low salary versus what his friends made as peddlers and the ailing state of his factory), we probably would expect him to have chosen to leave his job to start a small business.

In contrast, the narrative approach expects Mr. Gong to emplot his options through stories which focus on specific pieces of information and ignore others, and which assign moral weight to different options. In fact, the stories that he constructed implicitly argued that people (and occupations) should be judged by how well they serve society, by their level of contribution (*gongxian*). For example, when recounting his career history, this is how Mr. Gong described entering the Chinese Communist Party (CCP):

> I got in [to the Party] in 1990. I first applied in 1967, when I first came to this work unit. I really wanted to get in all these years. In China, it was only the Communist Party which could lead the country to where it is now, such a big and populous country. Of course you can work for the country without being a Party member. But you can do more if you're in the Party because they teach you policy, point you on the right path. Your understanding is deeper. But in those years, it was hard to get into the CCP. It was competitive and there were limits on the numbers allowed in.

When asked whom he respected in Chinese society, Mr. Gong replied:

> People respect those who have real intellect, such as high level engineers, members of the Chinese Academy of Science, people in high technology.

To develop, you need cultural quality. Without culture, you can't have technology. China developed so slowly before because it was closed, refused to learn from foreign knowledge. Deng opened everything up and it's developed so fast. We had to research it all out ourselves. . . . [Scientists'] skills are higher, and what they do the rest of us can't do, and what they produce is so valuable it's priceless.

In both of these narratives, people in certain positions (Party members) or occupations (scientists) deserve respect because they contribute to the common good and/or help Chinese society in its project of "development" (*fazhan*). When market reforms legalized private businesses in Chinese cities, Mr. Gong applied the narrative of contribution (gongxian) in such a way as to conclude that private businesspeople did not serve society or aid China's progress. In his stories, businesspeople were oriented towards personal profit, rather than communal good. Not only did their work fail to serve society, most of them made their money by taking advantage of others. Mr. Gong explained, "Common people look down on cheaters, like those who take money but don't have the goods. Or those who sell false goods, like false medicines. Common people are really upset about these things, furious." Businesspeople who "worked hard" were successful, but those "who used bad methods, such as cheating people" would soon lose their wealth.

In the world depicted by Mr. Gong's stories, the realm of private business was populated by immoral people who were willing to cheat innocent customers for the sake of money. Driven by the crass pursuit of profits, those in the private sector neglected the values that made life meaningful: serving others and contributing to China's development. He also described the market as "risky" though "exciting." The private sector was a place where Mr. Gong obviously did not belong. In fact, it was so obvious that he did not have to think about it. He, like many of the people I interviewed in the state sector, claimed that he never even considered leaving his work unit for the market. Far from calculating the pros and cons of all possible career options, Harbiners used narratives to frame a world in which one choice was obviously right, and most alternatives would never seriously cross their minds.

To return to my previous analogy, social actors use narratives first to determine which paths are actually options. Most potential paths, or potential practices, will fail to garner any attention at all. There are many possibilities that Mr. Gong never mentioned, such as working for a private firm or for a friend's business, or transferring to a different state firm as a contract worker. These options are rendered invisible. When determining which paths are chosen for consideration, narratives help people construct a moral frame for judging among them. By directing people to one path over another, these narratives help shape which practices will become institutionalized. Since the content of the narrative shapes action, the content also influences the eventual form of the institutions.

Collective Narratives and Collective Action

Mr. Gong's stories may have shaped his decisions, but in order for narratives to shape institutions, they must affect collective action. To understand how they do this, we must examine the concept of *collective narratives*.

So far we have been discussing *ontological narratives*, the stories that Mr. Gong and each individual social actor construct all day long in order to know which course of action to take. By their nature, stories are made to be told to other people. The narrator adjusts the tale to fit the audience, and the listener makes connections and puts the story together, with the result that narratives are always co-constructed between the teller and an audience in a collaborative effort. Even when people tell stories in their own heads, they do so to an imaginary audience, justifying and explaining themselves to potential listeners. Therefore, narratives cannot be constructed out of thin air. In order to connect to the audience, they must be built out of narrative components (characters, settings, plot devices, and so on) which feel familiar to the listeners.

In other words, narratives work when they draw upon shared repertoires. Producing narratives is a process of innovation which utilizes these models in ways ranging from "servile repetition" to "calculated deviance" (Ricoeur 1991:25). Even so, the content of the collective narrative repertoire constrains the types of stories which can be told—and in doing so, it constrains the kinds of actions and choices that social actors can make as they shape new institutions. Shared narratives are resources for creating social "rules," in Anthony Giddens's sense of the word (Giddens 1986:66–68). These rules generate and reproduce practices, which can become institutionalized. As people follow rules and participate in practices, their actions and experiences become emplotted as new stories for the collective narrative repertoire. Narratives play a vital role in the production and reproduction of what Giddens calls "systems" and what I would term institutions (Giddens 1986).

Personal narrative repertoires contain both *public* and *collective narratives* (Somers 1992:604; Steinmetz 1992:490). *Public narratives* are published or disseminated by actors in the public realm, such as political figures, government organizations, journalists, television producers, political activists, and experts, including social scientists. In contrast, *collective narratives* are anonymous, commonsensical stories which "everyone" knows. They would include the plots of folk tales. Just as Russians would understand a reference to magic fish or Emelya's spells, Americans know what a "Cinderella story" or an "ugly duckling" is, and Chinese are familiar with the adventures of young girls who disguise their sex in order to become scholars or warriors ("The Ballad of Mulan" 1994).

Especially under conditions of significant social change, such as the postsocialist transformations, people will need new collective narratives to make sense of these new circumstances. Needless to say, collective narratives are not created the same way that ontological or public narratives are; they are not constructed or written by individual social actors with an audience in mind. Instead, collective narratives emerge much more organically from the accumulated conversations of many social actors trying out different stories on each other in an attempt to make sense of the new circumstances surrounding them. Eventually, certain themes, characterizations, plot components, settings, and moral logics will become more commonly used than others, more resonant, more familiar, and more established. These will evolve into a new set of collective narratives for the shared repertoires. Because the content of these new collective narratives will shape collective action, perhaps for years to come, they will influence the shape of institutions.

Just as the process of narrative construction is always both individual and collective, it is also both local and national (and even global, as we shall see). It is also a constant process, a continuous re-narrativization which negotiates contemporary conditions by drawing upon the past. Because Harbiners could draw upon a history that was both specific to their city and shared across China and other post-socialist nations, their ontological and collective stories reflected both national and international trends in narratives and local variations, as did their economic practices.

Narratives in Action: "Inside" Versus "Outside"

To illustrate the way that public, ontological, and collective narratives influence new institutions, let me examine one way that narratives shaped stratification practices in Harbin. The Marxist-Leninist regimes of the twentieth century set out to transform their society's stratification system by decreasing the value of economic capital and lowering the status of private businesspeople, while at the same time increasing the value of political capital and raising the status of workers and cadres in heavy industry. To these ends, they propagated public narratives based on the moral argument that professions should gain occupational status according to how much they contribute to the collective good (as defined by the party-state, of course). Mao Zedong's regime, which gained control of China in 1949, followed this template. Newspaper stories proclaimed that state-led industrialization was China's road to wealth and power, while the 1952 Five-Anti Campaign taught people to see capitalists as exploitative, selfish, and immoral.

When the market reforms reintroduced private sector occupations into socialist societies, such as in China in the 1980s and 1990s, citizens had to decide how to interpret these new career options. To do so, they created collective narratives, stories to make sense of confusing information, which would allow them to make decisions, take actions, and judge other people's decisions and actions. Even as late as 1998, many Harbin residents still constructed collective narratives which borrowed heavily from socialist public narratives of stratification propagated under Mao. First, they divided all work options into two, mutually exclusive settings: "inside" the state work unit and "outside" in the market.

For example, a middle-aged professor, offering his historical description of businesspeople in Harbin, insisted: "people who had stable lives and set salaries would never leave their jobs. Instead it was those who did not have stable jobs who were willing to go outside into business. Those were the ones who got rich, the people who were willing to run around—people without culture, who were willing to do anything."

A mid-level cadre in a government organization imagined her fate if she were ever laid off: "For me to go outside to work, I think I'd do okay. I'd make it. As a government official, well, I think management work would be pretty suitable. And also, my writing's pretty good. At least I think I'm pretty okay! But I'm not ready to 'plunge into the sea.'"

Similarly, a former engineer offered this explanation when describing her decision to leave her work unit job to start her own business: "I felt the world outside looked better than in here." Although these represent different types of stories, told for different purposes, in all of these narratives and many more like them, there were only two settings for social mobility options. Option 1 was to stay inside the state-managed work unit, and Option 2 was to go outside into the uncontrolled and chaotic world of the market.

Working "inside" meant "staying inside a work unit" (*liu zai danwei limian*). In urban China during the socialist era, a work unit was not just an organization; it was also a physical place, ideally a self-sufficient compound with workers' housing, cafeteria, health clinic, schools, a market, and so on, usually all located within a surrounding wall. "To stay in a work unit" evoked the image of being in a protected place, where all of one's needs were met by a paternalistic state. The other common expression used to describe life on the inside was the "iron rice bowl" (*tie fanwan*). This image alluded to the permanence of the situation, the unbreakable promise of lifetime employment and welfare, care from the cradle to the grave. Marketization undermined the socialist work unit, but at least for the first two decades, many state sector workplaces managed to retain at least some work unit features. In the early 1990s, I worked in such a work unit as a teacher, and except for going to church once a week or doing an occasional bit of shopping downtown, my entire life took place within those walls.

According to the narrative, to leave the safety of the state sector was to go "out into society (*waimian de shehui*), as though work units were completely separated from the wider social environment. In Chinese urban slang, people who went "outside" were said to be "jumping into the sea" (*xia hai*), quite an evocative image in dusty, landlocked Harbin. In fact, "jumping into the sea" was such a common phrase that by 1997 it could no longer be classified as slang, but instead was simply taken for granted as a useful verb. In everyday conversation, people would say to one another, "I'm thinking about jumping into the sea next spring. Does that sound like a good idea?" or "That was the year she jumped into the sea." If working on the "inside" was connected with an idealized image of a socialist work unit, life "outside" was associated with self-employment and entrepreneurship.

In reality, by the 1990s, China's urban workplaces did not fit neatly into these two categories of "inside" and "outside." As in other socialist-capitalist "mixed" economies, there had been an explosion of new hybrid forms, such as state enterprises which had been reformed to mimic market organizations. People could also work for foreign companies, Chinese-owned private companies, or joint ventures. Yet many Harbiners continued to use the same oppositions in their own stories—state versus the private sector, the work unit versus self-employment—which Maoist public narratives had set up decades before.

The narratives of "inside" and "outside" shaped Harbiners' response to marketization. Maoist state narratives had been constructed purposely to denigrate the "outside" option, and this prejudice was reflected in 1990s' discourse in Harbin. When narrating their career histories, many of my "inside" subjects would describe with pride how the state conscripted them into their work units because of their skills and abilities. According to the plots of their stories, their labor and talents contributed to the collective good and earned them the paternalistic care of the state, as manifested through the work unit. The flip side of these success stories, of course, was the tales of those who were unable or unwilling to act correctly and selflessly and who were refused entry into the work unit system or cast "out into society" to fend for themselves. Only within this narrative context can we understand the full professor, dean of her prestigious department, who could say to me with pride, "I don't know about anything outside in society." Yi Zhongtian, a Chinese author, declared in 1996:

> The work unit is one's rice bowl but it is also one's face. So if a person doesn't have a work unit then they will have no face. Not only does the lack of a work unit exclude the possibility of a person having a face, but even worse, without a work unit they are often pigeon-holed as being "suspicious characters" or "dangerous persons." One can even go as far as to say that, without a work unit such people come to be regarded as "unemployed idlers" (Bray 2005:4).

Those who went "outside" were associated with low-status characteristics: low level of education, moral weakness, and poor family background. Stories about private businesspeople often featured former criminals as the main characters. Of course, people with criminal records probably did go into private business, since their chances in the state sector were slim to none. However, the idea that the private sector was populated entirely (or even substantially) with ex-cons is demographically ridiculous. In reality, business owners were more likely to be innocent retirees than former felons (Li 1997). Also, the narratives focused on the most unpleasant, uncomfortable, undignified, and unsafe aspects of "outside" work—which was usually defined as street peddling. One of their favorite phrases for life on the "outside" was "standing on the corner with a cart of clothes," quite a potent image in Harbin's long, bitter winter.

In other words, the narrative settings of "inside" and "outside" trained people to focus only on the most extreme forms of private work options, and to focus on the riskiest aspects. These stories devalued economic capital vis-à-vis security. For example, in 1998, one graduate student said of a friend who was working for a world-renowned European multinational firm: "Sure she makes a lot of money. But it's not a permanent job. She could get fired any time." Her words implied that any job without the promise of an "iron rice bowl" was dangerously risky and insecure, even one in a historically stable, blue-chip firm. As a result, although people in the private sector made much more money than in the state sector, most Harbiners rejected the opportunity. According to the 1996 *China Statistical Yearbook* data for Heilongjiang province, 68 percent of people still remained in their work units, and another 14 percent worked in the state sector as contract workers. Only 16.6 percent had gone into business for themselves—a number that exactly matched the national average. Less than 2 percent were working for private firms. Those who did venture "outside" engaged in strategies to minimize their risks, such as moonlighting.

Yet Harbiners' narratives about "inside" and "outside" did more than simply discourage most people away from market practices. They also affected occupational status because work in the private sector was initially confined to those who had not succeeded well in the socialist system—those with lower levels of education or political capital. Until the early 1990s, only those Harbiners with little to lose took the plunge into the private sector.[2] Out of the 26 businesspeople I interviewed, only one "jumped into the sea" prior to 1989—a housewife from an ethnic minority who had only three years of education. She sold homemade pickles on the street to shore up her family's meager finances. Since those who went "outside" during this period had low levels of financial and social capital, private business became strongly associated with street peddling and other forms of petty capitalism. Indeed, although "*getihu*" is a Chinese legal designation referring to any owner of a private business with less than seven employees, in popular narratives the getihu was a stock character—a local street vendor or small dealmaker with low status, little education, and weak morals.

It is likely that some version of the narratives of "inside" and "outside" shaped behavior in other post-socialist states, or at least in other socialist-market hybrid states. In the last decade of Hungarian communism, for example, private business was permitted. Just like in Harbin, Hungarians treated the private sector with trepidation. "Most private activities were part-time and on the side, with people keeping one foot firmly in the state sector for security" even though "the small private sector had no worries about demands for its products and services . . . because demand always outstripped supply" (Rona-Tas 2002:47–48). Even in societies in which the state sector had been substantially dismantled, people constructed narratives to justify avoiding the private sector as much as possible. In Russia, people understood private business as a realm confined to those with *blat* (connections) (Ledeneva 1998:184–92). This taught non-elite households to focus on defensive strategies of survival, cobbling together sustenance from wages, garden vegetables, and government handouts, rather than venture out into entrepreneurship (Burawoy et al. 2000).

In China, research reveals that the discourse of "inside" versus "outside" and its attendant prejudices against entrepreneurship existed in other cities, especially in the 1980s, though it seems to have lingered on in Harbin longer than elsewhere (Gold 1990; Jankowiak 1993; Ikels 1996; Lu and Perry 1997:11). Yet even in Harbin, wholesale prejudice against businesspeople and the private sector eventually began to fade by the turn of the century, as the private sector expanded and the city's state sector was hit hard by *xia gang*—the Chinese euphemism for state enterprise layoffs. In the early years of the new millennium, the discourse of "inside" and "outside" was increasingly replaced by a new conceptualization of occupational status based on the rhetoric of "quality" (*suzhi*).

A number of China scholars have noted the rise of suzhi discourse in China (Kipnis 1997 and 2006; Yan 2003; Anagnost 2004). In the early years of the new century, the rhetoric of "quality" seemed to become ubiquitous; it was used to justify the need for "development" (on the individual, community, and national level), as well as to rationalize hierarchy, inequality, and exploitation. Despite the term's widespread popularity and apparent resonance, Chinese respondents were universally unable to define suzhi, or to clearly explain how one determined whether an individual possessed "quality" or not (Yan 2003:197; Anagnost 2004:496). However, in practice, suzhi was associated with educational credentials, high culture, science and technology, modernity, and progress. In other words, suzhi discourse offered a conceptualization of hierarchy and status centered on human capital. For example, instead of condemning all businesspeople as unworthy of respect because they work "outside" the socialist system, suzhi discourse divided them into two groups: respectable entrepreneurs who have "quality" and lowly getihu who do not.

Significantly, this new conceptualization of hierarchy and status emerged at a time when the socialist framework, based on political capital, was losing its explanatory power. This book traces this (incomplete, partial, and uneven) transformation from one basis of hierarchy to another, from one based on the logic of state socialism to one based on the logic of suzhi.

Political, Economic, and Human Capital: Three Paths

This book examines this dialogue between the state and its citizens and the global market which is constructing the institutions of stratification in Harbin. For example, it traces the unintended consequences of the public narratives Deng Xiaoping's regime propagated in pursuit of cadre reform in the 1980s. As part of his project of shifting the goals of the Chinese state away from political ideology and toward economic development, Deng argued that the current cadre corps was too large, too old, and had an insufficient level of education to carry out his Four Modernizations (Lee 1991). These narratives not only increased the value of human capital, but they also revised the moral logic of contribution into a moral logic of development. Status should be rewarded to people not just for contributing to the common good, but for contributing to the common good defined as economic development, and measured by international standards of meritocracy and progress.

Drawing upon these public narratives, Harbiners constructed collective narratives which criticized state sector stratification institutions for obsolescence, and eventually for corruption. These narratives not only implied that the value of human capital needed to increase in the market socialist era, but also insinuated that the value of political capital should decrease. Furthermore, a certain segment of urban Chinese citizens, the intellectuals who had been severely marginalized during the Maoist period, took these narrative themes even further. Combining the narrative of development with components from traditionalist narratives about the moral superiority of educated people, they published public narratives which insisted that intellectuals deserved more political authority than cadres. Although the intellectual political movement was largely quashed with the violent crackdown of the 1989 Tiananmen Protests, the public narratives of the activists entered the collective repertoires of Chinese urbanites, including those in Harbin. The narratives of development and the narratives of moral, contributing intellectuals were two of the many narrative streams which converged to create the discourse of suzhi (quality).

One result of these narratives was that Harbiners tended to view "intellectuals" as categorically distinct from "cadres." In fact, I discovered that people interpreted the occupational landscape of post-socialist Harbin through a tripartite division of paths associated with three types of capital: political, economic, and human. The first path involved participation in the socialist institutions of stratification (state sector work units, the Communist Party) and led ideally to cadre ranking. It was the "inside" path of power through the party-state. To say that these stratification institutions were in decline relative to their position under socialism (when they were practically the only viable path for social mobility in urban China) is self-evident. In chapter 4, I discuss how the "inside" path was under revision as cadres went from being the dominant occupation in society to being (in the words of one of my informants) just "one of 300 professions." And the people of Harbin were shaping this revision in part through their emerging collective narratives about the role of the state and its cadres in post-socialist society.

According to Harbiners, the antithesis to the "inside" path was to "jump into the sea" (xia hai) of the market. People on the "outside" path had abandoned the quest for power and sought money instead; economic capital trumped political capital. According to the stories, they quit their state sector careers to start up their own independent private businesses, though in actuality aspiring businesspeople were much more cautious in their strategies towards entrepreneurship. As I mentioned in the previous section, collective narratives based on contribution depicted businesspeople as morally suspect individuals with low levels of education, people who could not get a "real" job in the state sector. Their work did nothing to serve society. (It did not occur to Harbiners that "creating jobs" should be seen as a contribution, although anxiety about unemployment had reached almost hysterical proportions in the city.) In reality, of course, some private businesspeople, even in Harbin, were well educated. However, collective narratives depicted "intellectuals" as moral individuals whose work contributed to China's development, so these "quality" businesspeople could not be seen in the same light as ordinary (i.e., low-class) business owners. In chapter 5, I examine the rise of a bifurcated business class, divided by human capital and suzhi.

If the first path was associated with power and the second with money, Harbiners connected the third path with knowledge. This path focused on human capital and was often cited when parents discussed their hopes for their children. According to their narratives, this path would ideally involve testing into a "key" university (China's designation for its most prestigious tertiary institutions), going overseas for graduate school, and eventually attaining a position as a scientist, academic, or professional (such as a doctor). People in these occupations were designated "intellectuals" (*zhishi fenzi*), a term which contains the root word "knowledge" (*zhishi*). In chapter 6, I explore why intellectuals were seen as a separate occupational category from cadres (even when they worked in state organizations) and businesspeople (even when they owned or worked for private companies). I also analyze why the path of knowledge was in ascendence in turn-of-the-century Harbin, despite the failure of the Tiananmen Protests and intellectual dissident movement of the late 1980s. Human capital was valued, and intellectuals were admired, because they straddled the worlds of "inside" and "outside." According to narratives, they contributed to society, unlike businesspeople. Moreover, their contributions were moral and modern, unlike those of cadres. In brief, an unexpected convergence of narrative elements has led to the collective view that human capital was a key indicator of "quality," the true measure of human worth in post-socialist China as it sought its rightful place in the global order.

These three forms of capital—political, economic, and human—were all associated with formal institutions and publicly recognized. Yet a fourth form of capital, social capital, operated in the informal spaces beneath and between these institutions through the practice of guanxi. During the socialist period, guanxi connections, established through favors and gifts, became the common social mechanism for bypassing the onerous, often impenetrable, official channels. Guanxi practice operated on the principle of gift exchange and reciprocity: Person A helped out Person B in anticipation of being able to call in a favor at a later date. Perhaps the most common favor exchanged was simply an introduction. With a personal introduction from Person A, Person B becomes a social acquaintance (*shouren*) in the eyes of Bureaucrat C, someone worth aiding as a friend. Without such an introduction, Bureaucrat C would see Person B as merely a stranger (*shengren*), someone to ignore. In its more unpleasant forms, guanxi devolved into direct bribery. Despite the fact that the Chinese party-state explicitly condemned guanxi practice and social capital, they became (ironically enough) increasingly associated with cadres and political capital. In chapter 4, I discuss the implications of guanxi for the socialist institutions of stratification, and in chapter 5, I analyze its importance for developing entrepreneurial practices.

Yet the core of the early post-communist stratification system was the tripartite schema, in which social mobility strategies were categorized into three paths, associated respectively with political capital, economic capital, and human capital. On the one hand, we must understand how the schema was grounded in history. The central categories were vestiges of former Chinese systems of stratification. The political path evolved from the socialist stratification system, just as the "intellectual" path reflected its roots in the imperial Confucian bureaucracy. Meanwhile, the "market" path carried the baggage of both Maoist-era anti-capitalist propaganda and pre-revolutionary petty capitalism, while absorbing the influence of global capitalism's own logic of stratification.

On the other hand, in its contemporary form, the schema was continuously created and re-created through the words and actions of ordinary people. It was their lived experiences which embodied the emerging stratification and status hierarchies, and it was their stories which shaped their practices. In Harbin, narratives constructed the category of "intellectuals," for example, so that it contained both a doctor at a state hospital and an engineer at a high-tech multinational, crossing the divide between the state and private sector. As a result, human capital could act as a bridge between "inside" and "outside," allowing some private businesses to borrow some of the respectability usually associated only with state organizations, and some state firms to capture a little of the cutting-edge "modernity" of global capitalism. Stories also focused on private business owners as the icon of the market sector, but generally ignored their employees, unless they could be categorized as "intellectuals." In doing so, Harbiners' narratives made it difficult to even imagine a fulfilling, lifelong career working in a private firm; they rendered that entire category of work invisible. As a result, those who did work in the private sector almost all viewed their jobs as temporary positions, one step on the path either to an "iron rice bowl" job in the state sector, or to "jumping into the sea" as an entrepreneur.

A cautionary note: for analytical purposes I tend to examine the different forms of capital (political, economic, human, and social) separately. Yet we must never forget that forms of capital only have value because of their mutual convertibility and interaction. In practice, everyone in Harbin, regardless of occupation, used multiple forms of capital in their daily strategies of action.

When I associate the cadre path with political capital, this does not mean that aspiring cadres did not accumulate human capital or were disinterested in economic capital. Indeed, we shall see that in the 1980s and 1990s educational credentials became an increasingly important prerequisite for political capital and that political capital was coveted by many because it was easily converted into useful social connections and money. Yet those on the cadre path chose political capital as their primary investment, a strategy which (at least in the short term) meant that they had to forego certain practices which would have procured other forms of capital. Moreover, cadres were associated with political capital, and the status of cadres reflected the value of political capital, and vice versa.

Methods

In order to study emerging collective narratives and to analyze how they affected collective behavior in ways which shaped the emerging institutions of stratification in post-socialist China, I turned to the qualitative research methods of ethnography, participant-observation, and open-ended interviews—intensive methods which all require large investments of time. The study focused on one city, Harbin, located in northeastern China. I will discuss Harbin in more detail in chapter 3, but I should point out here that no place in China (or anywhere else) is "typical." Chinese urban areas differ greatly from the rural countryside, and regional centers like Harbin are unlike China's coastal boomtowns. Most scholarship on urban China has concentrated on four regions, centered on Beijing, Hong Kong, Chengdu, and (most popular of all) Shanghai (Jankowiak 2004a:118). This bias, which may reflect the Western scholar's preference for the PRC's most comfortable cities, skews our view of China by focusing on its most economically wealthy and globally connected urban areas.

My goal, then, was to collect narratives which addressed different forms of capital (political, economic, human, and so on) in terms of value and exchangeability. I also needed to know what kinds of stories Harbiners were using to talk about different occupations and their status in the occupational hierarchy. In both cases, I was interested in discovering not just the content of the narratives, but also which forms of capital and which occupations were not mentioned. In other words, which "paths" were being ignored and neglected? I also sought the different types of moral logic which underlay the stories.

Of course no one in Harbin talked about "stratification institutions," "forms of capital," "occupational hierarchies," or "moral logics." My first task, then, was to find out what language they did use to talk about these issues. I spent the first few months of my time in Harbin conducting participant-observation fieldwork at twenty work sites (listed in appendix 1), making connections, and chatting informally with people about different workplaces and occupations, about their own career histories and their hopes for their children. Through this work, I eventually uncovered the three "paths" discussed above (political capital versus economic capital versus human capital).

In these endeavors, and later in my more structured interviews, I was aided by some characteristics of the Chinese urban workplace which may seem unusual to anyone unfamiliar with the PRC. First, despite the walls which surround traditional socialist work units, Harbin workplaces tend to be very open to non-employees wandering about. Chinese social institutions of personal connections (guanxi) make it perfectly acceptable for a stranger to be in an office or factory as long as she is a friend of an acquaintance of a friend (and so on) of someone who works there. Second, in every workplace I visited, people dropped whatever they were doing to chat with me for an hour, or even much longer. The Maoist legacy of full employment in urban areas combined with China's enormous population has conspired to create a situation of underemployment where too many employees have too little to do at work. This situation was exacerbated during the time of my research by economic difficulties affecting Harbin, drying up the supply of contracts, clients, and customers. It was also common for people to invite me out for long meals, which would inevitably consume a large part of the afternoon or evening. In some cases, I was able to participate in some work at the research site, such as translating menus or contracts, debugging computers, or watching over a retail booth while the proprietor ran an errand. More often, I participated in the nonwork activities being performed at the workplaces: playing ping-pong or cards, watching a chess game with master critics, or (most commonly) gossiping and discussing current events.

Interviews and Narratives

After eliciting from my respondents the salient categories of the stratification schema (power and money and knowledge; cadres and businesspeople and intellectuals), I needed to reveal the narratives which were being used rhetorically to create these three paths and the moral logics which supported them. Of course the ultimate goal was to discover how these narratives were shaping people's actions and patterns of participation, and thereby affecting the value of various forms of capital, the status of various occupations, and the mechanisms of stratification in Harbin. My strategy was to collect stories which touched on these topics. Although I continued to gather data through informal conversations while observing workplaces, I also conducted more formal interviews with eighty-two working adults. (See appendix 1.)

In these interviews, I asked people to tell me the story of their own career history, and (if relevant) to talk about their aspirations for their children. I then asked questions designed to elicit narratives about forms of capital, occupations, and mechanisms of stratification. For example, I asked what was the most important factor for success in Chinese society today, which occupation was most respected, and what were their views of cadres, businesspeople, or intellectuals. In all cases, I would request both their own personal opinion on the subject, as well as their thoughts on what "common people" (*laobaixing*) believed. My goal was to find recurring moral themes, plots, characters, and settings to determine the new collective narratives emerging in the postsocialist era. I also compared the stories people told and the actions they took (or planned to take) in their own career choices and child-rearing decisions.

My interview outline is available in appendix 1, but since the interviews were conducted as conversations, these questions were used as guidelines rather than as a formal structure. The interviews were informal and open-ended, and usually lasted between forty-five minutes and two hours. Most interviews were conducted in one sitting, though in several cases I returned to ask more questions on a second occasion. Most of the interviews were conducted in Mandarin Chinese, which is the common speech in Harbin.[3]

The majority of interviews were conducted in the workplace, though some were also conducted in my apartment, in the homes of my interviewees, or in restaurants. In most cases, these interviews were not confidential. In a few work units, and often times in the markets, people would wander in and out, listening in until they became bored. In a few cases, subjects would even draw others into the interview: "Weren't we just talking about this the other day?" "Don't you remember when that happened?" A few interviewees, when impassioned about a topic, such as cadre corruption, would actually play the surrounding audience like a Baptist preacher working a congregation. "Am

I right?" they would call out, and the rest would answer, "Yes, you're right!" In such cases, the resulting narratives were the product of not just a two-way conversation, but a multi-vocal discussion.

Reflexivity, Relationships, and Research

By the very nature of the project, eliciting collective narratives presents its own dilemmas. I assert that narratives are developed and honed through conversations, real and imagined, as people justify their actions to other members of society. However, a tape-recorded interview is not merely a conversation, and a data-collecting American researcher is not merely a social acquaintance, no matter how innocuous she tries to appear. According to Human Subjects regulations for my university, all of my subjects had to sign detailed consent forms. Before I began my research, I worried about how formal and unnatural this ritual would appear in a Chinese context, where people rarely sign the kind of legalistic forms that are so common in the United States. Fortunately, almost none of the people I approached were put off by the form or the tape recorder, and most of my subjects did seem quite comfortable and were willing to treat the interview as a conversation. Many would interrupt me in the middle of my "legal rights" speech to assure me that they weren't worried and that they were willing to say anything into a tape recorder. Out of eighty-two interviewees, only two or three seemed observably nervous and self-conscious, while the vast majority were surprisingly candid. More often than not, they cheerfully brought up those topics I assumed would be too "politically sensitive" to discuss in public. If they noticed me glancing nervously at the tape recorder while they ranted about cadre corruption or the Tiananmen Protests, they would laugh at me.

Obviously the fact that my ethnic background and fluency in Mandarin allow me to "pass" as a Chinese national helped to make my interviewees feel comfortable around me, as did my gender and relative youth. On the other hand, if the production of narratives is a collective project, co-created by all the participants of the conversation, then as one of the participants, I could not help but affect the resulting product. After all, in mobilizing narrative explanations, people determine what is necessary to explain depending on their evaluation of the audience. To my interviewees I was a foreigner, someone who needed more explanation than their usual social acquaintances. This, of course, worked in my favor, since people felt obliged to explain in greater detail and to leave less to assumption. However, they also saw me as an "intellectual," a member of one of the occupational categories under consideration. This is a problem for my study, especially since one of my key findings was the growing importance and value of human capital. Since I cannot erase my intellectual status, my recourse was to correlate my respondents' words with their actions.

Another issue that researchers in the PRC must contend with is the importance of the practice of guanxi—the art of personal ties and favor exchange. Without practicing guanxi, conducting fieldwork and interviews in China would be difficult, if not impossible. Trying to obtain access to organizations or people through official channels produces few actual refusals, but a great deal of frustrating silence. However, using guanxi creates its own problems, not the least of which are the ethical issues involved. Guanxi involves the exchange of gifts and favors, but I could not bring myself to offer material gifts, or bribes. Fortunately, I had other resources to draw upon with a clean conscience. I translated and copyedited English documents, offered descriptions and advice about life in North America, and gave people the opportunity to practice their English conversational skills. Ironically, my other source of guanxi was as a relationship broker. I became a link between Harbin's population of foreign students and scholars and the Chinese eager to befriend foreigners. Moreover, since my research allowed me to meet quite a number of people in Harbin, by the end of my time there I found myself in a position to introduce locals to each other.[4]

By working through guanxi connections, I could often bypass difficult official protocols, but this also had its risks. When I used guanxi to access a work site, although direct superiors would usually know about my presence, often the higher levels of management were never informed at all. This led to one extremely awkward situation in a factory, when the public security personnel wandered in during an interview and demanded to know what was going on. Although my tapes were temporarily confiscated, and I was given a stern lecture on official protocol, in the end everything was resolved without any problems. In fact, in the midst of the incident, my embarrassed contact simply escorted me to the next department to conduct an interview there—with the department head, no less.

Chapter 2

NARRATIVES AND THE SOCIALIST STRATIFICATION SYSTEM

In China, the rise of stratification institutions in the early post-socialist era was ad hoc, piecemeal, and incomplete. In contrast, the socialist stratification system which preceded it was planned and intentional. One of the central projects of twentieth-century Marxist-Leninist party-states, including the PRC's Maoist regime, was the deliberate creation and legitimation of their own systems of stratification. Narratives were an integral part of the process. They provided the motivation for the project and shaped the results. Moreover, the propagation of narratives was one of the key techniques used by elites to institute new stratification practices, just as the co-optation and adaptation of state narratives were two of the primary mechanisms for citizens to resist and revise those institutions.

In the endeavor to construct a socialist stratification system, which began when communist forces "liberated" China in 1949, Mao Zedong and his followers were aided by the wholesale disintegration of Chinese institutions in the early twentieth century. Even before the fall of the Qing Dynasty in 1911, economic dislocation and rampant inflation had eroded the value of economic capital. Human capital also suffered: the Qing had dismantled the state Confucian educational system, but failed to establish a replacement before the regime collapsed. With the end of the imperial state, the land formerly known as China first fragmented into warring territories under local strongmen, and then coalesced into civil war between the National Party (Guomindang or GMD) and Chinese Communist Party (CCP).

In 1949, the Chinese Communist Party emerged victorious, reunited China (with the notable exceptions of Taiwan, Hong Kong, and Macao), and gained for itself the Herculean challenge of constructing functional institutions for this society. Adopting the institutions of a classical Marxist socialist system, it was able to accomplish this goal with surprising speed. Within a few short years, the People's Republic of China had political institutions to impose order and manage the country, economic institutions to provide relative prosperity, and educational institutions to train people. Along the way, the regime had constructed a coherent stratification system, one which deliberately elevated the value of political capital at the expense of economic, human, and social capital. Yet in 1978, less than thirty years after it had gained control of the country, the CCP began dismantling many of these socialist institutions in the name of market reforms. To understand why this happened, we need to examine both the general characteristics of Marxist socialist systems and the specific conditions of the Chinese case, as well as the logical consequences of the narratives which served as both of their foundations.

From Budapest to Beijing, the revolutionary leaders of the early twentieth century were invested in the same Marxist meta-narrative. Moreover, they were trying to apply this meta-narrative to societies which shared key characteristics: predominantly agrarian economies seeking a magical formula for catching up with their industrial neighbors as quickly as possible. These conditions inspired similar reactions to (and revisions of) that Marxist meta-narrative. For these communist leaders, the salient narrative plot in Marxism-Leninism was that which depicted the apparently powerless classes rising up and changing the world. Marx's theory was not taken to be a description of economic transformations driving social and political changes through history, but a prescription for transforming economies and societies through politics.

Given these points of convergence, as well as the role of Soviet advisors in establishing many of these states, it is hardly surprising that these regimes engineered similar political and social institutions, including the institutions of stratification. And, in a collapse which seemed almost choreographed, these institutions by and large fell apart in the last two decades of the twentieth century. Yet for all these similarities, socialist institutions were in many ways very locally specific phenomena. People made sense of new stories and institutions through the lens of their narrative repertoires and institutional experiences. As these repertoires and experiences differed from locale to locale, the interpretation of—and response to—socialist institutions also diverged. In terms of social stratification, all Marxist socialist systems sought to monopolize the paths to power and status by establishing the dominance of political capital over all other forms of capital—economic, human, and social. But local narrative repertoires affected how political capital was defined and assessed. They also determined the resources that adherents of economic, human, and social capital could use to resist and undermine the socialist stratification system.

The Marxist Socialist System and
the Dominance of Political Capital

Marx himself never argued that a socialist state should increase the value of political capital vis-à-vis economic and human capital. Yet this was a logical consequence of his narratives, after they had been reinterpreted and revised by the socialist leaders of the twentieth century. For the communist revolutionaries who found themselves in a position to set up Marxist societies, one of the most important narratives for making sense of their world was the narrative of capitalist exploitation. According to this story, the ills of the industrialized world, from economic depressions to child labor to colonialism, were due to private ownership, which led inevitably to exploitation. To attain an industrialized prosperity without private ownership, one should establish a "dictatorship of the proletariat," or a workers' state. In practice, this led to the centrally controlled redistributive economy, in which the state collected and redistributed the bulk of the society's resources, including its labor. People were allocated into jobs according to state needs, rather than their own desires. In China until the 1990s, these state job assignments (*fenpei*) were actually coveted, even though employees had no formal control over the process, because only low-status, poorly compensated positions were available on the free labor market. Because the state literally controlled almost all economic resources, it could dictate which forms of capital would gain and lose value (White 1978).

The second key narrative for shaping the socialist stratification system was the narrative of socialist paternalism, which claimed that the advantage of Marxist socialism over all other alternatives was higher standards of living for all. This narrative taught people to measure progress in economic terms. It was reiterated in countless tales that compared past poverty and exploitation (under "bourgeois rule") with present progress and prosperity (under the Communist Party). For example, in 1957, Mao Zedong proclaimed:

> In 1949, national steel output was only a little over 100,000 tons. Yet now, a mere seven years after the liberation of our country, steel output already exceeds four million tons. In old China, there was hardly any machine-building industry, to say nothing of automobile and aviation industries; now, we have all three. When the people overthrew the rule of imperialism, feudalism, and bureaucrat-capitalism, many were not clear as to which way China should head—towards capitalism or towards socialism. Facts have now provided the answer: only socialism can save China (Mao 2001 [1957]:444).

Such narratives were not confined to state discourse. Citizens were taught to "recall past bitterness" and to describe the miseries of life before Liberation compared to the prosperity of the present. It was a staple plot for history books, fictional stories, films, and even personal, ontological narratives. In her memoir, Wang Zheng reminisced about her childhood in late-1950s Shanghai, including the time her older sister took her to see a film about the Long March of the Red Army. Afterwards, eating fruit soup for a snack, Wang cried out, "The Red Army soldiers never had such delicious soup!" Her sister replied, "No, they never had it. They endured all the hardships and sacrificed their lives for the sake of our happiness" (Z. Wang 2001:33).

The narrative implies a contract between the party-state and its citizens: as long as the latter behave obediently, the former will act as a benevolent parent and provide them with everything they need. This is the logic which animates the narratives of "inside" and "outside" described in chapter 1. Good people, who serve society through the party-state, will be rewarded with paternalistic care "inside" good work units. Consequently, one of the primary functions of the workplace was as a site for the redistribution of state resources to households and individuals. In fact, state firms in socialist China were not called businesses but "work units" (*danwei*). This terminology reinforced the perception that the purpose of the firm was not to sell products or make profits, but to provide urban residents with their "iron rice bowl."

Despite its strong repertoire of narratives defending egalitarianism, even Marxist narratives could be used to justify the unequal distribution of resources. The narrative of class struggle argued that some classes, such as workers, contributed more to society than other classes, such as capitalists or peasants. In China, urban firms in significant sectors were nationalized into state work units; less important workplaces were designated as collectives and given fewer resources. In Chinese parlance, collectives received "wooden rice bowls" rather than "iron rice bowls." Even in the state sector (which employed 78 percent of the urban workforce in 1975), firms were hierarchically ranked and given different levels of compensation. Inequality also existed within work units, where persons of higher rank received better material compensation, usually not in terms of pay, but in benefits in kind, special prices, and access to scarce goods and services. Even with all these perquisites, a high-level cadre's standard of living in a Marxist state was quite meager compared to the elite in a capitalist society.

Given the stranglehold the party-state had on the stratification system, it was clear that the qualifications most valued by the political leadership would become the most important form of capital in society. By and large, they chose to reward loyalty to the Party, earnest enthusiasm for its ideology, and disciplined obedience to its instructions. Janos Kornai points out that this emphasis on fidelity and compliance are nowhere apparent in Marx's writings, but instead grew out of revolutionary military experience, where guerilla warfare required discipline, fervor, and obedience (Kornai 1992). The result was that the Marxist socialist systems tended to promote "virtuocracies," in which political "virtue" was more valuable than skill or knowledge. The simplest way to ensure these traits was to select and reward Communist Party members, since the Party recruited with these criteria.

The Chinese Case

Despite sharing many characteristics with other twentieth-century stratification systems, the Chinese Communist Party also constructed narratives which responded to local historical circumstances and shaped local institutions. One issue which profoundly shaped the understanding of political capital in China and exacerbated the tendency towards "virtuocracy" was the almost total absence of urban proletarians in the Party during the revolutionary years. None of the states where communist parties triumphed had a very large working class, but China's proletariat was particularly minuscule, well under 1 percent of the population (Lieberthal 1995:40). To make matters worse, the CCP had almost no access to these few urban workers from 1927, when the Nationalists drove the Communists out of China's cities, until 1945, when Harbin came under CCP rule. To deal with these circumstances, Mao Zedong offered his own revision of Marxism-Leninism, a set of narratives which became known as Mao Zedong Thought. These stories used relative disadvantage, rather than relations of production, as the criterion for revolutionary identification (Mao 1954 [1926]), allowing the CCP to become an organization populated by young, uneducated peasants during the 1930s and 1940s.

Mao also claimed that ideological fervor, rather than economic conditions, was the motor behind social transformation. Military success only added to the narrative repertoire of tales which described the triumph of the lower classes (motivated by fervent beliefs) over the rich and powerful elite. These narratives led the CCP leadership to devise the institution of the political campaign: a carefully choreographed series of events designed to transform beliefs in order to institute new practices, including ones designed to reshape the stratification hierarchy. Trained activists would infiltrate villages, workplaces, and neighborhoods, where they disrupted the normal routine. They led emotional rallies, where some aspect of the current system would be harshly criticized. Then they taught people the new ideological line through "political study," which often involved reading or listening to stories.

Mao also offered the narrative of perpetual class struggle, which led the regime to wage continuous war against the party-state's own stratification system. He directed his rhetoric of class struggle against not only those who inherited "bad" class designations from the pre-revolutionary era, but also those of "good" class backgrounds who "served the interests" of the enemy classes, such as cadres who used the new bureaucracy to serve themselves and their children, thus creating a new system of stratification (Kraus 1981). However, until the Cultural Revolution, Mao was also unwilling to directly challenge the structural roots of bureaucratized inequalities (Kraus 1981:82), thus guaranteeing that China would always have different "classes," and that those at the top of the stratification hierarchy would always be the potential object of class struggle.

Relative wealth and privilege were considered suspect in most Marxist socialist systems (Kornai 1992), but in China they triggered traumatic political campaigns. Beginning before 1949 and continuing periodically throughout the Maoist era, "rectification" campaigns against cadre privilege and corruption threw Chinese society into disorder. From early on, Chinese citizens also learned how to use the rhetoric of Maoist class struggle and political campaigns to their personal advantage. Bai Di recalls that, as a schoolgirl in 1967 Harbin, she tried to "seize power" from her parents at the dinner table. "With some revolutionary mumbo jumbo, I managed to make my point. I wanted to have some power, economic power, which boiled down to money. Yeah, I needed some pocket money" (Bai 2001:82).

Maoist narratives of ideology and class struggle exacerbated the socialist tendency toward "virtuocracy" and drove a wedge between political and human capital. Although official policy required that people in the state hierarchy be recruited and promoted on the basis of both "virtue" (*de*) and "ability" (*neng*), the peasant revolutionaries who "liberated" China in 1949 used these narratives to reinforce their prejudices against educated people and to justify recruiting people like themselves into the Party and cadre ranks. "Virtue" was also operationalized as seniority, measured not in age but in tenure as a Party member, though these two numbers are obviously correlated. Mao argued that social practice and experience were vastly more important than book learning (Mao 1954 [1937]), and this was interpreted to mean that years of service could be translated as ability. Since older people tended to have less schooling, higher education levels actually correlated with slower promotion rates (Kau 1969:266; Oksenberg 1969:175). Despite these recruiting policies, the cadre corps always retained a substantial minority of members who had strong educational credentials but poor political standing. These people were kept out of positions of authority, as political capital trumped human capital (Walder 1995b).

Ironically, this practice of rewarding seniority dovetailed well with imperial era state Confucian narratives, which argued that younger people should respect and obey their elders. Nor was this the only sign of pre-revolutionary cultural influence on the Chinese definition of political capital. As in other socialist states, the Maoist regime implicitly justified socialist inequality with the logic that those who served more deserved a bigger share of the benefits. In China, this argument was made using language which hearkened back to the Confucian narrative of contribution (*gongxian*).[1] In Chinese, Confucianism is not called "Confucianism" but the "scholars' school" (*rujia*), and the Confucian canon purports to contain the core of "pure knowledge" ordering and underlying all other knowledge areas (Zhu 1992:11; Confucius 1998:162). The men who studied and understood this knowledge were believed to understand the world in a way which ordinary people could not comprehend. As a result, they served society to a greater degree than their uneducated counterparts, and they deserved higher status and better rewards.

The Maoist regime transformed the Confucian narratives of contribution by arguing that Marxism-Leninism (and later Mao Zedong Thought) constituted the core knowledge underlying reality. Therefore, those who absorbed this new, revolutionary wisdom contributed more to society than ordinary people and deserved positions of leadership. Yet, regardless of the criteria, the narratives of contribution still justified a system of inequality: those who know more, do more, and therefore deserve more compensation. This tendency toward hierarchy inevitably triggered Maoist narratives of egalitarianism and class struggle, which led to another round of disruptive political campaigns. Because both the Party and the cadre corps recruited for and rewarded political purity and ideological fervor above all else, these campaigns grew increasingly intense, culminating in the national debacle of the Cultural Revolution, which shut down many of China's political, economic, and educational organizations for several years in the late 1960s.

Ordinary People and Narratives about Political Capital

The Maoist party-state was quite successful in embedding the narrative of contribution into popular discourse. When I asked a forty-two-year-old Party cadre why he wanted to join the CCP, he explained: "When you're young, you want to develop and make a contribution to society. The CCP's purpose represents these deepest human desires. Service to people is its central tenet, to bring communism to the majority of the people. So it matched my own goals and desires to struggle to liberate the masses."

A sixty-year-old cadre at a state enterprise agreed, "Money isn't important; it's what you can contribute to society. At least that's what we thought in my generation." Harbiners would relate movie plots about heroic officials who served the people with sacrificial care.

Yet many of the ordinary collective and ontological narratives which supported political capital were far less idealistic. For example, many of my interviewees found Party membership worth obtaining simply because the competition was so intense. CCP members relished describing the long odds and arduous effort of gaining membership. One thirty-eight-year-old former cadre boasted several times in one interview that he entered the Party as a college freshmen, in the very first round of competition. This man said nothing to me about the ideological aspect of Party membership but did mention that gaining the credential improved his living standards.

Indeed, the most common narratives about political capital in Harbin were those which described its usefulness for getting the good things in life. A fifty-year-old professor explained to me, "Before the Cultural Revolution, to be a Party member meant that you had a sweet life, better work, better benefits and everything. Without membership, you couldn't be any kind of cadre." The forty-eight-year-old cadre at the Post and Telecommunications Bureau reminisced:

> No matter where you went, Party membership was good for you, so you could move up into management levels. . . . You didn't pursue money then, you just wanted to rise high in the work unit. Back then, it was the first thing people would ask you if you were trying to meet a girl—are you a Party member? At that time, the Party was in people's hearts, and to be a member was a kind of glory, to be better than others. And also there were more activities then just for members, like films to see.

Indeed, by the 1970s, when asked about their criteria for mate choice, Chinese urban males listed "class label and political record" first (before "good looks"), while women listed it second (Whyte and Parish 1984:127).

Ironically enough, Chinese citizens were willing to comply with the Maoist institutions of stratification in large part because they desired the very perquisites—the "sweet life"—that Maoist ideology condemned. Although Mao Zedong's regime had succeeded in establishing the dominance of political capital, its citizens were learning quite a different lesson than the one the party-state intended to teach. They understood that life was "political" but translated that to mean that Party membership was helpful "no matter where you went," whether for gaining a promotion, attracting a mate, or seeing movies.

Economic Capital

In establishing the socialist institutions of stratification, communist parties not only sought to raise the value of political capital, but to undermine other forms of capital. The primary target was economic capital, given its centrality in capitalist systems. Despite the fact that the Chinese industrial bourgeoisie in 1949 was tiny, it still had a disproportionate amount of power, as well as control over the resources the new regime coveted the most—China's few industrial factories. Furthermore, they possessed the expertise to manage these concerns—expertise which Party members by and large lacked. Examining how the CCP successfully co-opted these resources and this expertise into the new socialist system reveals the efficacy of the Maoist political campaign and the power of Maoist narratives. In 1952, the Maoist regime launched the Five-Anti Campaign, a political campaign against business owners guilty of the five "poisons": bribery, tax evasion, theft of state property, cheating on government contracts, and stealing state economic information. The urban economy slowed to a halt as workers were pressured to denounce their employers and capitalists were forced to confess their crimes. Nationally, only 24 percent of all businesses were judged to be law abiding (Cheng 1963:67).

How did a relatively new regime manage to mobilize the urban population to engage in campaign activities? First, it had to propagate a new set of stories. Public narratives were mobilized to explain the nature of the enemy and the need for a struggle against it. Premier Zhou Enlai declared that the national bourgeoisie had "the nature of seeking only profit, benefiting at the expense of others," (Barnett 1964:155). An article in *Xuexi* (*Study*) declared: "The bourgeois class is an exploiting class. The exploitation of the toiling masses on the basis of the system of private ownership under capitalism, and the making of profits, constitute the material living condition on which the bourgeois class exists. The bourgeois class must undermine the material interests of the working class and other toiling masses for its own existence and development" (quoted in Barnett 1964: 155–56).

These narratives of exploitation allowed the party-state to reinterpret activities which had been considered acceptable into egregious sins against "the people." One of the most common accusations during the Five-Anti Campaign was "illegal earnings," a vague term broadly interpreted to include any "excessive" profits. If the bourgeois class existed to exploit the people, how could its profits be anything other than "excessive"?

The party state also propagated narratives describing how upstanding citizens should react to these exploitative capitalists. *Jiefang Ribao* (*Liberation Daily*) offered a tale about a young accountant named Chang. Although his boss indulged in illegal activities, Chang was initially reluctant to denounce him because the man was a relative who "did small favors" for his employee. However, during the Five-Anti Campaign, he was able to reinterpret the situation with a narrative of class struggle. His new ontological narrative translated his former qualms from loyalty into "sentimentalism," and his boss was recast from his role as a kinsman into the character of the harmful capitalist. With the story revised as a tale of class struggle, Chang was able to denounce him (Gardner 1969:514–15). Such stories taught Chinese urbanites not only the dangers of economic and social capital, but also the benefits of political capital. In their happy endings, obedient and active characters like Chang were rewarded by the new regime with Party membership and cadre status. These narratives were broadcast through loudspeaker systems set up by the hundreds on city street corners (Gardner 1969:512). Activists also organized newspaper reading teams so that the illiterate could have access to published narratives.

In the war of words, China's capitalists did very little to counter the onslaught of negative propaganda. In traditional Chinese stories, wealth is not associated with virtue, so economic capital does not carry moral weight. Instead, in Chinese narratives, people gain and lose fortunes for no apparent reason, with no connection to hard work, intelligence, or righteousness (Kuhn 1984:23; Niu 1996 [Tang Dynasty]; "Tu Tzu-Ch'un" 2000). In folk stories, businesspeople tend to be greedy, selfish, and immoral (Chi 1996; Ling 1996 [1628]). Urban businesspeople did complain that the Five-Anti Campaign was just an excuse for the state to appropriate their honestly earned wealth (Barnett 1964:150, 157). But without a strong narrative repertoire to draw from in their defense, they were unable to articulate a moral argument explaining why their wealth was honestly earned. For example, one bewildered businessman admitted that he may have suffered from a "profiteering ideology," but he tried to explain that he was simply trying to accumulate capital to expand production (Gardner 1969:507). These words, though sincere, were hardly persuasive to his hostile audience.

Although in fact few capitalists were arrested, the Five-Anti Campaign disrupted economic production and reduced capitalists' assets considerably through fines and "returned funds" (Barnett 1964:163). To rescue these weakened private firms, the state stepped in and took over, transforming former owners into state-employed managers and businesses into work units. Although private businesses never completely disappeared from China's cities, they were relegated to the margins of the economy. By 1965, only 3.6 percent of the urban workforce was not employed in either a state or collective organization, and by 1975 that number had dropped to .01 percent (Davis 1990:86).

The work unit system allowed the Maoist state to undermine the cash economy and further erode the value of economic capital. By 1978, urban residents were receiving only 26.3 yuan per month in wages from their work units, but 22.7 yuan worth of rationed commodities alone (You 1998:5).

Ordinary People and Narratives about Economic Capital

At least in Harbin, the party-state was quite successful in diminishing the status of private business. The collective narratives of "inside" and "outside" described in chapter 1 reveal that even in the post-socialist era, people generally looked down on entrepreneurs. Listening to my interviewees describing their lives during the Maoist years, one would assume that the private sector did not exist. Only once did an informant mention it: a forty-four-year-old woman who ran a small market stall told me that her father "was a worker, but did business on the side. They called it 'walking the capitalist road' back then, but he was never caught."

Harbiners also internalized, to some extent, the party-state's devaluation of economic capital. This is not to say that they neither wanted money nor coveted the things that money could buy; as mentioned above, part of their desire for political capital was for the material perquisites it brought. Yet in the 1990s, Harbiners were constantly telling me that money had little value in the Maoist years. A sixty-two-year-old retired professor complained about his students seeking jobs in the South after graduation because the salaries were higher there. "In my day, we never talked about salaries—because they were all the same!" he ended with a laugh.

When asked to detail their work histories, my respondents could usually remember their monetary salary at any stage of their career, but they could also recall with great specificity the structure of the non-monetary benefits. They thought it was common sense that status, rank, work conditions, and nonfinancial perquisites mattered more than cash income. If anything, Harbiners tended to use narratives which focused on what money could *not* buy. In *Chinese Lives*, a collection of oral histories from the early 1980s, a woman describes how she opened a private restaurant outside Harbin with her sister, but eventually merged her firm with a collective enterprise three years later. As part of the collective, they earned 25 percent less money and lost control of the business, and yet her narrative depicted the move as a step up. She explained that they had acquired sick leave, disability coverage, and days off, and the police had stopped harassing them: "When we had our own business we didn't see a film for over a year. Now the state gives us free tickets and even time off to go. We've got a higher social status, too. We're official employees now. My sister's a cadre, and she's in the Party. That would never happen if we were self-employed" (Zhang and Sang 1987:97).

Although Chinese urbanites craved material comforts for themselves, when confronted with other people's economic capital, they reverted to communist narratives which associated wealth with immorality. In *Chinese Lives*, a thirty-six-year-old train conductor confesses that he could not help disliking the people who could afford the luxury "soft-sleeper" berths in their twenties (Zhang and Sang 1987:304). A seventy-three-year-old retired English professor told me he despised "social climbers" who wanted wealth so badly they used "dishonest" means to get it, though he admitted that their methods may not be in any way illegal.

Through political campaigns and socialist institutions, the Maoist regime managed, to a great extent, to de-institutionalize private business occupations and to make economic capital, in terms of cash, significantly less valuable than in a capitalist society. Yet they did so by sending mixed messages about the value of economic benefits. On the one hand, the Party propagated a message of equality and asceticism, but on the other hand it justified the value of political capital by linking it to economic perks and using it to substantiate a system of economic inequality. No wonder Chinese urban citizens talked constantly about their economic compensation, endlessly dissecting and comparing their benefits and their salaries (Zhang and Sang 1987:111, 154–56). Under the Maoist system, Chinese urbanites still wanted a materially comfortable life; they had just learned that political capital was more useful than economic capital for obtaining it.

The Complications of Human Capital

Although twentieth-century Marxist regimes clearly sought to raise the value of political capital, and to decrease the value of economic capital, the party-states' relationship to human capital was more complicated. In every state in which communist parties triumphed, educated personnel were in short supply. But the Marxist socialist systems tended towards "virtuocracy," valuing party loyalty and ideological purity above education and expertise. In China and elsewhere, intellectuals tended to come from pre-revolutionary upper classes and had little reason to be grateful and loyal to the party-state. Instead, these people had the resources to set up a basis of power to compete with the new order.

Although these were issues in every socialist society, these problems were exacerbated by China's pre-revolutionary conditions. First, the CCP's rural history meant that Party members there had even lower levels of education, and even higher levels of hostility to "book learning," than in other socialist states. Second, until 1911, China was run by an imperial state with a meritocratic civil service bureaucracy. For hundreds of years, China's stratification system had been based primarily on human capital, and these institutions and the cultural narratives which supported them were inextricably intertwined with notions of Chinese identity. As a result, Chinese intellectuals (unlike Chinese capitalists) had a rich and resonant repertoire of cultural resources to draw upon to resist the CCP's attempts to lower the status of their occupations and devalue their form of capital. In the socialist era, although educated people were not considered a class per se, they were seen as enough of a special group to merit their own label: "intellectuals" (*zhishi fenzi*, literally, "knowledgeable elements").[2]

Cultural Narratives and Institutions in the Late Imperial Era

A common theme in Chinese historiography—ancient, modern, and contemporary—is the idea of a culturally unified state called China. Even the revolutionary communists who established the PRC in 1949 saw their new nation-state as the culmination of this long story. They expected their new subjects to hold certain "feudal" beliefs about "traditional Chinese society," many of which would be rooted in narratives based on Confucianism, and many of which would support the dominance of human capital. After all, Confucianism, or the "scholars' school" (*rujia*), propagated narratives which inextricably linked education and high culture (*wenhua*) with wisdom, righteousness, and contribution to society (*gongxian*) (Zhu 1992:7; Confucius 1998:15–16, 156).

These themes were reflected in collective narratives. In folk tales, the stock character of the scholar was distinguished by his morality and often cast as the righteous judge (Lung and Comber 1964), or the innocent victim ("The Boot that Reveals the Culprit" 1996). In Chinese historiography, good emperors listened to learned advisors (Sima 1994:657), while bad rulers exiled and executed scholars to avoid hearing the truth (Jia 1994:229). In fact, if the state deviated from Confucian principles, scholars did not just have the right but the responsibility to expose its errors (Goldman 1981:3; De Bary and Lufrano 2000:124–29). From the thirteenth century to the early twentieth, Chinese schoolboys learned to recite the Three Character Classic (*Sanzi Jing*):

> If you do not study/How can you become a [true] human being . . .
> Learn while young/When grown up put it to practice
> Influence the ruler above/Benefit the people below (Wang 1999:807).

These narratives shaped the central stratification institutions of the late imperial period. Outside the imperial family, the members of the ruling bureaucracy were selected through a series of meritocratic examinations, which tested knowledge of the Confucian classics. These narratives and institutions combined to make human capital, as defined by the state, the most valued form of capital in late imperial China. Significantly, in Chinese folk tales, a happy ending is often one in which our hero (or our heroine's husband or son) becomes a successful scholar ("The Oil Peddler Courts the Courtesan" 1996; P'u 1996a [18th Century]; P'u 1996b [18th Century]).

The Collapse of the Imperial System, and Maoist Narratives about Human Capital

The military debacles and economic crises of the late nineteenth century and early twentieth not only took down the Qing regime; the ascendence of the West also irrevocably undermined the legitimacy of the Confucian meta-narrative itself. Despite all this, Chinese scholars continued to believe that a true "core knowledge" existed, and that mastering this knowledge was the key and foundation for constructing and maintaining a powerful and prosperous state. Although the content of their learning changed from Confucian classics to Western texts, Chinese intellectuals still combed through their books seeking a new, true meta-narrative which would explain China's conditions and offer the correct script for its revival. They studied everything from Social Darwinism (Schwartz 1964) to Western "science and democracy" (Anderson 1990:36) to fascism (Eastman 1972).

Of course the meta-narrative which won out was Marxism-Leninism. Mao Zedong revised the Confucian narrative of culture so that Marxism-Leninism/ Mao Zedong Thought constituted the core knowledge underlying reality. In contrast, non-regime intellectuals, who tended to come from "bad" class backgrounds, did not possess this knowledge and culture, and in fact understood less than the uneducated classes (White 1981). These new narratives essentially bifurcated knowledge between the "core knowledge" of politics and morality, and merely technical knowledge—between political capital and human capital, "Red" versus "Expert" (White 1981). Under the Maoist regime, institutions reflected this bifurcation. Political and moral knowledge, or "Redness," was certified outside the educational system through institutions controlled by political elites, most notably the Communist Party. Meanwhile, the newly established educational system, which contained the institution of nationwide college examinations reminiscent of the imperial civil service exam, concentrated on purely technical expertise for all but a very tiny elite (Hayhoe 1989:20).

Yet even if non-regime intellectuals were supposed to be mere technical experts, they were still a scarce commodity and therefore an elite group in Maoist China. Although the Chinese government succeeded in establishing universal primary education and eventually most urban residents had access to some secondary school (Whyte and Parish 1984:60), the state only expected to educate a small percentage of students to expert status. As late as 1980, only 2 percent of the adult population had access to postsecondary education ("World Development Indicators" 1998). The contradiction between the CCP's suspicion of intellectuals and its need for their expertise can be seen in the shifting official categories used for educated personnel, which changed from "petty bourgeoisie" to "workers" to "agents of counter-revolutionary restoration" (White 1981:6–15).

Intellectual Resistance and Ordinary People's Narratives about Human Capital

Although the party-state aimed for intellectuals to become compliant functionaries in the centrally managed state structure, educated people could draw upon an older repertoire of collective narratives to argue for a more significant and autonomous role as state servants and the government's moral conscience. Mobilizing narratives of culture and contribution, they tried to reclaim (and revise) their traditional positions as respected, semi-independent, moral critics of the state and as intermediaries between the state and its subjects. During the Hundred Flowers movement of 1956, these intellectuals published stories depicting young and idealistic intellectuals who can see the flaws of the socialist system clearly, but are thwarted from their desire to serve the people by incompetent or cynical "Red" cadres (Liu 1981 [1956]; Wang 1981 [1956]).

These pieces explicitly echo socialist stories about idealistic heroes who battle on behalf of the masses. Yet their intellectual heroes are also like the state servants of imperial-era stories, who use their wisdom to sway their unrighteous leaders from the wrong path, risking their lives to speak the truth on behalf of the people.

The Hundred Flowers movement ended with the Anti-Rightist campaign, and state narratives were disseminated to refute these "misguided" and "dangerous" stories (Li 1981 [1957]). However, this did not end the tension between "Red" versus "Expert." As the regime "sought to establish a balance between the opposing forces of orthodoxy and creativity," it oscillated between emphasizing ideological purity (or "Red"-ness) at the expense of productivity, or seeking productivity ("Expert"-ness) at the risk of losing political control (Goldman 1981:9; Henze 1984). In the periods when ideological purity was embraced at the expense of expertise, human capital was often attacked. With contribution redefined in political terms, stories portrayed intellectual learning as false knowledge or Western or bourgeois lies, and intellectual competition as elitist and hierarchical. Clearly, the most extreme swing to "Red"-ness was the Cultural Revolution (1966–76). The hierarchical organization of schools was toppled, students attacked their teachers, the entrance examination was abolished, and the entire project of producing expertise was condemned.

The tensions between state narratives and intellectual narratives, combined with the oscillations in the party-state's policies, made it difficult for ordinary citizens to assess the value of human capital. At least during the Cultural Revolution itself, many ordinary people followed the state's lead and denigrated intellectuals as useless and arrogant. In *Chinese Lives*, a Beijing worker describes how his illiterate father, a Party activist, harangued professors at one of China's top universities during the Cultural Revolution:

> The old man can't read a word, but there he was giving all those university people shit. The Cultural Revolution screwed me up from when I was a kid, but that's just how it was: "All power to the proletariat." "Studying to become an official" was criticized, and everyone was talking about studying being useless. You should have seen all us little seven-year-old farts running around criticizing this stuff. We were full of crap! But what use is studying? My teacher only made fifty yuan a month, half of what my dad got, and he was much older than Dad (Zhang and Sang 1987:135–6).

Yet during the rest of the Maoist era, urban citizens seemed to retain the view that intellectuals were virtuous and respectable, attitudes which owed more to Confucian than Maoist narratives. In the 1970s, when her fellow hotel waitresses saw Lihua Wang reading during breaks, they reacted with admiration: "'It's good for you to read during breaks,' a married waitress told me. 'You can learn something rather than just waste your time at the restaurant.' Another advised me, 'Don't be like one of us, spending all your spare time worrying about the family business. Reading is education that will bring you a better future.' 'We should call her "little intellectual,"' someone else said" (L. Wang 2001:127).

Although the Maoist regime did not succeed in erasing the narratives of high culture and contribution, Chinese urbanites did learn to question the utility of human capital. A good school performance raised a person's chances of being assigned to an "iron rice bowl" work unit. As an intellectual, however, one might be the target of the next political campaign. These tensions became extremely acute during campaigns, like the Anti-Rightist Movement and the Cultural Revolution, which pitted the state against intellectuals. Students (and their families) had to debate whether to obey their teachers or denounce them, whether to invest in human or political capital (Shirk 1982).

Social Capital

The Maoist regime successfully brought a stable political system, social order, and economic growth to a beleaguered Chinese society. However, the structural flaws of the Marxist socialist system soon became evident. The redistributive economy required an enormous amount of state oversight and management. As a result, economic institutions were ponderous and inflexible, unable to move personnel and materials around as quickly as necessary (Liu 1981 [1956]; Kornai 1992:223). Because the socialist system orients firms to the state, rather than to customers, consumer products were given low priority and consequently were in short supply. Difficulties with scarcity led to hoarding, which exacerbated the problem. These economic irrationalities were worsened in the Chinese case by the disruptive nature of political campaigns, which destabilized institutions and undermined any incentive to invest in skills or technology for the long haul.

In response to the hoarding, scarcity, and irrationalities of the socialist economic system, citizens in every socialist state developed informal practices of favor exchange which bypassed official channels (Pawlik 1992; Verdery 1996:27; Ledeneva 1998). Using the idiom of gift exchange, favors and friendship, these practices allowed people to bypass official channels to obtain scarce resources, including coveted consumer products, good job assignments, and access to powerful people. To use the Chinese phrase, they allowed social actors to "go through the back door" (*zou houmen*). As a result, the value of social capital was quite high; skill at manipulating favors, expanding networks, and culti-vating "friendships" with useful people had a serious impact on an individual's standard of living. Although the Marxist regimes condemned these practices, those who benefited the most from favor exchange practices were cadres, who could take advantage of their gatekeeper status in the redistribution process.

Despite similarities in each socialist society, local narratives shaped the dis-tinctive nature of its favor exchange practice. As a result, Russians understood *blat* to have evolved from petty crime (indeed, the word was considered not "polite") (Ledeneva 1998:12–13), while the Polish saw their favor exchange practice through the lens of *srodowiska*, a bounded circle of friends. In China, socialist-era favor exchange practices were understood to be an extension of the "traditional" practice of guanxi, rooted in imperial-era Confucian narra-tives about relationships and reciprocity (Yang 1994: chapter 4).

In Chinese guanxi narratives, human beings are defined by their relation-ship to others. Each social role is understood in terms of dyadic relationships (daughter to mother, wife to husband, subject to ruler, etc.), not member-ship in a group. Each relationship is supposed to be reciprocal (Lo and Otis 2003:137). Although the paired obligations are different for each dyadic rela-tionship, in general the superior member is expected to take care of the in-ferior member, while the inferior member is supposed to respect the superior member. According to the Confucian meta-narrative, when all people perform their roles properly in all of their relationships, the entire society will be char-acterized by harmony and prosperity. This proper behavior includes manifest-ing emotional affection materially though ritual and gift exchange (Tong and Yong 1998:80; Lo and Otis 2003).

According to the rules of gift exchange, gift givers cannot act as though they expect anything in return; the performance must exclude explicit recognition of instrumental goals (Mauss 1967). On the other hand, to act properly, gift recipients have to reciprocate. Because the narratives recognize the relation-ship, rather than the material items, as the central focus of the exchange, it would be considered unspeakably rude to "pay off" the gift with a return gift of equal value. The proper response to a gift is to reciprocate with greater munificence, reflected in these two common sayings: "You honor me with a foot; I honor you with a yard," and "Receive a droplet of generosity; repay like a gushing spring" (Hwang 1987:954; Yang 1989:143). Each gift transaction is considered a step in a continuing relationship, one which is growing closer (Hwang 1987:954; Yang 1989:143; Tong and Yong 1998:81; Wu 2001:30). To "help friends," according to guanxi narratives, was simply manifesting "human feeling"(*renqing*). A person who ignores his or her relational obligations has "no face" (*meiyou mianzi*).

In reality, however, guanxi gift exchange offered a mechanism for obtaining useful resources. As long as the interaction followed the form of the gift exchange, and both parties acted as if the relationship was the most important matter, it was not seen as wrong to "pull" guanxi to get something necessary or desirable. Even in the imperial era, guanxi practice did not just involve the exchange of gifts and banquets in formal rituals, but also the exchange of more practical favors in more informal settings. In the Maoist era, guanxi practice became a key strategy for surviving the scarcities and irrationalities which plagued the socialist economy.

After 1949, Maoist narratives and institutions undermined the patriarchal clan and Confucian relational hierarchy, thereby de-institutionalizing the original basis for guanxi relationships. Yet the narratives about "helping friends," "human affection" (renqing) and reciprocity lived on. When guanxi was revived in the socialist era, it became a practice used by individuals to construct relationships with non-kin (Lo and Otis 2003:139). Nor were guanxi ties limited to colleagues or classmates; a guanxi relationship could be started with nothing more than an introduction from a mutual friend—or a friend of a friend of a friend. True to the Confucian narratives in its history, guanxi relationships were always understood as dyadic pairings. Person A could ask his friend B to ask her cousin C to ask her classmate D for a favor. Each person did her part for the sake of the immediate "friend," not for the stranger at the end of queue, but the result was that person A received what he needed from a veritable stranger (Yang 1994:125).

Of course the Maoist party-state tried to undermine the value of social capital by offering counter-narratives. Recall the newspaper stories during the Five-Anti Campaign which praised the young workers for realizing their guanxi ties to their capitalist relatives were nothing but "sentimentalism," and then (freed from the constraints of feudal narratives) denouncing their bourgeois kin (Gardner 1969:514–15, 530). State narratives associated guanxi practice with corruption, especially during rectification campaigns against cadres (Hsu 2001). Yet all the features of the Maoist system which allowed it to effectively attack the value of economic capital were liabilities in its battle against social capital. The centralized redistributive economy undermined private business owners, but it also put the state's own cadres in the perfect position to gain social capital, thereby removing most of their incentive to fight against guanxi practice. Political campaigns not only forced people to find ways to bypass state institutions during disruptions, but the sheer number of campaigns eventually drove Chinese citizens into political cynicism and retreat from state-controlled public life. It was during the Maoist era's most intense and fanatical political campaign, the Cultural Revolution, that socialist guanxi practice became most widespread and developed into its most elaborate form (Yang 1994: chapter 7).

Moreover, Chinese urban residents were armed with a repertoire of narratives to justify their guanxi practice against state condemnation. In the USSR, people were embarrassed to admit they ever used blat or even say the word in polite company (Ledeneva 1998:13), but in socialist China, guanxi practice was associated with renqing, a strongly positive term denoting the emotional and ethical bonds people should feel toward one another. Renqing motivates social actors to behave with proper warmth and care for each other, which includes reciprocating guanxi transactions. As a result, Chinese could talk about guanxi without shame. Take, for example, the oral history (recorded in 1984) of Han Xiaozu, an aviation engineer trained in Germany who returned to China in the late 1940s and worked with the former roommate of Zhou Enlai. Zhou eventually became China's premier, and Han's guanxi with this powerful man served him well during the rectification campaigns of the 1950s:

> When I was being hunted as a "tiger" during the "three-anti" and "five-anti" drives, Zhou Enlai put in a good word for me: "Han Xiaozu couldn't possibly have done things like that. If he were like that he'd never have come back [from Germany]." The outcome was that from one day to the next the "tiger" became the deputy chief of the tiger-hunting team. When I met the Premier he'd always shake me by the hand and address me by name before I could say a word. He fixed for

me to work in Tianjin, because there weren't any western-style houses in Beijing then, and he was worried that I wouldn't be able to adjust to life here (Zhang and Sang 1987:258–59).

Far from condemning Premier Zhou for favoritism or corruption, this narrative portrays him as an admirable man for remembering renqing even after he rose to high position.

Chinese urbanites did absorb state narratives to the extent that they learned to condemn guanxi if it was practiced by officials in an excessive or exploitative way. Yet thanks to the narratives of renqing—and to the institutional irrationalities of daily life in a Marxist socialist system—they still felt justified in participating in "ordinary" guanxi practice themselves. Social capital animated a stratification system which operated parallel to (and parasitically upon) the official stratification system, but just outside of state control.

Conclusion

Given China's condition in 1949, the accomplishments of the socialist system over the following two decades are genuinely impressive. As part of that project, the communist regime set up institutions of social stratification which established the dominance of political capital and put party-state cadres at the top of the occupational hierarchy. Yet the Marxist socialist system sows the seeds of its own destruction, and the Chinese incarnation was no exception. Its stratification institutions were rife with "contradictions" (to borrow one of Mao's favorite terms) which undermined the authority of its elites and eventually of the whole socialist system.

First, the party-state explicitly promoted an ideology of egalitarianism and asceticism, while at the same time raising the desirability of political capital by connecting it with economic perks. On the one hand, the regime (successfully) denigrated the value of economic capital in the form of cash, but on the other hand it continuously promoted the importance of economic products in daily life through narratives of socialist paternalism and contribution. The result was an inevitable cycle of political campaigns, as Chinese urbanites were tempted into the elite with economic perquisites, and then punished in rectification campaigns for enjoying those perquisites. Second, the bureaucracy's need for human capital was contradicted by the Marxist socialist system's tendencies toward virtuocracy. This tension led to periodic campaigns against intellectuals, which increased fanaticism and worsened the bureaucracy's problems with a scarcity of talent. Lastly, the Marxist socialist system condemned favor exchange practices but made it close to impossible for citizens to operate without them. Moreover, it inadvertently rewarded their cadres with high levels of social capital. Once again, this contradiction led inexorably to political campaigns targeting cadres, this time for "corrupt" behavior.

These recurring political campaigns against cadres had the unintended effect of arming China's citizens with a repertoire of narratives to judge, criticize, and condemn political elites. They also exacerbated the systemic economic flaws inherent in socialism, thereby eroding the party-state's ability to fulfill its promises of socialist paternalism. Repeated campaigns left Chinese social actors emotionally exhausted and politically cynical, driving them to withdraw from the public, state-controlled sphere of socialist stratification institutions, into the private, informal world of personal relationships, guanxi transactions, and the second economy—which in turn only contributed to the problems of hoarding, low productivity, and cadre corruption.

Chapter 3

HARBIN: FROM PARIS OF THE EAST TO THE RUST BELT

Harbin, the capital of China's Heilongjiang Province, is located in the area once known as Manchuria, now simply termed "the Northeast" (*Dongbei*).[1] In fact, as China's northernmost major city, it is associated with bitter cold and ice in most Chinese people's minds, especially since the city's most famous tourist attraction is its magnificent annual ice festival. Harbin's population of about 3 million residents would rank it as a major metropolitan center in most countries, but in populous China most residents assured me that it was merely a "mid-sized" city.

Harbin in Historical Context: From Competitive Colonialism to Soviet Industry

In a country where inhabitants pride themselves on the deep roots and millennia-long histories of their cities, Harbin is a mere century old and populated exclusively by immigrants. Moreover, it was founded by Russians and is located north of the Great Wall, the traditional demarcation between "civilized" China and the "barbarian" lands. The very name of the city, Harbin, sounds jarringly foreign to Chinese ears. Because of the weak presence of the Chinese state in the area, both Russia and Japan were able to implement de facto colonization of Manchuria without overt military conquest. Founded in 1898, the city spent its first thirty years under Russian, then Soviet, control through the China Eastern Railroad (CER). After 1917, Bolshevik and counterrevolutionary forces struggled over control of the CER, and Harbin became a haven for White Russians who fled to the city with all the wealth they could carry. Meanwhile, China fragmented under rival regional warlords, and Japan stepped up its position in Manchuria (Lensen 1974).

Despite political uncertainty, the city gained fame as the "Paris of the East" for its glamorous style. An American scholar visiting in 1929–30 declared Harbin more "modern" than either Beijing or Nanjing (Lattimore 1932:260). Even today, the fanciful European architecture of Harbin's Central Avenue echoes those glory days, or (to switch to a socialist narrative) serves as a reminder of the oppression and exploitation that maintained that glory. Harbiners like to tell visitors that each of the cobblestones on Central Avenue cost a worker's monthly wage.

In 1932, the Japanese army captured Harbin—a coup which paved the way for the establishment of the Manchukuo puppet state (Young 1998:58). To provide labor for Japan's industrial and military needs, by 1947 the city's population had grown to 800,000. Most of the immigrants came from Shandong and Hebei, and many of Harbin's current residents will still call themselves "Shandong people" or "Hebei people" even if they have never set foot in those provinces. My own family also emigrated from Shandong Province at this time (though in a completely different direction), which was a point of connection between my informants and myself.

After Japan's surrender in 1945, Harbin was quickly claimed by the Chinese Communist Party and used as a base in its civil war against the Nationalists. In fact, Harbin was the first large urban center under significant CCP control. As a result, the city became a "testing ground for the new stage of the Chinese revolution," the place where the Party tried out its policies and plans for urban management and transformation (Clausen and Thogersen 1995:151). Under state socialism, Harbin enjoyed its second "Golden Age," though one which contrasted starkly with its former glory as the "Paris of the East." In the 1950s, Harbin became one of China's main centers for heavy industry, benefiting from its geographical and cultural proximity to the Soviet Union, as well as from Heilongjiang's abundant natural resources, which include oil, natural gas, lumber, and coal. By 1965, Heilongjiang ranked fourth among China's twenty-five provinces and "autonomous regions" in terms of wages for workers and staff.[2] It also ranked fourth in overall state investment, despite the

Figure 1. Location of Heilongjiang Province (SOURCE: LARA SCOTT)

fact that it ranked twentieth in the size of its working population (Hsueh et al. 1993).

Since Harbin had a disproportionate number of state-owned heavy industry work units, its residents enjoyed some of the best jobs available in the socialist economic system. In the decade following the revolution, Chinese migrants doubled the population to 1.6 million, as "Southerners" poured in to fill Harbin's enormous industrial factories. Meanwhile, the non-Chinese population emigrated out. By 1964, there were only 900 Russian residents left, and for the first time in Harbin's history, it could be seen as a thoroughly Chinese city.

Harbin in the Reform Era

As Heilongjiang province and Harbin benefited from the socialist economic system, it is not surprising that they suffered when market reforms undermined that system. State enterprises in heavy industry were designed to produce for the state, not to sell to customers, and as a result they faced insurmountable obstacles in adjusting to the new market economy. By the 1990s, Harbin's industrial factories, once the source of the city's pride, had become symbols of economic inefficiency and backwardness. Of course, these problems were not unique to Harbin or to China. Even in the capitalist West, there has been a shift from Keynesian or Fordist state-regulated corporations to smaller, more flexible, customer-driven, niche-based enterprises (Harvey 1990; Storper 1990, 1992). The Northeast is China's Rust Belt.

In the late 1990s, for the sake of reform, uncompetitive state enterprises began to lay off (*xia gang*) large numbers of workers. Technically, xia gang is not the same as a layoff. (The term itself was borrowed from the military, and would be more accurately translated as "furlough." It had never been used in this context before, and my informants admitted that they initially had no idea what the strange word meant.) Work units are still responsible to their xia gang employees; they are supposed to put them back to work, for example, if the firm is able to support them again. In reality, however, Harbiners understood that xia gang was pretty much the same as a layoff, no matter what euphemisms were used. Xia gang anxiety reached a feverish pitch in 1998, when rumors spread through the city that not only were state enterprises poised to xia gang huge numbers of employees, but that government agencies would suffer a 30 percent reduction in staff.

In 1997, the proportion of Heilongjiang's urban residents still working in the state and collective sectors was higher than the national average, though not the highest in the nation (see table 1). Moreover, only 4.1 percent of the province's urban workforce was employed in foreign, joint venture, or private companies (the so-called *sanzi* firms), in contrast to the national urban average of 5.4 percent. Statistics from 1995 reveal that the proportion of contract employees was also quite low in Heilongjiang, a sign that fewer state and collective enterprises had taken on market characteristics than in other areas. However, the number of household businesses, or *getihu*, matched the national average (16.6 percent of the working population), indicating that Heilongjiang residents were neither especially reluctant nor unusually eager to take advantage of the new business opportunities (State Statistical Bureau 1998).

Once the economic powerhouse of industrial China, by the 1990s Harbin found itself in second place even in the economically depressed Northeast, after the port city of Dalian. Many of Harbin's residents felt some pain at the thought of their city's lost glory, as well as a bit of "red eye disease" (i.e., jealousy) toward their wealthier neighbors in the South. One small business owner described their subservience to the South in terms of economic flow: "This is how it works. There's some product that goes out of style in Hong Kong, so they sell a pile of it off to the Southerners. Then it goes out of style

Table 1. Percentage of Urban Employees by Sector, 1997

Province	State	Collective	*Sanzi*
Guangdong	48.1	15.7	15.0
Zhejiang	48.3	24.4	8.9
Fujian	51.3	12.9	20.4
Anhui	56.8	18.8	4.4
Liaoning	57.9	23.0	5.4
Shanghai	58.4	15.1	14.8
Jiangsu	58.7	24.3	7.5
Chongqing	59.3	16.9	4.5
Hunan	59.6	13.9	1.9
Henan	61.4	19.1	6.1
Tianjin	61.5	18.2	10.9
Jilin	61.5	16.2	4.0
Shandong	61.7	17.3	7.4
Hubei	61.9	13.8	5.2
Heilongjiang	**64.4**	**16.4**	**3.1**
Jiangxi	65	13	1.4
Sichuan	65.3	16.7	5.3
Nei Menggu	66.9	13.4	2.7
Hebei	68.1	14.1	4.1
Guangxi	70	10.4	3.9
Beijing	70.9	13.7	10.8
Guizhou	72.2	11.3	1.9
Hainan	72.4	6.8	6.5
Shanxi	72.5	16.1	1.8
Shaanxi	73.4	11.3	1.8
Yunnan	74.4	11.6	2.6
Gansu	75	12.6	1.1
Ningxia	75.2	10.4	2.0
Tibet	75.9	5.3	—[a]
Qinghai	76.5	10.2	1.1
Xinjiang	79.2	7.7	1.4
National	*54.6*	*14.3*	*5.4*

Source: *China Statistical Yearbook 1998*, Table 5-4
Note: The percentages do not add up to 100 since the figures do not include the self-employed or those working in very small family firms.
[a] Data unavailable.

in the South, so the Southerners sell it to us hick Northerners here in Harbin. Then it goes out of style here in the Northeast, and we try to sell it to the Russians. But it's out of style in Russia, too, so we're stuck with a big pile of junk."

In the 1990s, Harbiners told me with absolute conviction that Heilongjiang was the second poorest region in China, next to Tibet. During that decade, I heard the exact same claim in several other provinces, including Shaanxi, Jiangxi, and Anhui. In fact, I began to wonder whether people in every region of China were convinced that they lived in the "second poorest" area in the country. Although people in Heilongjiang were convinced that they had been bypassed by the benefits of reforms, their economic position was actually closer to the middle of the pack.

In the mid-1990s, household income in Heilongjiang was somewhat lower than the national average, but as the province's wealthiest city, Harbin clearly had benefited from China's recent economic boom (see table 3). The city had its share of gleaming department stores. The average citizen was enjoying a higher standard of living than before, dining on seafood and investing in washing machines and English lessons. Meanwhile, the nouveaux riches were visible everywhere, clad in designer clothes and clutching tiny cell phones as they drove their Jeep sports utility vehicles. Harbin had even begun to recapture its "Paris of the East" reputation as one of the most fashion-obsessed cities in China. On warm days, beautifully made-up girls once again strolled down Central Avenue's cobblestones just as they did in the 1930s, flaunting the latest fashions.

I chose to study Harbin in part because it was not one of the PRC's post-socialist boomtowns, not Shanghai, Shenzhen, Guangzhou, or even Beijing, the cities which habitually attract popular and scholarly attention. The fact that my respondents were overwhelmingly positive about the reforms and optimistic about their futures was more striking because of Harbin's position in China's Rust Belt, and its position as a target for massive state enterprise layoffs. Moreover, 1997–98, when I did the bulk of my research, was when Harbin's economic woes were at their worst and when xia gang anxieties reached their peak, at least according to the perspective of informants three years later. On the other hand, Harbin is also not an isolated mountain village in China's western regions, where market reforms have decimated the local economy. Instead, Harbin lies somewhere between the two extremes of the

Table 2. Regional GDP, 1997 (in 100 million RMB)

Province	GDP	Rank
Guangdong	7,316	1
Jiangsu	6,680	2
Shandong	6,650	3
Zhejiang	4,638	4
Henan	4,079	5
Hebei	3,954	6
Liaoning	3,490	7
Hubei	3,450	8
Shanghai	3,360	9
Sichuan	3,320	10
Fujian	3,000	11
Hunan	2,993	12
Heilongjiang	**2,708**	**13**
Anhui	2,670	14
Guangxi	2,015	15
Beijing	1,810	16
Jiangxi	1,715	17
Yunnan	1,644	18
Shanxi	1,480	19
Jilin	1,447	20
Chongqing	1,350	21
Shaanxi	1,326	22
Tianjin	1,240	23
Nei Menggu	1,095	24
Xinjiang	1,050	25
Guizhou	793	26
Gansu	781	27
Hainan	410	28
Ningxia	210	29
Qinghai	202	30
Tibet	77	31

Source: Data from *China Statistical Yearbook*, 1998

Table 3. Average Urban Annual Household Income, 1995 (in yuan)

Province	H. Income	Rank
Guangdong	7,445	1
Shanghai	7,196	2
Beijing	6,238	3
Zhejiang	6,225	4
Tianjin	4,931	5
Guangxi	4,809	6
Hainan	4,803	7
Hunan	4,705	8
Jiangsu	4,647	9
Fujian	4,511	10
Shandong	4,265	11
Xinjiang	4,184	12
Yunnan	4,113	13
Hubei	4,032	14
Sichuan	4,005	15
Guizhou	3,935	16
Hebei	3,923	17
Anhui	3,797	18
Liaoning	3,708	19
Ningxia	3,387	20
Jiangxi	3,381	21
Heilongjiang	**3,377**	**22**
Qinghai	3,320	23
Shaanxi	3,311	24
Shanxi	3,307	25
Henan	3,302	26
Jilin	3,176	27
Gansu	3,156	28
I. Mongolia	2,873	29
Tibet		30
Average	*4,288*	

booming coastal cities and the suffering inland regions, experiencing both the advantages and disadvantages of the market reforms.

In addition, Harbin's international connections can be seen as both unique and representative of a larger trend. Its experiences with international trade differ from those of cities with strong connections to the wealthy capitalist centers of Hong Kong, Taiwan, Japan, or even South Korea, and they also differ from inland cities located far from international borders. However, these experiences also illustrate the growing role of international linkages in everyday life, as ordinary Chinese citizens become more connected and vulnerable to international networks and events. Local businesspeople, even peddlers, were increasingly attuned to the flow of goods and people between Harbin, Russia, South Korea, and (to a much lesser extent) Japan, Taiwan, and eastern Europe.

Profiles of Harbin Work Organizations

So far I have described Harbin from a historical and demographic perspective. But how did the city look from the perspective of an ordinary resident contemplating career choices? In this section, I describe five workplaces, ranging from a government agency to an open street market, and the stratification institutions, forms of capital, and common narratives associated with each one.

Government Agency

The Provincial Disability Services Agency, a government organization, was founded in 1988, when the state became more concerned about extending welfare services to disabled people. Most of the employees were conservatively dressed by contemporary Harbin standards. The women wore their hair tied back in buns or cut pragmatically short. The higher-ranking cadres dressed slightly more fashionably and colorfully; the head of the organization favored vibrant red sweaters with lipstick to match. The cadres at the Disability Agency enjoyed many substantial non-cash benefits: 100 yuan of free telephone service each month, excellent medical coverage, shuttle transportation to and from work, and highly subsidized housing. (The largest and most luxurious apartments I saw in Harbin inevitably belonged to cadres.) Also, the work unit often sent members back to school to further their educations.

In China, as in many other societies, serving the disabled is not a high-status endeavor. Consequently, the physical infrastructure of the Disability

Agency compared poorly to some of the other government organizations I studied, especially the Public Security Bureau (PSB) and the Harbin Communist Party Headquarters. The work unit was located in a slightly dilapidated wood and brick building in a courtyard hidden from the street and almost impossible to locate without a guide. Although the agency provided a full array of socialist benefits to its employees, geographically it was not a self-sufficient compound, and many benefits had to be obtained off-site. The offices were comfortable, even cozy, outfitted with armchairs and couches, and there was a rather elegant conference room on the top level. However, the halls were dark with uneven wooden floors, the furniture worn, and the canteen was a dimly lit, gray concrete box serving rather plain fare. One of the employees was so embarrassed about the quality and quantity of food available to me at lunch that (over my protests) she ran back to the kitchen to fix an omelette.

Also, a much higher proportion of female employees worked at the Disability Agency, whereas men predominated at the PSB and Party Headquarters. Not surprisingly, compared to those high-status agencies, this work unit had fewer resources to distribute to its employees. Although I was told that all state cadres of the same rank should receive comparable salaries, this was clearly not the case. The department head (*tingzhang*) at the Disability Agency earned only 800 yuan a month, while a cadre of the same rank at the Heilongjiang Province Discipline Supervisory Committee earned 1,200 yuan, with 500 extra tacked on for "extra duties." Both of these cadres were of about the same age and had similar levels of education and experience. Branch-level cadres (*kezhang*) at the Disability Agency made between 600 and 750 yuan a month, depending on experience, about twice as much as a low-level factory worker.

To achieve their current occupation, the cadres at the Disability Agency depended on political, human, and social capital, in descending order of significance. All of my interviewees there were Party members. Although I was told that Party membership was no longer a requirement for a cadre career, clearly it had been in the recent past. With Party membership, it was possible to gain cadre position even with very low levels of education. Two of the cadres at the Disability Agency were unable to finish middle school before starting their careers, due to the Cultural Revolution. After stints of rural labor, one entered the military, while the other was assigned to an administrative organization in a county town. Both rose through the ranks by performing their duties well, eventually joining the Party and achieving cadre status. After they joined the

Disability Agency, they were both sent back to school to earn vocational college degrees.

Even though political capital was sufficient to gain cadre status in the past, human capital was becoming increasingly important in the government sector, and this was reflected at the Disability Agency. Respondents in their thirties had bachelor's or vocational college degrees. One thirty-five-year-old woman from a county town explained that she entered college in order to obtain a city job and residency. After graduating, she did indeed get assigned an urban job as a middle-school teacher. However, as she found teaching difficult and low paying, she and her parents used *guanxi* connections to engineer the difficult switch to the Disability Agency. Although she was a Party member, clearly it was her educational credentials, especially her English skills, which had made more of a difference in her career. Although uneducated people could become low-level cadres, a college or vocational degree was the prerequisite for higher positions. Most cadres at the division level (*chuzhang*) and above had tertiary educations which they had obtained by testing into college (or vocational college) as adolescents, rather than from being sent back to school as adults by the work unit. I should note that the chuzhang or division level was "the rank that matters, the level at which your life gets better," according to my subjects, who compared it with getting tenure as a professor.

Overall, the people at the Disability Agency seemed to be content with their work unit. They believed that they were doing something worthy, contributing to society in a meaningful way. They complained a bit about their low salaries, usually with narratives focused on the market sector, where "peddlers" (*xiao fan*) made a disturbing amount of money "through dishonest means"—or so the cadres claimed. Although the possibility of layoffs (xia gang) did hang over the Disability Agency, it did not seem to be a source of great anxiety. Several of the interviewees insisted that there were no plans to lay off anyone at all at the organization. However, others admitted that it was quite likely that this work unit would be a target of government downsizing.

Even those who were convinced that their work unit would be hit by layoffs claimed that they were not afraid of the possibility. For example, a former military man declared, "I'm not nervous. Even though this time they're saying there's going to be xia gang in the government administration, I'm not nervous. Because I'm at the right age. If I get laid off, let's say, at my age, it's still easy to find another job. Maybe I can't find an ideal job, but I can find one. So

I'm not worried." Since he was forty-two years old, I was not sure I shared his optimism. His supervisor, the department head, was also contemplating her chances "out in society":

> For me to go out to work, I think I'd do okay. I'd make it. As a government official, well, I think management work would be pretty suitable. And also, my writing's pretty good. At least I think I'm pretty okay. But I'm not really ready to "jump into the sea." I'd have to work for someone. The best case is that I'd get a higher position working for someone. If it's not the best case, if it's really low work, well, I'll just go home. Let my husband support me. [Laughs]

Traditional State Enterprise

The Agricultural Machine Factory was located in a semi-suburban section of Harbin. The factory was started in 1956 by combining several small factories together. At full strength, it employed 2,000 workers, ranking it as a mid-sized enterprise by Harbin standards. During the Maoist era, as a heavy industry enterprise, the Agricultural Machine Factory was considered a good place to work. Even in the late 1990s, the setting was still attractive. Within its surrounding wall, this self-sufficient work unit had a surprising amount of green space and trees. It almost felt like a college campus, except that in the middle of the grass lawn a sample of their enormous products was displayed: five gigantic pieces of agricultural machinery, gleaming in Crayola-bright primary colors.

The Agricultural Machine Factory had experienced hard times during the reform era. Over 1,600 employees had already been "furloughed" (xia gang), leaving only several hundred. As a result, the work unit had an abandoned air. The buildings were run-down, and (as I ruefully discovered when I needed to use a toilet) the facilities had not been renovated in decades. In contrast to the Disability Agency, where people were quite energetic and optimistic, the Agricultural Machine Factory seemed enveloped in a feeling of quiet resignation, even despair. The remaining employees had seen their friends and family members laid off and were understandably anxious about the future of their own jobs. Their salaries ranged between 350–500 yuan. In theory, they would receive bonuses of up to 200 additional yuan depending on sales, but no one was expecting to receive any bonuses at all. Also in contrast to the Disability Agency, almost all the employees were male, reflecting both the Chinese bias against women in heavy industry, and the common practice of laying off women before men.

All of the employees I interviewed had been at this work unit for their entire working lives, but their career trajectories depended on their age.[3] For example, the fifty year old had been assigned to the Agricultural Machine Factory after middle-school graduation to be a factory worker. During his thirty-three-year tenure there, he had been moved all over the organization, from engineering to sales and back again, all according to the work unit's needs rather than his own desires. At the time of the interview, he was back in sales, traveling all over the country to drum up interest in the factory's products. He wore a slightly shabby sport coat, in contrast to the dark blue cotton work suits on all the other employees.

Workers who were in their forties had their careers disrupted by the Cultural Revolution. They spent their youths "sent-down" to the countryside, and obtained their jobs in the work unit through the institution of "substitution" (*dingti*), i.e., by taking a parent's position upon retirement. As one worker put it, "Now that's no longer allowed, but at that time, there was no choice. Now there is a lot of choice, so no one would want to do it." With children in school and more years until retirement, they were very concerned about xia gang (layoffs). Unlike the cadres at the Disability Agency, these workers had little human capital, and their work unit could not provide them with more schooling opportunities. They assumed that their political capital (Party membership) would not help them. Utilizing narratives of "outside" to contemplate their opportunities "out in society," they could only conclude that they had no chance to succeed in the wild and risky world of the market.

I also interviewed one worker who was still in his twenties, who displayed an energy and ambition that the older workers lacked. He had been assigned to this work unit after graduation from vocational high school. He recalled that at that time, in 1990, "I wanted this job because at that time it was considered a good job, state enterprise. This was the time before xia gang, after all. And everything was new, so I liked it here. It was considered good work, though not the best." Although the work unit had not lived up to his expectations, he was doing his best to improve his situation. Since the factory could not send him back to school, he tested into vocational college by himself and was currently taking night classes for a degree in economic management. Also, he was applying for Party membership and aiming for cadre status.

Unlike the older workers, who felt that their personal fortunes were tied to their sinking work unit, this young man's ambitions were not confined to the Agricultural Machine Factory:

> I want to be a cadre! A good ambition, right?. . . . But not necessarily in an enterprise. I'll see what kind of opportunities come up. But I'll work hard to make it happen. I've done okay here so far. Last year, I got a Harbin City Pioneering Prize, second honors, for intensely doing my cadre work, for intensely pioneering. . . . I just want to find a place where I can develop my own good qualities, where I can work hard and do a bit of something. It doesn't matter what it is, as long as I have the opportunity to develop.

Although his ambitions were to become a cadre, his strategy was quite different than it would have been before the reforms. Like the other young people I interviewed at other workplaces, he treated work organizations like steps on his own individualized career path. Despite his socialist rhetoric ("intensely doing my cadre work," "intensely pioneering"), it was clear that, in his mind, the real purpose of work was his own personal development (*fazhan ziji*).

Hybrid State Enterprise

The University New and High Technology Park and Business Group was the result of a market socialist experiment. In order to shore up dwindling state funding in the 1990s, the regime encouraged, even pressured, state organizations ranging from the post office to research institutes to start for-profit business ventures. The results could be disconcerting: for a few years, the hottest discos in Beijing were managed by the People's Liberation Army. Prior to the late 1980s, the University had been completely dependent on state funding. In 1992, to seek the funds necessary to maintain its position as one of China's preeminent science and technology schools, the president decided that the University needed a market venture. At that time, he approached a state enterprise cadre to head up the project for him.

Although the original idea was to capitalize upon the "synergy" between the school and the Park to develop, produce, and market technologically advanced products, this plan went almost immediately awry. The Technology Park was to be constructed on land located adjacent to the University, donated by the city. However, the Technology Park leaders immediately realized that this land was prime commercial real estate along one of Harbin's major traffic arteries, near one of the city's key retail centers—and that technological factories can be built anywhere. Consequently, in the mid-1990s, by a large sign proclaiming "The University New and High Technology Park," the firm constructed a large department store; two gleaming office towers over twenty stories high; an upscale hotel, restaurant, nightclub, and bowling alley; and acres of multilevel apartment buildings. (While doing my research, I lived in one of the apartment buildings, shopped at the department store, and bowled at the bowling alley.) The "Technology Park" also purchased several vacation resorts outside the city, and, in 1998, the enterprise built a large underground mall under a major intersection near the University.

In an attempt to live up to its "Technology Park" name, beginning in the mid-1990s, several industrial parks were constructed in Harbin's suburbs to manufacture "high technology" items. Despite some minor early successes, these factories were generally both costly and unprofitable. Meanwhile, a "Science and Technology Market," developed to showcase products from the Park and University, completely failed. By 1997, the space was being used by ordinary peddlers to hawk combs and underwear. In other words, the venture was not a "Technology Park." In 1998, as if to confirm this, the firm changed its name to the "University New and High Technology Business Group." In that year, the Business Group employed over a thousand people. But, unlike a traditional state enterprise with the same number of employees, the Business Group could not be seen as a single work unit, but a collection of disparate workplaces connected only at the top. The maids in the hotel, the engineers at the factories, and the legal advisors in the administrative building experienced completely different work conditions.

Because the venture had been founded by a state enterprise cadre unattached to the University, most of the Technology Business Group's leadership came from political, rather than academic, backgrounds, and few had genuine college degrees. University intellectuals were unimpressed with these cadres' political capital and considered them uneducated and crassly opportunistic, reliant on shady connections rather than real competence. Professors developing products would deliberately avoid marketing them through the Technology Business Group. As a result, by 1997, the University and the Business Group were two separate entities, yoked together uncomfortably by the same name and geographic proximity.

Figure 2. One of the University Technology Business Group's hotels, ca. 2004 (PHOTO BY AUTHOR)

Given the sprawling nature of the Technology Business Group, it would be impractical for me to describe every enterprise it managed. Instead, I will focus mainly on the administrative building and one of the industrial factories. In sharp contrast to the decrepit air of the Agricultural Machine Factory, the Business Group clearly had a great deal of money to spend. The central administrative offices were housed on the top floors of one of the twin looming office towers, gleaming white, which it had built near the University. Inside, the administrative offices were pristine with chrome and marble trimmings, and they offered views of Harbin from the perspective of a conquering giant. The industrial factory was not as opulent, but the buildings were also bright with newness, a shining white compound in the midst of a field, its modernistic shapes hinting at technological wonders within. Both areas were under construction, with builders scurrying to and fro with materials. Upon closer inspection, it was clear that the facilities were not as well built as they should have been, but from a distance they were quite impressive, and they offered the impression that the unfinished areas under construction would no doubt be even more impressive.

At the administrative building, men (predominantly) and women in fashionable suits rushed about, working longer and harder hours than I saw anywhere else in Harbin. There was a general air of feverish ambition, and people seemed to feel that they were part of something big, something new and exciting. In contrast, beneath the glossy exterior, the industrial factory was almost dead. Construction delays and equipment snafus meant that the factory was not producing anything, one whole year after it had been scheduled to open. Engineers (all male) and support staff (mostly female) were on the payroll but had very little to do most days besides attending an occasional meeting or modifying the factory plans. One engineer studied English through books and tapes, the secretary knitted some clothes for her daughter, and everyone battled boredom and frustration. Employees did not even bother to suit up in their bright blue work uniforms. However, a nearby factory (also managed by the Business Group) was up and running, and morale was much higher there.

Was the Technology Business Group an "inside" organization or an "outside" one? Basically, it was neither, or both. Employees, including both managers and workers, would smile and call it a *sibuxiang* ("four-not-like"), a mythical Chinese beast which was made up of parts from four different animals and therefore "not like" any of them.

On one hand, the Business Group was clearly profit motivated and had a great deal of autonomy from the state. In contrast to the government agency and the traditional state enterprise, it seemed to operate more or less in a free-labor market. Although it was possible for employees to be assigned a position in the enterprise, or to be transferred here formally from another state work unit, these cases were rare. Instead, many of the Technology Business Group's employees had found their jobs on their own, most commonly through newspaper advertisements, and were hired according to human capital: their skills, educational degrees, professional credentials, experience, and scores on enterprise-administered examinations. Alternatively, employees gained their position through social capital, using guanxi connections. This was especially common for upper-management positions. In contrast to government agencies and traditional state enterprises, Party membership and other forms of political capital did not seem to matter at all here.

Like a private work organization, the Business Group did not offer an "iron rice bowl" for its employees. In fact, it offered less security than most capitalist firms. Most employees had no formal contracts at all and had been hired in a most ad hoc fashion. "If the boss doesn't like you one day, then you're out," explained an administrator. It was unclear if the Business Group would ever manage to organize its retirement and pension system. Employees had no illusion that this would be lifetime employment, and many were making contingency plans. In fact, most of the employees under the age of thirty-five not only expected their positions to be short term, but they wanted them to be that way. They saw their careers as a series of steps to take, one by one, and each job was simply one of the steps—a place to gain experience before moving on to bigger and better things. A technician in his twenties explained: "I've already worked in this industry for three years. There are still some things that I haven't learned yet. What I have to think about is when I've just about learned all I can learn from here, when I've progressed as far as I can go. Then if there's an opportunity, I'll go."

On the other hand, there were work features which definitely stemmed from the state sector. For example, the salary structure was distinctly "socialist." In 1997, workers and shop clerks earned between 350 and 500 yuan a month, and engineers between 500 and 750. Managers at the Technology Business Group made between 800 and 1,200 yuan, and the Chairman of the Board took home 1,800. These salaries were only slightly higher than those at the Disability Agency and Machine Factory. Among my interviewees in the private sector, even low-level managers earned 3,000 or 4,000 yuan, while engineers could make 5,000 or more. While the Technology Business Group's salaries were low, it offered more socialist work benefits than would be available at private firms, such as on-site housing, canteens, commuter shuttles, and even bags of groceries and bolts of cloth. The industrial factories were self-sufficient, walled-off work units, reminiscent of their traditional socialist predecessors.

Employees in their forties and fifties tended to see the Business Group as an "outside" organization. For them, coming to this enterprise was *xia hai*—"jumping into the sea." For example, a fifty-eight-year-old administrator described his move from the University to the Technology Business Group as a xia hai narrative:

We're all one work unit, the school and the Group. One work unit, but there is a regulation: if you come over here, you have to burn your bridges. Because the school still eats from the iron rice bowl. . . . Because this is a totally outside enterprise, while the school is run by the state. There, your salary comes from the state. But out here, you prosper or fail with the enterprise. So if you want to do that, you have to throw away your iron rice bowl. You can't go back.

In contrast, younger people employed at the Business Group saw themselves as still working on the "inside," while "jumping into the sea" would require doing something more drastic. For example, a thirty-five-year-old manager at the department store insisted: "I don't feel any need to jump into the sea. Also, if you do, you have a 50 percent chance to either succeed or fail. The risk is too high. I never really thought about going to a private or foreign company because I've always had good opportunities to develop. So I haven't had the need to go outside, or else I would have." Other young people explained that working at the Business Group was an opportunity to gain skills and prepare for "jumping into the sea."

Private Company

I now turn to the world of the market, to work organizations which were undoubtedly on the "outside." In Harbin in the late 1990s, there was a social distinction between "good businesspeople" on one hand, and *getihu* ("individual businessperson") on the other, a bifurcation which I will analyze in chapter 5. In the popular narratives, getihu were street peddlers, "standing on the corner with a cart of clothes," while "good" or "real" businesspeople wore suits, carried briefcases, and worked in offices. In this section, I will be focusing on one such "real" businesswoman and her business, the Pizza Parlor, a large and flourishing restaurant serving foreigners and the nouveau riche. I will address petty bourgeois getihu in the next subsection.

In comparison to the Agricultural Machine Factory or the Technology Business Group, the Pizza Parlor was a very small workplace, with about two dozen employees. When I interviewed the owner in 1998, the restaurant had been open for only five months. Fortunately for her, the new restaurant had an excellent location, on a major intersection close to one of the city's major shopping districts and within walking distance of the Russian Market. It was also not far from the university with the highest concentration of foreign students in Harbin. The restaurant was the kind of contemporary organization that begs to be used as an example of "globalization" or "postmodernism." The

Figure 3. The Pizza Parlor, ca. 2004 (PHOTO BY AUTHOR)

Pizza Parlor was a franchise member of a South Korean chain, and it served supposedly Italian food to mostly Russian customers in a Chinese city. To top it off, the restaurant was located in a Japanese-style building which had once housed Japanese officials during Harbin's Manchukuo days. The menu, which offered pork chops and Indonesian curry along with pizza and pasta, described its wares in Chinese, Russian, and (thanks to my translation) English. A meal for two here cost between thirty and eighty yuan, too costly for Harbin's working class.

In 1998, the restaurant was brightly lit and sparkling clean, decorated in a fair imitation of a North American pizza place, with Budweiser signs and an exposed kitchen fronted by a counter. There were twenty-six tables in two rooms. On TV sets MTV played, competing with U.S. top-40 pop music blasting over the speakers. The Chinese wait staff was young and attractive, dressed smartly in white shirts, black tuxedo vests, and bow ties. The clientele was young, sophisticated, and dressed in the latest style. By 2004, the restaurant had been renovated in a more sophisticated bistro style, though the menu was the same.

Besides Russians and foreign students, its customers were Harbin's new money. In fact, it immediately became an informal club for the city's business elite, making it an ideal place for me to meet and interview entrepreneurs. As these businesspeople discovered that I could translate and edit English-language documents, I became one of the unofficial services offered by the restaurant. The entrepreneurs I interviewed had founded and were currently managing private companies worth hundreds of thousands to millions of yuan. The smallest firm had five employees; the largest had hundreds. Most of their owners were between the ages of thirty-five and forty-five, though there were people as young as twenty-three who were clearly on this path. All of these businesspeople had either bachelor's or vocational college degrees, and all but one had tested into their tertiary institutions rather than getting in through their work units.

The owner of the Pizza Parlor was in her mid-thirties, though she looked much younger than women of comparable age at the Disability Agency because of her long unbound hair and trendy clothes. Like most of the other entrepreneurs I interviewed, she had a high level of human capital, with a bachelor's degree in engineering. After graduating from college in 1985, the owner had worked as an engineer at two highly ranked state enterprises for five years. Similarly, all the entrepreneurs I interviewed had once had good jobs in the state sector, either as cadres in government agencies, or as intellectual "experts" in state enterprises or universities. Most were members of the Communist Party. In other words, these people had both human and political capital (and no doubt social capital as well), and had enjoyed relatively high positions under the socialist system. They chose to "go out into society" voluntarily, and did so from a position of relative strength.

When they chose to become entrepreneurs, they tended to do so in careful stages, as though they were loath to give up their state-sector guarantees until they were absolutely certain of success. Several worked for private or foreign companies to gain experience and guanxi ties before starting up their own business. For example, the owner of the Pizza Parlor worked as a tour guide for a large hotel for four years before starting her own travel agency in 1994. Her connections in the travel industry led her to open a Chinese restaurant in Russia. Moving back to Harbin in 1996, she started a development corporation to work with Russian entrepreneurs, but then became involved with the pizza franchise in 1997. During this entire period of time, she never officially quit her engineering position at the state enterprise. Instead, she strung together a series of fake sick leaves and "study" leaves so that her name remained on the employee roster—and so that she could return there if life out in the market did not work out.

Such leaves of absence (both formal and illicit) were common, as was the practice of moonlighting. As a matter of fact, a number of these entrepreneurs were still working at their state-sector jobs, even though their private companies had obviously succeeded. They explained that their state-sector positions required very little effort to maintain, often as little as one day of work a week. Not only did this provide them with a safety net, but in many cases it actually helped their businesses. For example, one professor kept his university position because it enhanced his intellectual credentials—manifesting his human capital through symbolic capital. Two of my respondents worked for state trading companies and ran their own private trading companies on the side, a situation which was obviously advantageous for obtaining business opportunities. When I asked if this could be construed as a conflict of interest, they seemed honestly surprised.

When these people finally decided to start their businesses, they turned to personal connections for financing. Everyone in Harbin agreed that bank loans were impossible to obtain unless one had guanxi with someone at the bank. Presumably after one had achieved success, it was possible to acquire such a special relationship. Because these entrepreneurs had more social capital than most people, they were able to raise larger amounts of economic capital through friends and kin than the getihu described below.

Besides the owner, there were a number of other people working at the Pizza Parlor. As I mentioned before, the staff was young, mostly in their early twenties, and so uniformly good looking that I was convinced that they were hired at least in part for their appearance. They earned 500 to 550 yuan a month, but received no non-cash benefits other than one meal a day at the restaurant. Clearly, the restaurant was a workplace, rather than a work unit. Most of the employees were not from Harbin but from the smaller county towns surrounding the city. Because they did not have urban registration permits, they were forced to find their own housing arrangements with friends and relatives or in college dormitories.

All of the staff members I interviewed were hoping to someday become entrepreneurs. In their words, they wanted to "be my own boss" and to "depend on myself" (*kao ziji*) rather than the state. Their ambitions, then, focused on economic capital. This put them in conflict with their parents, who wanted them to settle down with a "real" job in a "proper work unit," to choose political capital and security over economic capital. In fact, a number of these young people had state-sector positions waiting for them at home. One explained to me that her father was the head of a state enterprise and was holding a job for her. "I feel conflicted," she told me. "I want to go home. But I also want to choose to do the work that I like. . . . I want something where my work time isn't set and controlled. If I had the opportunity and the ability, I'd go into business for myself."

To pursue their dreams, their strategies focused on human capital; most were enrolled at vocational high schools or colleges, while others engaged in self-study courses. In general, they saw political capital as irrelevant. None of these young people were Party members, nor did they think joining the Party was particularly important, though some saw it as a nice honor. Their studies focused on those subjects that they believed would be useful in the market: English, computer programming, accounting, and public relations. They treated their jobs like courses as well, jumping from one position to another to pick up skills and knowledge. Although they were quite pleased to be working at the Pizza Parlor, which they saw as a "modern" establishment with high standards, they saw their jobs there as steps along a path to greater things. For example, one young man, of Korean descent, had already switched careers once, even though he was only twenty years old. He had worked for two years as a computer technician at a Korean joint venture. He explained, "I actually liked the work there, but I felt that I should change my environment, change my place. Other people also told me this, said that young people shouldn't have a set job. They should start new things." He added, "I plan to stay here for a period of time. When I meet another opportunity that I think is fresh and new, I'll take it." Someday, when he had gained enough "social experience," he would be able to consider "jumping into the sea" and starting his own business.

Street Market

Of course, a street market is not a work organization in the sense that a government agency or a business firm is. Instead, it is a geographical space and a nexus in the circulation of goods and people. In the late 1990s, Harbin had all kinds of street markets, ranging from the neighborhood food and vegetable markets to more elaborate retail centers. In all cases, Harbin's markets were filled with independent operators, who brought in their own goods and sold them, and rarely contained chain stores.

The Russian Market was not as glamorous as the underground malls or fashion markets, but it occupied a niche well above the local food markets. As its nickname indicates, it catered primarily to Russian traders, who purchased large batches of goods to carry back to Russia in gigantic sacks. After the Soviet Union fell in 1991, a number of Russians came to the city to look for trade opportunities. They congregated in the old Russian neighborhood, often staying at the Daqing Hotel. Soon, the Daqing Hotel became the center of an informal market where Chinese and Russians traded goods. In 1992, the local district government took over the area and made it an official market, with rented stalls and tax collectors. Over the next several years, the Market became a central clearinghouse for Russian goods entering Harbin and Chinese goods leaving for Russia.

By the late 1990s, the tottering Russian economy, increasing trade regulations, and border difficulties were diminishing the Russian trade, and the flow of Russian customers was often reduced to a trickle. Fortunately, as the Asian Financial Crisis had forced many South Korean firms to seek new markets, South Korean traders and products became a presence in the Russian Market in 1997–98. The getihu in the Market liked to joke that they were all "multinational companies," selling South Korean goods to Russian customers, who sometimes carried their products all the way to eastern Europe.

In the 1990s, there were two arches marking the entrances to the Russian Market, with its official name ("The People's Trade Market") stenciled in gold calligraphy. Two streets, one of which was completely closed to traffic, were lined with numbered green metal stalls. Between the stalls, in the middle of the street, more merchants set up their wares. In 1998, the stalls could be rented for about 450 yuan a month, when all the fees were included. Since every possible space was rigged to display goods, potential customers were attacked by a visual barrage of color: neon-bright swimsuits, gaudy watches and binoculars, knockoffs of Nike and Adidas sports bags, garishly painted Russian dolls and gleaming silver tea sets, leather jackets, and fur stoles with little paws and plastic eyes. During Harbin's bitter and long-lasting winters, the getihu behind the stalls huddled in fur caps and the ubiquitous padded green army overcoats of the poor and working class. However, not everyone at the Russian Market was forced to work out in the cold. Some of the retail areas were located inside. There were several buildings which rented out booth space, essentially a few meters of counter top and a wall where goods could be displayed. Although they had the advantage of shelter and heat, there were

Figure 4. Harbin's Russian Market, ca. 1998 (PHOTO BY AUTHOR)

fewer customers. Merchants complained that customers did not know about the location or did not bother to come in.

In 1997–98, the Russian Market was clearly suffering from lack of business. Only a handful of Russians wandered about, and it was common for the merchants not to make a single sale all day. The local getihu complained that the Russian border crossing had been closed for political reasons they did not understand. With little selling to be done, the merchants wandered away from their stalls, asking a neighbor (or a visiting sociologist) to keep an eye on their merchandise. All over the Russian Market, getihu visited one another, often sitting down for a game of chess or cards, or just a long chat. Over the following years, business declined further as Russian traders began buying their goods directly from cities farther south like Beijing, bypassing their Harbin middlemen. When I returned to Harbin in 2004, the Russian Market had disappeared. A handful of shops selling Russian tchotchkes (which I cynically suspect were "made in China") was the only trace that it had ever existed.

Although the businesspeople I described in the last section would never identify themselves with these getihu, the merchants in the Russian Market did identify with those high status entrepreneurs. They saw "businesspeople" (*shangren*) as one group, just with different degrees of economic success. When getihu were asked about their role models, they would tell stories about businesspeople who had made it big through their hard work and creativity, who had become entrepreneurs. The most ambitious and youngest getihu had such hopes for themselves. Even their appearance referenced the elite business class: the men tended to wear suits or, alternatively, blue jeans and a sweatshirt with a designer logo, while the women wore brightly colored clothes and make-up and permed their hair—cheap imitations of the styles favored by wealthier businesspeople.

However, the getihu in the Russian Market had very different backgrounds than the businesspeople described in the last subsection, with much lower levels of human and political capital. First of all, very few of them had more than a high school education, and some of them had substantially less. None were Party members. Moreover, prior to "jumping into the sea," many had worked at the lowest levels of the socialist economy, such as in collectives or in the despised service sector. None had been professionals, and only one had been a very low-level cadre in a low-status local bureau. In these positions, they would have had less access to powerful people, and their levels of social capital were correspondingly lower.

On the other hand, the majority of my respondents had possessed jobs in "real" work units, no matter how lowly, and had chosen voluntarily to "go out into society." Like their high-status counterparts, they had tested their chances carefully before entering the market. They had taken leave from their work units, moonlighted in their spare time, or worked for other private enterprises before striking out on their own. Most of them were attracted to the market for the money, especially since their state incomes had been so low. Many flitted from deal to deal, taking part in whatever business transaction had become available. Consequently, their earnings fluctuated wildly from month to month and person to person. The most successful could take in ten thousand yuan in the month prior to Chinese New Year's (China's major shopping holiday), but others were barely breaking even or losing money. Those who were doing poorly tended to be new to the market; more established getihu seemed to make between a few hundred and a couple thousand yuan a month—quite good money given their levels of human and political capital.

A few of the merchants and traders in the Russian Market had never had a work unit position. One such woman, of Korean descent and from a peasant background, had only two years of schooling and no job prospects in the socialist economy. For her, the market reforms had provided an unprecedented opportunity for success. About a third of the getihu I interviewed had been forced out of their work units by xia gang. For some of the younger workers, being laid off actually offered them the chance to do what they had always wanted: to "go outside" against their parents' wishes. But older workers had a much more difficult time adjusting to life without an "iron rice bowl."

Conclusion

After its tumultuous early history, Harbin experienced stability and economic prosperity under Maoist socialism as a center for heavy industry. However, the economic institutions supporting Harbin's position were undermined by the market socialist reforms, turning the city's image from that of an industrial showplace to a Rust Belt dinosaur. By the 1990s, Harbiners were confronted with the reality that the reforms were affecting and destabilizing everyone's work life, and not just the careers of those brave enough to "jump into the sea" of private business. In formerly "safe" organizations like the Agricultural Machine Factory and Disability Agency, xia gang had broken the "iron rice bowl" and introduced feelings of insecurity. In hybrid organizations like the University New and High Technology Park, work practices could not be invented and implemented fast enough to keep up with the pace of expansion and change; without contracts or pension plans, employees lived in a precarious state of uncertainty. Regardless of their position in society, Harbiners making career decisions were negotiating a world in flux, with few stable institutions.

Chapter 4

THE PATH OF POWER: REVISING THE MEANING OF POLITICAL CAPITAL

It's not like before when people wanted jobs in state enterprises or in the government, to be cadres or leaders. Now the good jobs are in private companies—so what's the point of joining the Party? You'd just have to pay fees, go to boring meetings. Those people who still want to get into the Party, who think it's a big deal, are crazy.

—An employee in a foreign firm

Narratives play a vital role in social change because they provide the frame through which social actors make sense of surrounding conditions and through which they create strategies of action to respond to those conditions. The relationship between narratives and institutions is both path dependent and local. In every Marxist state in the twentieth century, the conflict between the narrative of socialist paternalism and the narrative of revolutionary equality led to institutional contradictions. Yet in China, due to Mao Zedong's own interpretation of these narratives, there was a ten-year detour for the Cultural Revolution, more than a decade after Stalinism had released its grip in the European socialist states. In both cases, however, these traumatic swings to the left inspired a new generation of leaders to emplot narratives emphasizing economic pragmatism and downplaying ideological purity. These similar narratives inspired similar reforms, including the shift from virtuocracy to meritocracy. Once again, however, local differences emerged. In Europe, the narratives of "reform communism" were eventually rejected and superseded, while in China the market socialist project survived 1989 and evolved from there.

Why did the Communist Party survive in China, and what did it mean to be a party-state cadre in an essentially post-communist state? To answer these questions, we must understand how market socialism, and the role of cadres in the market socialist project, were narratively constructed in a dialogue between party-state elites, local cadres, political dissidents, and the ordinary citizens who constituted the audience courted by each of those other groups. In China in the 1980s and '90s, party-state elites, informed by their own narrative interpretations of their nation's circumstances, issued policies to revise the meaning and content of Communist Party membership and cadre rank. Local bureaucrats, more invested in Maoist ideology and the institutions of virtuocracy, resisted these new definitions with their own narratives, even as they took advantage of the new opportunities by drawing upon their social capital through *guanxi* practices. Political dissidents offered their own narratives, labeling new cadre behaviors as corrupt.

Ordinary citizens reacted to the mixed messages they received from state and dissident actors by constructing their own collective narratives, which borrowed elements from all of the above. These collective narratives allowed many Harbiners, especially young people, to amass sufficient evidence to avoid the cadre corps. In addition to shaping social mobility practices, these narratives also provided Harbiners with shared criteria to assess their political leaders. Ironically enough, despite the radical nature of the reforms, my respondents continued to judge cadres with the criteria of socialist paternalism—and then used narratives of corruption to explain how those cadres were found to be sorely lacking. As a result, collective narratives not only informed the status of cadres, but had wider implications for the party-state itself, by redefining its role and its claims to political legitimacy.

Narrative Sources
The Cultural Revolution and its Effects on Political Narratives

Despite its accomplishments, the Marxist socialist system sows the seeds of its own destruction with its contradictory narratives and the institutions they engender. On the one hand, communist party-states legitimize their rule with narratives of socialist paternalism, promising economic prosperity and increasing standards of living. On the other hand, they promote institutions and ideologies which undermine their ability to fulfill that promise, including a ponderous economic system which stifles innovation and encourages hoarding, and narratives which condemn inequality, wealth, and consumerism. In the 1970s and '80s, in many socialist states, the people who came to power were those whose narrative repertoires negotiated this contradiction by prioritizing the requirements of socialist paternalism and economic growth over either ideological purity or protecting the party-state's monopoly over economic resources. In the Soviet Union and eastern Europe, this political shift was facilitated partly by loans from capitalist states, which were trying to negotiate the recession of the 1970s by lending poor nations cash to buy capitalist technology (Verdery 1996:31–32). Unable to sell enough goods on the world market, these socialist states could not pay back those loans—which both precipitated economic crises and highlighted the weaknesses of the socialist redistributive system.

Meanwhile, China was almost completely isolated from the world, politically and economically, as it underwent the throes of the Cultural Revolution and its aftermath. The Cultural Revolution, the most violent phase of which lasted from 1966–69, can be seen partly as a logical outgrowth of the contradictions of the Maoist system. The socialist system inevitably produced a stratification hierarchy, which inevitably triggered Maoist narratives condemning inequality, "bureaucratism," and "intellectualism." As a result, Mao "periodically went to battle against his own creation" (Lieberthal 1995:119), launching political campaigns in a vain attempt to offset the social, political, and economic results of the very institutions he established. Deeply invested in the narrative that ideological zeal could transform institutional reality, Mao launched the Cultural Revolution in part to level inequalities between the urban and the rural, the educated and the uneducated, the bureaucratic elite and the ordinary citizen. He also wanted to give the younger generation, which had never tasted the bitterness of pre-socialist life, an experience of revolution before they succumbed to petty economic concerns. These were all longstanding concerns which had been addressed in previous political campaigns.

Yet the Cultural Revolution was also a hideous and unnecessary aberration caused by Mao Zedong's megalomania and paranoia. Throughout his life, Mao became increasingly prone to emplotting any criticism against him as conspiratorial plots. On an ontological level, he had constructed a story in which

China could be saved by no one but himself. Consequently, he launched the Cultural Revolution in part to address specific issues of succession and to consolidate his *personal* power (rather than the power of his party) to formerly unimaginable heights. Previous campaigns had been choreographed and controlled from above, but this time Mao used the power of his personality cult to whip up China's young people into a wild and fanatical frenzy, instructed them to organize themselves into groups of Red Guards, and told them to attack the system on their own initiative. Whereas campaigns had always been designed to consolidate and legitimize the authority of the party-state, in the Cultural Revolution, Red Guards were encouraged to assail both government and Communist Party organizations.

Moreover, Mao also made certain that neither the army nor the police would be permitted to intervene to protect their victims—which included many of his colleagues and potential rivals. Red Guard factions eventually descended into open warfare against each other. Millions of people were abused, maimed, and killed before Mao officially ended the Cultural Revolution in 1969 by putting the nation under military control and shipping 18 million former Red Guards into the remote countryside (Lieberthal 1995:115). The institutional effects lasted at least until Mao's death in 1976, if not until Deng Xiaoping came to power in 1978.

If the central contradiction of the Maoist era can be seen as the tension between the pragmatic narrative of socialist paternalism and the utopian narrative of class-based revolution, the Cultural Revolution can be seen as the triumph of the latter over the former. Mao Zedong was willing to shatter the economic and political institutions of the socialist system for the sake of a massive movement toward revolutionary purity. Given the painful price of that vision, it is not surprising that the Deng Xiaoping regime, which came to power in 1978,[1] chose the opposite side of the calculation: investing in the narratives of socialist paternalism and economic growth rather than ideological fervor. The personal experiences of the Cultural Revolution provided much evidence to reinforce the moderate narratives of many of China's post-Mao leaders, who were attacked by the radicals during the Cultural Revolution because of their moderate views. Deng Xiaoping himself was not only exiled, but Red Guards threw his son out of a window, crippling him for life. Those moderates, like Deng, who survived the Cultural Revolution naturally turned to narratives which denigrated mass movements and fanaticism. Persecution and exile had also given them plenty of fodder for emplotting stories recounting the flaws of bureaucratic over-centralization and the failure of socialism to alleviate poverty in China's hinterland.

Drawing upon these experiences, these moderates emplotted narratives which both explained the disastrous road to the Cultural Revolution and offered a new script for the party-state. These narratives argued that economic development and social stability were the true goals of socialism and the way to return China to her glory. Deng proclaimed: "We are a socialist country. The basic expression of the superiority of our socialist system is that it allows the productive forces of our society to grow at a rapid rate unknown in old China, and that it permits us gradually to satisfy our people's constantly growing material and cultural needs. After all, from the historical materialist point of view correct leadership should result in the growth of the productive forces and the improvement of the material and cultural life of the people" (Deng 1984 [1978]-a:139).

According to Deng's narratives, political upheaval only undermined this project, and there was no better example than the Cultural Revolution.

> Our people are undertaking the historic mission of modernizing our agriculture, industry, national defense, and science and technology with the present century, in order to transform China into a modern and powerful socialist state. We have waged a bitter struggle against the Gang of Four[2] over the question of whether the four modernizations are needed or not. The Gang made the senseless statement that "the day the four modernizations programme is realized will make the day of capitalist restoration." Their sabotage brought China's economy to the brink of collapse and led to a constant widening of the gap between us and the countries with the most advanced science and technology. Did the Gang really want to build socialism and oppose the restoration of capitalism? Not in the least. On the contrary, socialism sustained grave damage wherever their influence was the strongest (Deng 1984 [1978]-c:98).

Party-state Elites after Mao: Narratives and Policies

Following the logic of the narratives condemning over-politicization, the Deng Xiaoping regime avoided political campaigns. Exhausted and disgusted by the excesses of the Cultural Revolution, people, even within the Party, welcomed this policy. A minor campaign against "spiritual pollution" in 1983 only highlighted the ineffectiveness of the institution. Instead of active persecution and struggle sessions, the CCP focused on milder methods of persuasion and education, such as political study classes.

Motivated by narratives of economic pragmatism, Deng and his followers were willing to look outside of socialist orthodoxy for techniques to promote economic progress. During the Maoist era, Chinese citizens were taught to construct narratives opposing the glories of New China with the miseries of life before Liberation. In contrast, Deng Xiaoping told narratives which explicitly compared the PRC's economic conditions with Western capitalist nations, and found it sadly wanting. He snapped: "If the rate of growth of the productive forces in a socialist country lags behind that in capitalist countries, how can we talk about the superiority of the socialist system? We should ponder this question: What have we really done for the people?" (Deng 1984 [1978]-a:139). Deng's purpose was not to cast doubt on the economic superiority of socialism over capitalism; he sincerely believed that the only reason for the lag was the CCP's failure to implement socialism correctly. But he also made it clear that China's narrative point of comparison should be the richest nations of the world, including the United States, and the content of the comparison should focus on material conditions, rather than ideological purity. Through his stories, Deng rhetorically re-imagined China as a player in a global marketplace, one nation among many in an interconnected world, rather than as an isolated character.

Significantly, Deng Xiaoping and leaders in other socialist states were opening their societies to outside influences at the very moment that capitalist states were undergoing an economic transformation of their own. The economic recession of the 1970s had revealed the weaknesses of the Keynesian system, in which economic growth stemmed from economies of scale and was facilitated by a three-way partnership between Big Business, Big Government, and Big Labor. As a result, capitalist economies were beginning a painful (and still incomplete) shift to "flexible accumulation," where smaller, quicker firms sought niche markets on a global, rather than national, scale (Harvey 1990; Verdery 1996: chap. 1). Deng Xiaoping agreed that China could no longer rely on increased production capacity to develop its economy; economic progress depended on technological advances (Deng 1984 [1978]-c:100). These narratives justified new policies, such as those encouraging the Chinese to learn technological and economic information from those capitalist states. Deng famously quipped that it did not matter if a cat were white or black, as long as it caught mice. In the same vein, he argued that "science and technology have no class nature; capitalists make them serve capitalists, and socialist countries make them serve socialism" (Deng 1984 [1978]-b:122).

When Marxist-Leninist states experimented with market reforms in the twentieth century, human capital increased in value at the expense of political capital. This was true in eastern Europe beginning in the mid-1960s, with the rise of the technocratic intelligentsia after the rejection of hard-line Stalinism (Eyal et al. 1998:23). In China, a decade later, Deng Xiaoping's regime began offering narratives complaining that the party-state's cadre corps was too large, too old, and not nearly educated enough to carry out its new economic vision. For example, a 1980 *Renmin Ribao* (*People's Daily*) article explained that only cadres with vocational college degrees or higher were really capable of "leading the masses in achieving the Four Modernizations." Unfortunately, "for historical reasons and due to mistakes previously made in directing work," many current cadres had a "low cultural standard" ("*Renmin Ribao* on Standard in Selecting Cadres" 1980:L23).

While the European socialist states had spent the 1960s and '70s filling their bureaucracies with technocrats, China had been mired in its most militant period of virtuocracy: the Cultural Revolution. Thanks to narratives of seniority and an insufficient retirement policy, older cadres could not be easily removed from the bureaucracy, where they clustered at the upper levels. By the late 1970s, the average age at the higher echelons was well into the sixties and even seventies (Lee 1991:267). In terms of human capital, 60 percent of those employed by the party-state, and 71 percent of leading cadres, had never attended senior high school (Lee 1991:224). This is not surprising since CCP members, the main source of cadre recruitment, possessed a low level of education. In 1984, even after a concerted effort to recruit educated candidates, only 4 percent of Party members had a college degree, while 82 percent had only a junior high school education or less ("*Renmin Ribao* on Recruiting Intellectuals for the CPC" 1984). Moreover, the bureaucracy was growing larger and larger. In 1958, there was one cadre for every eighty citizens, but by the early 1980s there was one for every fifty (Lee 1991:206).

In order to ameliorate this situation, the regime proposed a series of policies in the early 1980s to retire old cadres, shrink the bureaucracy, and recruit and promote new cadres based on human capital, rather than political virtue (Deng

1984 [1978]-d). According to the new narratives of meritocracy, leaders were to be chosen on the basis of their "adherence to the socialist road," "possession of technical knowledge and organizational abilities," and "being in the prime of life" ("*Renmin Ribao* on Standard in Selecting Cadres" 1980). Similar standards would be used for recruiting Party members, while family background and personal history were no longer to be factors. In other words, political capital was redefined, shifting away from "virtue" and toward "ability," with human capital and youth conflated with "ability." By 1998, the Xinhua News Agency could report that 43 percent of Party cadres had some college education (Miller 2000:21–22). In a further blow to political capital, Deng Xiaoping sought to de-institutionalize the Party command system in state enterprises and install a "manager responsibility system," in which enterprise cadres would be given increased freedom of action and incentives based on economic performance.

In both China and the European socialist states, elites reacted to the contradictions inherent in the Marxist socialist system by developing narratives which demanded a less ideological, more pragmatic socialism. These narratives motivated similar institutions, an attempt to create a "reform communism" or "market socialism." Yet, in Europe, a critical mass of people eventually concluded that market socialist institutions were an untenable dream, and they collectively constructed narratives which claimed that liberal capitalism and democracy were the only solutions to the woes inflicted by Marxism. Meanwhile, in China, the project of market socialism has survived into the twenty-first century. To understand why, we must look beyond the elite to see how ordinary citizens mobilized narratives and shaped market socialist institutions.

The Response of Local Cadres and Political Dissidents

Even if Deng Xiaoping and his followers were not seeking to undermine the socialist stratification system, their policies nevertheless constituted an attack on political capital as it had been defined for at least a generation. Moreover, to implement these new policies, the regime had to rely on the very people most invested in the virtuocractic institutions which were being assailed—local rank and file cadres. One can imagine how those cadres with a "low cultural standard" felt about these narratives, which basically dismissed them as "mistakes." Not surprisingly, they resisted the reforms, and they were well armed with a rich repertoire of narratives to defend their point of view.

These virtuocratic cadres responded by drawing upon narratives which conflated ability with virtue, and equated virtue with class status and loyalty. According to their plots, these new policies threw away the hardy worker and peasant cadres who had conquered the evils of "Old China" and who had dedicated themselves to Chinese society for decades, only to replace them with feeble bookworms who knew nothing about the real world. They sarcastically asked whether the international symbols of communism were to be changed from the hammer and sickle to spectacles and a pen ("Policy of Promoting Intellectuals Examined," Beijing *Guangming Ribao* 1984). In *Chinese Lives*, a collection of oral histories from the 1980s, a county-level cadre with a middle-school education gave his assessment of a new cadre:

> But—just between us—do all those kids with diplomas work out so well? . . . We were sent a new deputy county head of thirty with a degree from the teacher's college. . . . They call it a "younger, more intellectualized leading group, with cadres whose ability and political integrity are equally matched," but how can you measure ability and integrity? He owes it all to his degree. . . . The long and the short of it is, they don't have what it takes to be officials. Do you think a middle-school teacher knows what happens in a county office? . . . He knows less than the Party committee's messenger. . . . The old cadres have the experience, but people ignore that. . . . In my opinion, there are some old comrades who're more willing to stick their necks out and take on responsibility than the young cadres, not to mention being less selfish and more upright (Zhang and Sang 1987:197).

Local Party cadres also repudiated attempts to remove them from enterprises with the "managerial-responsibility" policy. While Deng and his supporters constructed narratives which argued that political tasks harmed economic productivity, Party cadres emplotted political work as a necessary contribution to society and paternalistic care for the people:

> The Party committee must play a decisive part in the management of socialist enterprises. This is because a socialist enterprise is not simply an economic entity that is only directed by the market. It is also "a small society" taking care of a number of political and social welfare functions. Even though managers can take overall charge of production and sales, they can in no way deal effectively with the other functions a factory is endowed with. These are our responsibility (You 1998: 45).

Armed with this defense, local cadres refused to comply with the new policies. The very top levels of the bureaucracy, where Deng and his allies could exert direct control, did become significantly "smaller, younger, and better educated," but at the provincial level and below, the anti-virtuocracy reforms were much less effective. Local bureaucrats, refusing to accept intellectuals as members of the working class, would block their applications for Party membership (Lee 1991:232). Despite repeated attempts, Deng was unable to implement his "managerial-responsibility" system until the 1988 Enterprise Law, and even that did not end resistance on the factory floor. As late as 1998 in Harbin, most people told me that there was no hard and fast rule determining whether the Party secretary or the head manager had the real authority in a state firm; instead the situation depended on the specific case.

Old cadres even complained, though less vociferously, about the regime's abandonment of political campaigns. In the new, de-politicized era, some Party cadres keenly felt a loss of purpose, power, and respect. Political study did not inspire the kind of zeal and excitement that had come from political campaigns. (From 1991–93, I worked at a Chinese university, where students spent their political study classes reading novels, passing notes, sleeping, and even listening to music on headphones. During one class, a student played a handheld video game which beeped so loudly that even their apathetic teacher, the Party cadre, was roused to annoyance.) Consequently, some Party cadres began to construct narratives which defended the institution. They argued that the cynicism and corruption of the reform era could be blamed on the lack of political campaigns. According to an old cadre:

> In the 1960s and 1970s whenever a campaign was waged by Chairman Mao, Party members would become very busy. Everyone wanted to show he was a fighter. I remember that our shop was given the task of printing a large number of Mao portraits. All Party members were working non-stop for two days. Now look at our Party secretary! He organized mahjongg when the Party branch is supposed to conduct political study. He would not dare if there were still political campaigns (You 1998:92).

One of my interviewees, a fifty-year-old laid-off enterprise cadre turned businesswoman, argued angrily: "Why is there so much corruption in Chinese society today? Well, it's Deng Xiaoping. In Mao's time they used political campaigns to straighten out these people. Those leaders and leaders' kids who use special privileges and personal power to do some improper things. Mao prohibited these things. . . . There should be a big campaign against corruption, just like in the old days! A political campaign!"

Yet for most of my subjects, the political campaign was an obsolete, embarrassing practice. One of her business acquaintances, a man in his thirties, interrupted her diatribe: "You don't want a political campaign! We need better laws." Startled, the woman said, "Right! Laws to stop corruption. That's right." Clearly, he had absorbed the state's new narratives, even if she had not.

Although low-level cadres resisted some reform policies, many cadres also took advantage of the opportunities which became available. One of the ways that the reform policies affected the occupational status of party-state cadres was through social capital, though the effects were not straightforward. The reforms inadvertently increased the value of social capital, especially cadres' social capital, but cadre prestige was eroded by the backlash against the increasingly blatant use of guanxi practice, articulated primarily through narratives against corruption.

In the interest of speeding up economic growth, in the 1980s the Deng Xiaoping regime introduced a number of market mechanisms to complement the redistributive economy. To counteract the inflexibility and slowness of the bureaucracy, state enterprise cadres were permitted to sell extra products (above and beyond their allocation to the state) on the open market. The regime also made it clear to enterprise cadres that they were now to be judged by economic, not political, criteria. This message was not only reinforced by the cessation of political campaigns (which had been used to punish cadres for political crimes), but also by the implementation of economic incentives, such as bonuses based on profits.

Ironically, in mixed command-market economies, state cadres have an enormous economic advantage. In urban areas, they are just about the only social actors with access to products to sell on the market. In fact, they have access to the very products which had been most scarce and most hoarded under the socialist system, and they could obtain these at low state prices. Market reforms allow them to sell these coveted goods at market value, a recipe to make an easy killing. Some version of these "cadre-entrepreneurs," taking advantage of "political capitalism," arose in every socialist state experimenting with market practices (Verdery 1996:33; Ledeneva 1998: chap. 6), yet the specific form of their practices was shaped by local cultural repertoires. After all, when policies legalizing market transactions initially appeared, how would socialist citizens know how to respond? For decades, they had never thought about finding customers, hiring employees, advertising products, setting prices, setting up deals, or writing contracts. Capitalist societies have institutions to negotiate these tasks, and people in them have the skills in their cultural repertoires to use them, but these were alien to social actors who had spent their lives learning how to operate in a socialist redistributive economy.

As a result, in post-socialist societies, social actors had to adapt their socialist-era narratives to make sense of the new opportunities. In Russia, for example, new business opportunities were understood in the language of *blat*, the practice helping out members of one's circle (*svoim*) at the expense of public resources (Ledeneva 1998). Bureaucrats, who had learned how to exploit the state entrepreneurially during the late Soviet period, now used those skills to transfer the financial resources of their brigades or committees into starting capital for their new private businesses (Yurchak 2002). In China, people turned to the similar, but not identical, practice of guanxi. Guanxi practice, with its basis in gift exchange, its idiom of friendship, and its mixture of the expressive with the instrumental, may seem incompatible with marketization to neoliberal economists. Yet for the Chinese, it was a familiar practice which allowed people to expand their networks of contacts and to exchange goods and services outside the formal institutions of the socialist system. Furthermore, guanxi practice was already in their collective cultural repertoires; the rules of the game were common knowledge. As a result, social capital rose in value in the 1980s because the urban residents who could best take advantage of the reforms were either cadres who were skilled at using guanxi practice, or people who had good guanxi relationships with cadres.

Without the threat of rectification campaigns, guanxi practice became less risky, and concomitantly more blatant. Parents openly sought advantages for their children, cadres cheerfully offered their friends goods at ludicrously low prices, and upscale restaurants opened to cater to the growing need for fancy banquets. Although scholars argue that Chinese people are well aware of the difference between "normal" guanxi practice and bribery (Smart 1993), a flourishing guanxi culture opens up opportunities for corruption. At the university where I taught in the early 1990s, the cadre in charge of post-graduation job assignments (*fenpei*) routinely solicited bribes; everyone knew exactly how much one had to pay to receive assignments at various levels of desirability, as though the prices were posted on a menu.

Although bribery was clearly criminal, many other "political capitalist" activities, such as selling state goods at market prices, were legally ambiguous. Unlike their predecessors, the pragmatic post-Mao leaders eschewed heavy-handed ideological propaganda and concerned themselves less with shaping people's thoughts and more with economic results. Consequently, they were quite reticent in offering narratives to make sense of the growing wealth of "entrepratchiks."

The Dissidents Offer their Explanation:
The Power of the Narrative of Corruption

With the party-state unwilling, or unable, to offer clear-cut narrative explanations for the changing roles and practices of its own cadres, other actors were able to step into the breach with their own narrative explanations. While disgruntled intellectuals in eastern Europe couched their criticism of communism in the language of "civil society," China's political dissidents took this opportunity to label new cadre behavior as corruption (*tanwu, fubai*). In 1979, journalist Liu Binyan published the bombshell story, "People or Monsters?" in *People's Literature* (Liu 1983). In crisp but sensational detail, this long article describes the rise and fall of Wang Shouxin, an infamously corrupt Party secretary of a coal factory in Heilongjiang Province in the early 1970s.

The case was already well known before Liu's article, and on the surface, his piece was just another orthodox socialist tale which condemned "feudal" practices for harming the glorious Communist Party. Yet Chinese readers understood immediately that "People or Monsters?" was a scathing critique of the Communist Party and the cadre corps. For one thing, many of the crimes committed by Wang Shouxin had become legal practices under Deng Xiaoping: she had amassed a fortune selling state goods at (semi-)market prices; she had established a guanxi network for the exchange of goods and services which bypassed the state bureaucracy; and she had spent her (illegal) profits on elaborate banquets and other luxury goods. Deng was proclaiming that "To get rich is glorious," and Wang had certainly gotten rich.

In many ways, Wang Shouxin's experiences could be read positively as the type of entrepreneur that Deng's regime was promoting. Ambitious and hard working, she constantly sought out unfilled market niches and moved in (by illegally manipulating the movement of state goods) to make a profit. Yet Liu's article frames her tale as a narrative of political corruption. He depicts Wang as sexually loose, foul mouthed, short tempered, arrogant, rude, and insatiably power hungry. In his story, she is utterly unconcerned about the welfare of the people in her charge, mercilessly exploiting them to feed her prodigious appetites. Moreover, Liu laments, Wang is unique only in that she was caught. "The case of Wang Shouxin's corruption has been cracked. But how many of the social conditions that gave rise to this case have really changed? Isn't it true that Wang Shouxins of all shapes and sizes, in all corners of the land, are still in place, continuing to gnaw away at socialism, continuing to tear at the fabric of the Party, and continuing to evade punishment by the dictatorship of the proletariat?" (Liu 1983:68).

In invoking corruption, Liu was deliberately drawing upon a powerful narrative theme in Chinese political history. It has roots reaching back to the traditionalist Confucian political narrative linked to China's imperial dynasties. According to this narrative, the first emperors of each dynasty were pure and upright, concerned only with the welfare of the common people. Their successors, however, were distracted by the luxuries of imperial life, and their officials were able to indulge in corrupt behavior. Eventually, corruption became so prevalent that the entire empire suffered, and the decadent dynasty was overthrown by a righteous man, who founded the next dynasty. This narrative figures as a recurring theme in the Chinese political imagination and was a template for political historiography (Jia 1994). Corruption, then, was associated with regime failure, with dying dynasties (Lui 1979). By using the accusation of corruption, Liu and other political dissidents insinuated that the communist government, despite its ideology, could be as weak and illegitimate as the dynasties of old (Hsu 2001).

In 1988, when the television series *River Elegy* presented image after image of a decaying, degenerate regime, the producers made clear the connection between declining dynasties and the current Chinese regime:

> This distinctive social structure made China flourish greatly. But within this marvel of great unity, and beneath the glowing exterior of this overly ripe civilization . . . the core of that social structure was slowly rotting. This situation very much resembled the present situation in which the Yellow River dikes are silently being hollowed out by mole crickets, ants, and field mice. The Confucian bureaucracy had an irresistible tendency to corrode, power itself becoming a corrosive agent. Hence, once a dynasty reached its peak, collapse lay just ahead. . . . Bureaucratism, the idea that prerogative and privilege go with position, and corruption

continue to damage the "four modernizations" program. These persistent ancient social disorders are somewhat like the silt that the Yellow River carries each year, which clogs the lower reaches of the watercourse, gradually building up to a crisis (*River Elegy*, part V, quoted in [Ding 1994:157]).

Corruption narratives were so powerful, in part, because they offered a plausible explanation for social problems; the reason why the people are suffering is that the elites are corrupt. In imperial times, corrupt emperors and their officials were blamed for floods, famines, and bandits. Due to their immorality, they had lost the Mandate of Heaven which justified their rule, and the entire natural and human order of things responded with rebellion. With "People or Monsters?" Liu demonstrated that the plot worked just as well for making sense of the dislocations of market socialism. In the 1980s, urbanites found themselves confronting inflation, unemployment, and visible inequality—albeit at levels still much lower than in most developing societies. For Chinese residents who had not experienced any inflation in a generation, and who had been taught to abhor inequality and conspicuous consumption, this was shocking. "People or Monsters?," *River Elegy*, and other corruption narratives argued that these unpleasant phenomena were neither temporary growing pains due to the economic transition nor the reasonable price for economic growth, but instead were caused by the immoral deeds of corrupt cadres who had abandoned their loyalty to the people and were gaining wealth at their expense.

Needless to say, dissident corruption narratives undermined socialist institutions of stratification by linking political capital with political corruption. In addition, by arguing that the entire cadre bureaucracy was infected with this disease, these narratives offered a platform from which to attack the political legitimacy of the CCP itself. Corruption narratives played a central role in the Tiananmen Protests in 1989. While the movement's student leaders were savvy enough to talk about "democracy" and "freedom" to the Western press, they used corruption narratives to elicit support from their fellow Chinese citizens. For example, a Beijing University handbill colorfully titled "Soldiers, Look How Profiteering by Government Officials is Eating You Up" declared:

Why is China's economy such a mess? Why does the daily stipend of a soldier remain at 1.65 yuan after all these years, despite rocketing prices?

Nowhere else can one find the answer to these questions except in the word "official." One official takes the lead, another follows, and very soon each official acts as a protective shield for another's crimes. Now let me ask, in whose hands shall China crumble? "No corrupt officials, [then] no revolt," as the saying goes (Han 1990:31).

The party-state was forced to respond and to try to offer counter-narratives through political speeches and through articles in the state-run media. The state launched an anti-corruption campaign in 1982 with great media fanfare, which was followed regularly by similar campaigns every several years for the rest of the century. Initially, state narratives were quite confused, awkwardly forcing the problem into the frame of "class struggle," or blaming "feudalism," "decadent capitalist ideology," or "individualism," as though the CCP were trying on all its old villains for size (Hsu 2001). It was not until the mid-1990s that the state finally settled upon the economic development narrative to deal with the corruption crisis. Essentially, this plot argued that corruption hurt economic development by debilitating the party-state's ability to implement its policies of economic construction, economic reform, and "opening up" to the outside world (Hsu 2001). In these narratives, the CCP was once again the hero, striving to deliver rising living standards to its citizens, but impeded by the rather faceless forces of corruption.

These new official narratives offered a radically different conception of the role of the party-state—and the role of the party-state's cadres—than in Mao Zedong's day. A cadre's purpose was no longer ideological transformation or moral leadership or even paternalistic care; instead cadres were economic managers who served citizens by providing economic opportunities and social stability. Cadres were no longer revolutionaries or heroes, but bureaucratic functionaries.

Collective Narratives

Because of the debates between central leaders and rank-and-file cadres, between the state and political dissidents, Harbin residents received conflicting narratives about political capital and "inside" workplaces and occupations. Nor were their cultural toolkits confined to these public narratives. They also contained additional narrative resources: stories and plots and characters learned under Mao, from folk literature, and from collective narratives created to make sense of previous circumstances. Confronted with the problem of how to assess political capital and cadre status in the reform era, how did they mobilize these narrative resources? In their stories, were party-state cadres ideological leaders, paternalistic caregivers, corrupt criminals, or faceless economic managers? Choosing any one of these options over the others would have serious implications, not only for the occupational status of cadres, but also for the role of the party-state and its political legitimacy.

Social actors rarely discuss the status of an occupation or the relative value of a form of capital. What they do, instead, is to tell stories about utility, competition, and meaningfulness. That is, they tell tales which offer, implicitly, the answers to the following three questions about the occupation or form of capital: First, is it useful? Does it offer the opportunity to have a comfortable and pleasant life, however that is defined? Second, what is the competition like for obtaining this position or this type of capital? Is it weak or strong, fair or unfair? Third, does it provide a meaningful life? Will other people think that the work is important? Does it offer social status and prestige? In answering these questions about cadre status and political capital, what kind of narratives did Harbiners draw upon—narratives from the Maoist era (still defended by virtuocracy cadres), narratives of the reformist regime, narratives from political dissidents, or narratives from elsewhere?

How Useful Is Political Capital?

Under Mao, Party membership was the key to cadre status, and cadre status was the key to a good life, materially speaking. Despite the CCP's ideology of asceticism and equality, cadres were at the top of the redistributive food chain, and almost all other paths to (relative) economic prosperity were suppressed. Political capital, defined by the ethos of virtuocracy, was to a great extent the prerequisite for economic and social capital. As ontological and collective narratives from the Maoist era made clear, China's urban citizens were well aware that political capital was exceedingly useful for improving one's standard of living. After Deng Xiaoping and his followers began instituting economic reforms, however, it soon became less and less clear how useful political capital was, and would be in the future. In Harbin in the late 1990s, party-state cadres earned more than factory workers, but often considerably less than private entrepreneurs. Moreover, incomes in the private sector were increasing rapidly, while those in the state sector stayed flat. Cadres, however, also received generous non-cash benefits, and they had access to better guanxi networks. Yet by the end of the decade, there was also the threat of layoffs. To complicate matters, many of the reform policies affected cadres in enterprises differently than cadres in government bureaux.

Given all these contradictory factors, how could social actors determine the utility of political capital? Even the academic literature failed to reach consensus, with some China scholars convinced that the power of political capital was in decline (Nee and Lian 1994; Nee 1996), while others argued the opposite (Walder 1995b; Walder et al. 2000). Harbiners did not peruse the academic literature to make their decisions about socialist institutions. Instead, they emplotted information into narratives which served to simplify the data. For example, I was struck by the fact that, in their narratives, Harbiners rarely differentiated between cadres in state enterprises and cadres in government offices, despite the fact that the reforms policies were making those two occupations less and less alike. They used the term "cadre" to include even the administrators of hybrid organizations and privatized firms, like the University New and High Technology Park, who operated like managers of a capitalist firm.

In terms of narratives of utility, there was strong consensus in Harbin that Party membership had lost its ability to affect a person's standard of living. Only five respondents argued that Party membership was still useful for social mobility, while four times as many told me the opposite. Significantly, interviewees who were Party members themselves were more likely to claim that membership was not useful and less likely to argue that it still made a difference in Chinese society. A forty-two-year-old cadre turned international businessman told me that he joined the Party after college, but let his membership lapse after leaving the government. He admitted:

It's not important, not as important as it was before. No one cares about it anymore. Of course officials still need to do it. When I joined the Party, it wasn't very important either. I didn't really think about it. It was just that most people at work were Party members, so they wanted me to join, too. Actually, even without being in the Party, work would have been fine, fine either way. My parents hadn't cared much either way, whether I entered the Party or not.

A thirty-six-year-old professor and entrepreneur drew upon corruption narratives to joke that Party membership was useful—but only for criminal cadres:

If you already are an official, and you are a Party member, and you break the law, you would receive a different punishment depending on whether you had Party membership or not. Just a little. Because if you break the law, like you took 100,000 [yuan]. If you're a Party member, they punish you by taking away your Party membership. But if you don't have that membership to take away, then you go to prison. So it's a layer of protection over you. But it's not a thick layer—it's a very thin layer!

A waitress in her early twenties suggested that Party membership might even be detrimental to one's career:

Nowadays, young people don't care about getting into the Party. People used to think Party members were all good. But now know that they're good and bad, so it has no meaning. It's still useful to be a Party member. But rumor has it that *sanzi* [foreign, joint, and private] companies won't want you if you're a CCP member. It's because foreigners think Party members are too conservative. So now some young people aren't even willing to enter the Party.

These views contradict the findings of social science research, which indicates that Party membership was still a salient credential well into the reform era (Walder 1995b; Walder et al. 2000). Indeed, my own data indicate that Party members did better than non-members, not only in the state sector, but also as private businesspeople. Yet Harbiners, unaware of our sociological findings, were more persuaded by the anti-virtuocracy narratives propagated by the Deng regime, which argued that political capital was less important than human capital.

This theme was especially common in cadres' own narratives about Party membership. While non-cadres sometimes mentioned that CCP membership might still be useful for cadres (though it certainly made no difference for anyone else), cadres themselves insisted that what really mattered was a college degree. The forty-three-year-old head of the Disability Agency was a Party member, but her younger sister, also a cadre, was not. "The way we think about it now is that it doesn't affect her work," explained the elder. "You don't need to be a Party member to be a cadre. Oh no. Entering the Party is voluntary." All that mattered was the younger woman had a college degree, which was the requirement for the upper ranks of the cadre corps.

A forty-four-year-old manager at a state trading company reminisced happily about entering the CCP in his youth, but he added:

> Now my sixteen-year-old son, he's not thinking about the Party, just about studying to get into college. This is new. Before, people cared about the political, like Party membership. Now there is no more job allocation, and people have to find their own jobs. The first requirement at a lot of places is a college degree. Of course, after you have the job, your development isn't just about education. But you won't even get a chance to try without a degree. So every parent wants their kid to go to college. But there are too few colleges.

Although Harbiners disparaged the utility of Party membership, many believed that cadre status was still the path to material security, perhaps even prosperity. The exceptions were the cadres (and former cadres) themselves, who almost all bemoaned their low salaries. When I asked a forty-two-year-old Party cadre to describe his career history, he related a tale of declining power, switching from post to post, bureau to bureau, as his previous positions lost their authority. Although he claimed to agree with the reforms which gave power to economic managers over Party secretaries, he also admitted that he hoped his twelve-year-old daughter would choose a different career path. "It fit my condition at my time—that's what the nation needed at that time. But now it needs more direct contributions. . . . Maybe she can be a teacher or go into economic development." Later in the interview, he added, "There are also contradictions in cadres' lives. For the CCP, the nation asks a lot, but gives them a low salary. . . . There is not a match between what they give and what they get. This should be fixed." A forty-five-year-old woman described how she educated herself during the Cultural Revolution through hoarded books and surreptitious English broadcasts, then rose through the worker ranks to attain cadre status through the dint of hard work and ambition—only to watch her work unit, an electronics enterprise, forced to lay off 60 percent of its workforce. Although she was optimistic about her chances if she lost her job, a trace of bitterness appeared in her comments: "[Cadres] don't make any money. They say on the coast, 'If you don't study hard you'll be stuck in government.'"

Yet we must keep in mind that people in every occupation bemoan their inadequate compensation. (Would any gathering of professors be complete without a few erudite gripes about our supposed poverty?) When cadres complained about their low incomes, they ignored the fact that they received the best non-cash benefits available in China. Non-cadres were more apt to allude to these benefits. The most common stories on this topic were negative examples, which drew upon the "inside/outside" dichotomy. Harbiners disparaged jobs "outside" in the market for failing to offer the kinds of benefits available "inside" the state sector, especially housing and urban registration.[3] Indeed, the largest and most beautifully appointed apartments that I saw in Harbin inevitably belonged to cadres, who paid a fraction of the market value for their homes. A number of people in their twenties admitted that they took positions in the cadre corps, even when they loathed the job, in order to obtain an apartment or legal residence in the city. Members of their parents' generation told me that they wanted their children to have jobs which were "stable" and "secure," a "proper" job in a state work unit. Despite the threat of layoffs, they still believed that the cadre corps was a safer bet than the wild world of the market. These stories drew upon the narratives of socialist paternalism, where a "good job" was defined as one which offered "iron rice bowl" security and social welfare benefits.

Then again, I was surprised that many impressive cadre benefits were ignored in Harbin narratives. For example, people rarely mentioned that cadres received the best medical care, usually gratis. Work units often sent officials back to school for further degrees, paying full wages in addition to tuition. Many of my interviewees expressed a fervent desire to further their education, but few were able to do so. In my sample, over half of the cadres had gained an additional degree later in life. Yet no one mentioned this benefit when discussing the occupation. Instead, the most common utility narratives were about the benefits cadres enjoyed from guanxi practice, and from corruption. Because these narratives were drawn from corruption narratives, they served to condemn cadre immorality even as they lingered sensationally over the enviable details of cadre life. Harbiners relished telling stories about Chen Xitong (Beijing's former mayor) and the former deputy mayor of Harbin, both of whom had been arrested for corruption in the late 1990s. A thirty-five-year-old cadre at the Disability Agency asked,

> Have you heard of it? They were all people in Harbin's municipal government, assistant mayors or whatever. Taking the state's money in piles and piles! When the police were investigating [the deputy mayor], you

know, because they were following leads from another case and they found out his involvement, when they searched his office, even he had no idea how much money was in his desk drawer. It was a big pile! It was so much, it was uncountable! If you think about it, a deputy mayor's salary should only be 1500 a month. Where could all that money come from? It just doesn't match up. Isn't that bribe-taking?

Because of the scarcity of housing in cities, many Chinese urbanites were obsessed with the problem of obtaining apartments. In this context, the housing perks of cadres was a hot topic. A high-ranking administrator at the Technology Business Group related his quest to find apartments for his sons as a narrative of epic struggle. In contrast, he complained, officials could get palatial homes without even paying for them. (Ironically, people outside his office saw him as a cadre, though he clearly did not put himself in that category. And his position allowed him to receive fine apartments for all his family members.) The following excerpt reveals the fascination Harbiners had with narratives about cadre corruption. During the interview, the professor who had introduced us was also in the room. The professor paid little attention to the conversation—until the topic of cadre housing came up:

> *Administrator*: After I moved into this new house, I felt really content. But then [my wife] went to the house of a [high city official], and oh. . . . You know the living room in our new house is a bit under twenty meters square, a lot better than in our old house. But she saw this official's house and oh! Over fifty meters! [*The professor breaks in*: *"That's not possible! Do you know how big fifty square meters is?"*[4]] It was over fifty meters! She saw this because she treated that [official's] wife. [*Professor*: *"Aiya!"*] So she asked them—See, for our place we spent 30,000 decorating it.[5] But they said, oh, the work unit pays for that. That's how officials are. [*Professor*: *"Hmph!"*] If they had to reveal it. But they can take it without revealing anything. . . . Their salaries aren't very high, but their houses are so nice. And it's not just one house, it's a series of houses, everywhere a house! Common people are trying to squeeze their whole family into a few square meters, and they have multiple houses!

The cadre he was describing likely had done nothing illegal; his apartment and the work done on it were part of his compensation. The manager himself had received similar benefits on a lesser scale. But the speaker rhetorically transformed their actions into crimes by drawing upon the elements of the corruption narrative: political elites were wallowing in secret luxury at the expense of the common people they were supposed to serve. A fifty-four-year-old businesswoman was even more explicit, even though her own children were cadres.

> Look around, is there any factory head who isn't like this? Look at how many of them are committing transgressions! What I say counts, take the money, leave the factory poor. Why do you think people are saying, "Poor temple, but rich monks"? The temples are poor, the factories are bankrupt, workers have to xia gang, no more salaries, but go to the factory head's house and take a look—so wealthy. Right?

Harbiners were convinced that even those cadres who did not seek bribes benefited considerably from guanxi and gifts. The thirty-five-year-old woman from the Disability Agency said:

> Even if you don't want it, people will give it to you. It's hard to resolve. Especially since the people sending the gifts are all close to you, really good friends, asking for favors. Can you find a way to help me? And then if you achieve their task, they give you presents. Do you take it or not? These people giving aren't strangers. Even if you don't want to take it, you can't not take it. You don't even try, and you get rich. You say, "no, no," and wealth just comes.

Others pointed out that cadres' salaries were too low, so it was impossible to expect them not to take some advantage of their position. But even these comments were couched in narratives of corruption, and the speaker inevitably concluded that these practices, even though they were understandable, were detrimental to society.

Because these utility narratives were constructed as corruption stories, they condemned and denigrated cadre status even as they acknowledged its usefulness for obtaining a comfortable—even luxurious—life. It was impossible to conclude, after telling such a tale, that this was a good argument to pursue this profession. For one thing, one of the most popular forms of the corruption narrative is one where the criminal is caught and punished, with his or her decadent deeds exposed to the disgust of the world—hardly the stuff of a recruiting brochure. Many Harbiners believed that just about all cadres above a certain rank were at risk for arrest, partly because they could not avoid indulging in certain wayward activities, and partly because China's anti-corruption laws were unrealistically strict. A popular joke in the city, circa 1994, went:

SPEAKER 1: Given the new anti-corruption laws, shouldn't we just take out all the cadres and shoot them?
SPEAKER 2: Of course not! You would be executing innocent people!
SPEAKER 1: Then should we just shoot every other one?
SPEAKER 2: Of course not! You'd be letting too many guilty bastards off the hook!

A few of my respondents informed me that "other people" might find guanxi practice and bribes an incentive to become a cadre, but no one would admit to me that they personally found those aspects appealing. The "corrupt cadre" had become a stock character in Harbiner's narrative repertoires—interviewees told me that when they saw a cadre with nice possessions, they assumed that they were witnessing the fruits of graft, even when there was no other evidence for criminal behavior.

Overall, in the late 1990s, narratives of utility eroded the occupational status of cadres and the value of political capital. Harbiners drew upon the regimes' narratives against virtuocracy to disparage the benefits of Party membership. They adopted the corruption narratives of political dissidents to condemn any material gain that a cadre might enjoy. Although cadre status was still supported, often indirectly, by "inside" narratives of socialist paternalism, the benefits of the occupation were sullied by the taint of immorality and the risk of punishment.

Competition, Meritocracy, and Guanxi

In societies with fairly open systems of social mobility, an important method of assessing an occupation is through narratives of competition. An occupation will usually have higher status if social actors believe that many people are competing to attain it on an even playing field, yet few are chosen. Conversely, an occupation has lower status if the competition for positions is believed to be weak or manifestly unfair. The rhetoric of competition was ubiquitous in the PRC, both under Mao and Deng. Students were constantly subjected to competitions for "neatest dormitory room" or "most punctual class," work units competed for state commendation, and individuals competed for Party membership or "model worker" certification. Not surprisingly, Harbiners used narratives about competition to assess political capital, with both positive and negative outcomes.

Party members often told tales emphasizing the long odds they overcame to enter the CCP. A fifty-year-old worker at the Agricultural Machine Factory related: "Yes, I am a Party member. I entered in 1990. I first applied in 1967, when I first came to this work unit. I really wanted to get in all these years. . . . But in those years, it was hard to get into the CCP. It was competitive, and there were limits on the numbers allowed in. Also, I was young then, and there were older people who wanted to get in. Even now there are 80 years olds trying to get in." When I asked a twenty-seven year old who had recently started her own advertising firm why she applied to the Party, her reply veered almost immediately from ideology to competition: "I joined the CCP because I believed in communism. Also it was the competitiveness of the struggle to get in. A lot of people want to enter the Party, but only a few are chosen. . . . Being a Party member has not been actually helpful to my career, but I still feel like it's a sign of accomplishment."

Many interviewees believed that, while entering the Party had been competitive in the past, this was no longer true by the late 1990s. A thirty-eight-year-old cadre turned entrepreneur was clearly proud that he got into the Party in his freshman year of college, a rare feat. But he added, "But now young people don't want to join the CCP. After the reforms, it's no longer everything." An enterprise cadre was only twenty-five years old, but she was still nostalgic: "At that time [when I joined the CCP], I wanted to be better than everyone. Party membership was a prize to shoot at. But now, the government is trying to develop a lot of members among college students." Indeed, by targeting intellectuals for membership in the reform, the CCP was focusing on a much smaller potential population than it had during the Maoist years. Those with human capital were so heavily recruited that Party membership no longer felt special to them. In 1998, I went to a dinner party of graduate students where every attendee was a Party member, except myself, one of the students, and his (non–grad student) girlfriend, who was an employee at a private firm. Later, the girlfriend told me how disgusted she would feel if her boyfriend applied to join the CCP. She exclaimed, "Why would anyone want to enter the Party now? It's so hick (*tu*)! If he ever joins the Party, I'd break up with him."

For this young woman and many of my other informants, Party membership no longer symbolized competitive success. Most felt the same way about cadre ranking. Given the official and dissident narratives of the previous two decades, this view is hardly surprising. It was Deng Xiaoping and his followers, after all, who made it clear to everyone in China that they believed that the Party and cadre corps were too large, too old, and insufficiently educated. Some people were also well aware that local cadres were resisting the reforms, which meant that these unqualified people were still trying to run the country. After listening to a middle-aged cadre loudly proclaim his uninformed views, a disgusted young engineer turned to me and muttered, "That's what's wrong with China. That generation—they don't know anything because there wasn't any education during the Cultural Revolution. And now they're in charge of everything, and you can't get rid of them." In addition, dissident narratives like "People or Monsters?" showed cadres handing out positions and promotions as favors. In Liu Binyan's story, Wang Shouxin obtains her position by sleeping with a Party leader, and then manages to get every one of her family members into official positions, including one son who was both a rapist and a drunk.

Strains of both of these themes found their way into collective narratives. Many Harbiners portrayed the Communist Party as a not-very-exclusive club, and the cadre corps as infested with favoritism and guanxi. The twenty-five-year-old enterprise cadre explained to me, "[As a college student], even if you didn't know anything, you could get in. Now in society, Party members are not looked at as much different than others. It's no big deal. . . . In college, some people want to get in because it's not too much trouble and it might help in the future. Can't hurt, might help. Another group is totally against it."

A forty-eight-year-old cadre (and Party member) at the Post and Telecommunications Bureau explained that in the past, everyone wanted to get into the Party, but now, maybe only a third were still interested. The twenty-three-year-old cashier at the Pizza Parlor was ambivalent about whether she would apply to the Party, although she was the daughter of cadres. According to her, "Now to get into Party is not as big of a deal as before. It is not like before that you have to be excellent in every way to get in. The standard is not objective anymore but subjective. Of course you have to be OK, but now what matters is who likes you, such as the teacher."

A number of interviewees related tales of people who refused to apply to join the CCP, even though they had a strong chance of succeeding. A seventy-three-year-old retired English professor (and Party member) explained that his daughter refused to apply to the CCP, adding, "You know, one of the daughters of Deng Xiaoping is not a Party member. Each person has his own or her own reason." A thirty-five-year-old engineer also refused to apply, despite the urging of his superior. He mused, "It's ironic: those who want in, can't get in. Those who don't care, the Party comes after you." One of his colleagues at the University Technology Park factory, an engineer in his mid-twenties, admitted to me that Party membership was a source of family tension. His father kept putting the application on his desk, and he kept ignoring it.

In their narratives, Harbiners not only insinuated that the competition for political capital was weak, but that it was also unfair. Although my interviewees rarely claimed that cadre positions or promotions were easy to obtain, they often argued that the competition was not based on merit, but on guanxi favoritism. It is important to note that in the Chinese rhetoric, guanxi practice was not always seen as negative. However, in this context the stories echoed dissident tales of corruption and nepotism, and guanxi was used as a pejorative, in opposition to fair competition and meritocracy. A fifty-five-year-old art professor groused, "In government, if a high guy is your friend, then your work and future are ensured. For those who want to be officials, they can't leave the guanxi net." A forty-two-year-old manager at the Technology Business Group's department store sighed: "People used to think, 'oh he's a high official, he must have ability.' Now they just think that those officials must have had good opportunities. That's what I think, that high officials aren't necessarily better or smarter than lower officials. You don't actually rise on ability. . . . Also, there's the problem of guanxi; maybe people rise up because someone in a higher position likes them."

In fact, Harbiners were so willing to associate cadre rank with guanxi practice that when they encountered a situation in which a cadre or cadre's relative accomplished anything, they assumed that they were indulging in questionable activities. For example, I asked a thirty-nine-year-old social science professor to give me an example of someone who did not deserve their success, and he launched into a story about the governor's financially successful son. Although there was no outward indication of illegal or improper activity, my interviewee was sure that "the money's got to be from guanxi."

Non-cadres often claimed that their own field was much more meritocratic and competitive than the cadre corps. One forty-three-year-old physics professor explained: "There are government offices where the people are of low quality. There, people with guanxi get the jobs. People without connections can't get in, regardless of ability. But to get into college, it's still fair. Anyone can take the entrance test and get in." A twenty-four-year-old laid-off factory worker–turned-businessman condemned the entire realm of "inside" occupations: "In government or in enterprises, you'll need guanxi to rise up. . . . You can succeed in China with ability and hard work—in outside society." Even cadres were aware of these views. Without prompting, the forty-three-year-old department head of the Disability Agency burst into a defense of her profession: "Maybe common people will say, 'They used connections to get up there.' They have this impression. You can't say this doesn't happen. But in the end, if this leader is there, it's mainly because of real work, and because higher levels believed in them." But she also admitted, "Cadres used to be managed very strictly, but now the best people aren't getting into highest positions."

When Deng Xiaoping's regime launched its attack on virtuocracy, its goal was not to undermine the competitive prestige of the Communist Party or cadre corps. Yet that was the unintended result. In contrast, the political activists fully intended to cast suspicions on the cadre corps with their narratives about favoritism and corruption, and they were successful. Moreover, narratives about competitiveness tend to become self-fulfilling prophecies. An occupation perceived as competitive will attract more candidates, thus making it more competitive, just as a form of capital which is perceived as more valuable will become more valuable. But the more social actors believe that the competition for an occupation is weak or unfair, the fewer the people who will want to compete for those positions.

Narratives of Meaning and Prestige

In addition to good material benefits and a strong degree of competitiveness, high-status occupations are understood to offer meaningful work and widespread social prestige. In 1990s Harbin, these two concepts were rhetorically intertwined through the theme of contribution (*gongxian*). Narratives of contribution insist that the occupations which are meaningful are the ones which allow social actors to contribute to the social good, and that those who contribute deserve social prestige. Contribution narratives reach all the way back to the imperial era, when state Confucian rhetoric argued that the literati deserved respect because their knowledge allowed them to serve society to a greater degree than ordinary people. The Maoist state adapted these contribution narratives, propagating stories which claimed that cadres deserved their high status because they "served the people." Although Harbiners used contribution narratives to talk about the meaning and prestige of various occupations, these narratives came up most often when discussing cadres. Moreover, cadres used these narratives more than anyone else.

The salient issue behind contribution narratives was how to define contribution: What does service look like, and how should it be measured and assessed? This was a pertinent issue because, although Deng Xiaoping never directly criticized Mao Zedong, his reforms and rhetoric clearly implied that Maoist conceptions of contribution were wrong. Deng's policies specifically sought to transform the role of party-state cadres, and to change the rules of assessment. In addition, these policies affected different groups of cadres in different ways, so that a "cadre" at the head of a factory would have a completely different job than a "cadre" in a government bureau.

Despite the efforts of Deng Xiaoping and his followers to redefine the role of cadres, Harbiners generally turned to pre-reform narrative elements when assessing their party-state bureaucrats. Instead of differentiating between different types of government officials, bureaucrats, and enterprise managers, my respondents continued to lump them into one category: "cadres." The fact that the mayor of Harbin, a foreman at the Agricultural Machine Factory, a low-ranking bureaucrat in the Disability Agency, and the head of the University Technology Business Group had completely different job descriptions and worked for completely different types of organizations did not prevent Harbiners from seeing them as all members of the same occupation who should be judged by the same criteria. For my respondents, the salient issue was that all these people worked for "inside" organizations in positions of leadership. Even cadres themselves would make sweeping generalizations, though it was clear from their phrasing that a number of them exempted themselves from the category in these discussions. When I questioned them about this, a few insisted that they were not cadres (such as the administrators at hybrid firms like the Technology Business Group), while others explained that their statements only applied to government officials (if they were enterprise cadres) or to high-ranking leaders (if they had low-level positions).

Because cadre status was understood to be a single occupation, all cadres could be assessed by the same criteria. For Harbiners at the end of the twentieth century, those were the criteria of socialist paternalism. In the words of my interviewees, cadres were supposed to "work for the common people," "think of the people," "give themselves to the nation," "put common people first," and, of course, "care for the people." These were the traits which made the job meaningful and prestigious.

A number of them brought up the stories of Jiao Yulu and Kong Fansen as positive examples of cadres. Jiao was a Party member and cadre in Henan province in the 1960s who "led the masses" to combat and prevent natural disasters, until his death of liver cancer. Kong Fansen lived a generation later, serving in Tibet until his death in 1995. Significantly, both men's lives were the subject of both political campaigns and popular films. In 1966, Jiao Yulu's handsome face and signature v-neck sweater became known all over China as citizens were exhorted to study his example. In 1991, the film "Jiao Yulu" brought his story to a new generation, garnering China's top cinematic awards for best film and best actor.

The synopsis of the movie reveals its emphasis on Jiao's contribution and sacrifice:

> Jiao Yulu is a Communist Party member and county chief who devotes his life to helping his people become more prosperous during the 1960s. The setting is Lankao County in Henan Province, which has long been plagued by sandstorms, floods and poor soil. In 1962, the county suffers another natural calamity, but Jiao is determined to save the county from its poverty and backwardness. He works tirelessly, but dies of liver cancer in 1964. After his death he became well known nationally as a model worker (ShanghaiMe 2004).

Kong Fansen's campaign and film both came out in the year of his death, 1995, when the party-state needed to offer up a positive example of cadre virtue in response to popular anger about political corruption (not to mention international criticism of human rights abuses in Tibet). The film, which was nominated for Best Picture in China, depicts Kong leaving his family and comfortable life in Shandong for the stark barrenness of Ngari, Tibet, where he works tirelessly for the impoverished locals. He even adopts two adorable orphans. As an editorial in *Renmin Ribao* (*People's Daily*) states, "Comrade Kong Fansen was strict with himself and was just and honest. He never abused his functions and powers to seek private gain. On the contrary, he adopted Tibetan orphans over a long time, frequently helped sick Tibetan compatriots with medicine and helped needy Tibetan compatriots generously with money, despite his meagre income. His selfless service to the people made people's eyes fill with tears" ("Learn From Comrade Kong Fansen," 1995).

A number of my respondents had found these films emotionally moving and would refer to events or images which had been seared into their minds. Significantly, they often mentioned Jiao and Kong's ascetic lifestyles: the poverty, the cold, the discomfort. A thirty-five-year-old cadre at the Disability Agency related:

> [People] do respect some cadres a lot, like Kong Fansen and Jiao Yulu. . . . They gave their all to the public. Even though they had such high positions, their own families were so poor they didn't have anything. They would give to anyone who was needy, like if they met someone who was a beggar, or if they found out some family had a child who couldn't go to school, they would immediately reach into their pockets. And they weren't corrupt; they only lived on their little salaries. People give them respect, and wish that China's officials would be like them. They should be like this.

These stories drew upon Maoist narratives which implied that socialist paternalism and ascetic poverty were inextricably intertwined: loving the people means putting their welfare above your own, and even above the welfare of your family members.

Unfortunately, when using the measuring sticks of socialist paternalism and asceticism, Harbiners found their contemporary cadres sadly wanting. Instead of living in poverty and "caring for the people," 1990s cadres drove Mercedes Benzes and laid off their workers. Only a couple of my respondents pointed out that this discrepancy might stem from the fact that the requirements for the job had changed; cadres, especially enterprise cadres, were being asked by their superiors to focus on profitability rather than paternalism. The majority of Harbiners ignored these considerations and found a more persuasive explanation in the narratives of corruption propagated by political dissidents and publicized widely during the Tiananmen Protests. In capitalist societies, narratives about corporate leaders focus on profits and stock prices, with the result that an entrepreneur can be praised for firing employees if it makes the company more economically competitive. In contrast, the heads of Chinese state firms (or quasi-state firms) were assessed as cadres, who were supposed to protect their people even at the expense of losing money. As a result, Harbiners looked at the cadres around them and concluded that many, if not most, of them must be "bad" cadres.

A twenty-seven-year-old woman who worked at a branch of the Post and Telecommunications Bureau described herself as a manager and engineer, though many Harbiners would consider her a cadre. She explained to me that she and her college friends worshiped Zhou Enlai[6] because "he did a lot for the people, and worked hard his whole life for them." But cadres like that are now very rare, she said. "Nowadays, if a cadre isn't corrupt, if a cadre doesn't take bribes, that's all you can ask for. There are no heroes now, and we're losing our faith." A forty-two-year-old international businessman (and former cadre) quipped, "Out of ten officials, nine are taking bribes (*Shige dangguan, jiuge tan*)." Even cadres used this rhetoric; at the Disability Agency, a thirty-five-year-old cadre said: "Now, officials, the higher their position, the more money they have. Common people don't even have enough to eat, don't get their salaries for months, so they don't have a good feeling in their hearts. They feel like all the bitterness in their lives is due to those officials, from corruption and whatever."

For many of my respondents, the state sector layoffs (xia gang) were proof that cadres had forsaken their duty. According to corruption narratives, xia gang had to be the result of deliberate cadre neglect and immorality. A forty-two-year-old woman, laid off after fifteen years at a printing factory, explained:

> People respect government leaders who care for people and give them fairness. Like in a work unit, if leaders work hard and manage the factory well to keep workers from xia gang. But they just let it happen and let the factory crash. They were corrupt, too. How could people respect them? Before reforms, cadres were different. They cared about common people. Now some of them just do not care about people at all, just for themselves.

At the Russian Market, I interviewed a thirty-two-year-old woman who brought fashionable clothes from the South up to Harbin. It was a slow day at the market, and sellers at the nearby booths wandered over to listen in.

> Nowadays cadres are corrupt, don't work for common people. Let me give you an example, a work unit is laying off workers. It's in big trouble right? But the cadres are still eating big, carrying on. They're not even

considering what they're eating, how many people's salaries is that? They're not even considering that! How can the common people believe cadres? How can they believe their leaders? They're too corrupt, these leaders. [*All around, heads nod in agreement, and people murmur their assent.*]

The vivid image of cadres "eating" their workers' salaries is borrowed directly from the Tiananmen Protests (Han 1990:31). A forty-six-year-old janitor at the University Technology Business Group also expressed her ire: "I hate people who are corrupt. People who use power for themselves, not for the people. Now there are so many people xia gang who are middle aged, have no experience. How are they going to live? Raise their children? If the leaders were good, there wouldn't be this problem. The people I hate the most are those enterprise leaders who let their factories go bankrupt, but still eat and drink and party. Just hateful."

Some Harbiners believed that most cadres were corrupt, while others thought that only some of them were. Yet everyone agreed that cadre corruption was a very serious social problem and that a substantial number of cadres were failing to fulfill their obligations of socialist paternalism. Instead, they were abandoning the core duties which gave their occupation meaning and prestige. Over and over again, my interviewees told me that people used to respect cadres but no longer did so because of corruption. Some argued that "good" cadres still deserved high status, but "bad" ones did not. But by using the criteria of asceticism and socialist paternalism in an era of increased marketization, they were bound to find more and more cadres falling short of their standards.

Corruption narratives not only undermined the overall prestige of the cadre occupation, but they also inspired at least some people to conclude that the job had lost its meaning. Older respondents seemed more likely to believe that cadre work was inherently meaningful if done honestly; the problem was that cadres failed to fulfill their duties. Yet people in their twenties saw the occupation as inherently boring and pointless. This was especially true among those who had the best chance to become cadres themselves. I interviewed a twenty-three year old who was trying to decide between joining the cadre corps and going to the United States to study. Both of his parents were relatively high-ranking officials in the city, and apparently a cadre position was his for the taking. The interview took place in their home, possibly the largest and certainly the most beautifully furnished apartment I saw in Harbin. The young man expressed nothing but admiration for his parents, who had started off their lives as poor peasants. They were "talented and hard working and care a lot about those beneath them and the common people." Yet his ambivalence about following their footsteps was clear:

> My parents want me to go into government and be a cadre because it's stable. They are more conservative. But if I decide to go to the U.S., they'll support me. . . . Going overseas—the greatest pro is that I can practice and develop myself because my whole life has been at my parents' side. But my parents can't take care of me for my whole life. I could go out into society, take some initiative (*chuang yi chuang*), learn to take care of myself. Chinese people are too dependent. Chinese people are good at conforming, modeling themselves after others, but they are weak in creativity (*chuangzao*). The cons, well, maybe I'll go out and won't be able to deal with it, and won't be able to come back. And I'm afraid I'll go bad—the dangers of vice. If I stay here, the pros are that it's easier and more comfortable. I wouldn't have to work hard, just go to the office and maybe work, maybe just drink tea and read the paper. Do this until retirement. But it's boring. So if I do stay here, I've got to find something to do or I'll become weak, just eating OK and living OK. But a lot of Chinese are satisfied. A lot of government work is like this.

According to this young man, a cadre's job was essentially meaningless—drinking tea and reading the paper, staying safe and becoming weak. Although he believed that his parents served society, he also mentioned that many cadres were corrupt and harmed people. Since these two possibilities seemed to cancel each other out, the possibility of contribution (or of corruption) never came up in his own deliberations. For him, and for other young people in his position, the content of the job never came up. For them, the cadre occupation was not associated with doing anything productive; it was just an excuse to secure a safe and stable sinecure.

Implications for Personal Actions and for Cadre Authority

At the end of the twentieth century, Harbiners were offered a host of contradictory narratives about what the role of party-state cadres and the value of political capital should be in market socialist China. Collectively, they took elements from these different themes and constructed their own stories. In their narratives, Party membership was dismissed for losing its relevance, and, while cadre status deserved prestige for its contribution to society, it had been debased by the behavior of actual cadres. Although they used the criteria of socialist paternalism from the Maoist era to judge their cadres, they were now equipped with anti-virtuocracy narratives to question cadre competence, and corruption narratives to suspect their morality. What were the implications of these collective narratives for the relationship between the people and the party-state in market socialist China?

Most obviously, these narratives influenced the career choices of potential cadres. Those deciding whether this profession was worth pursuing came to mixed conclusions. For many parents seeking a good situation for their children, the cadre corps offered a "proper" job (*zhengshi de gongzuo*) with meaningful work and the potential for good connections. Although they were appalled at the problem of corruption, they were convinced that their own offspring would stay clean. Yet for my interviewees in the children's generation, corruption and favoritism were not seen as an avoidable problem, but as a permanent deterrent from "inside" workplaces. A twenty-three-year-old contract worker at one of the University Technology Business Group's factories stated: "There are honest officials too, but in a market society, they're hard to find. So it's better to avoid the 'iron rice bowl,' where you have to work for them, and go out to take care of yourself." He planned to start his own business someday. Indeed, almost none of my subjects under the age of thirty aspired to cadre position, and most felt ambivalent at best about working "inside." The only one who expressed an interest in cadre status was an incredibly ambitious twenty-five year old at the Agricultural Machine Factory who was simultaneously applying to the Party, running a small restaurant on nights and weekends, and taking classes in his spare time. In other words, he was covering all possible bases.

During the Maoist era, the party-state bureaucracy had its choice of the best and brightest young people that the nation had to offer, though it was hampered in its results by its own virtuocratic tendencies. By the end of the century, those virtuocratic constraints had been removed, but the best and the brightest (at least in Harbin) had less and less interest in joining the cadre corps. Those who became cadres usually did so because of parental pressure or a desire for security or one of the non-monetary benefits which came with the position, rather than any interest in the work involved. Many expected their time in the party-state bureaucracy to be short term, a stepping stone toward bigger and better things "outside" the state sector, rather than a lifelong commitment to a cause.

Yet collective narratives about cadres and Party members did more than just shape personal social mobility strategies or transform a job's position in the occupational hierarchy. They also limited the actions of actual cadres. Harbiners categorized all employees in the state system at the managerial level or above as "cadres," regardless of whether they worked in a government office or a market-socialist hybrid business. They even labeled managers of privatized firms in this way. They judged all of these "cadres" by the criteria of socialist paternalism. As a result, managers at state enterprises were constrained from taking actions to improve the economic competitiveness of their firms if they would also diminish the socialist welfare benefits of their workers. Throughout the 1990s, the state repeatedly announced that work units would no longer be permitted to distribute subsidized housing, and then repeatedly rescinded the order in the face of public outcry. At the University Technology Business Group, one administrator admitted to me that their department store was not profitable, and probably would never be profitable. But it employed over four hundred people in decent jobs, so the firm could not get rid of it. "It's our socialist contribution," he said with an ironic smile. By judging state enterprise cadres as political, rather than economic, actors, these narratives limited their ability to improve the economic competitiveness of the state sector.

Implications for State Legitimacy

These narratives also influenced collective views of the party-state and its political legitimacy—or lack thereof. Harbiners were willing to judge their national leaders with the same criteria they applied to local cadres, as is clear from the following joke, circa 1998:

> Jiang Zemin, Li Peng, and Zhu Rongji, and a small child were flying in an airplane. The plane hit some trouble and was heading to crash, when the four passengers realize that there were only three parachutes on board.
>
> Jiang Zemin says, "I am the President of China and the General Secretary of the Communist Party! I am needed to make important decisions!" He grabs one of the packs and jumps out of the plane.

Li Peng says, "I am the Chairman of the National People's Congress! I am needed to reform China's legal system!" He grabs a pack and jumps out of the plane.

Zhu Rongji looks at the child and says, "Little friend, I am already old. You are China's future, while I was its past. Please take the last parachute."

The child replies, "But Grandpa Zhu, there are two parachutes, one for each of us! Grandpa Li Peng jumped out with my backpack."

The joke condemns both Jiang Zemin and Li Peng for putting their own welfare above that of their people. Li Peng, who was universally loathed because he was blamed for the violent suppression of the Tiananmen Protests, is also skewered for being an incompetent idiot. A number of people told me that Li Peng was a fool who owed his power and position to his family connections—he was Zhou Enlai's informally adopted son. Thus, Harbiners emplotted Li Peng's life through a corruption narrative: through nepotism, an undeserving person is allowed to become a cadre, where he or she uses the position for personal benefit rather than to serve the people. In contrast, my interviewees saw Premier Zhu Rongji as an honest cadre who genuinely cared for the people. Over and over again, they expressed their belief that Zhu would straighten things out and solve China's social problems, such as corruption.

Another joke reveals popular concerns about the effects of corruption on the viability of the state:

At the National People's Congress, the topic was how to liberate Taiwan. One by one, each of the branches of the military make their presentations.

The head of the ground forces marches up and declares, "If you give me 10 million more troops and 100 million yuan, we could liberate Taiwan in two years!"

The head of the naval forces marches up and announces, "With 100 new ships and 100 million yuan, we could liberate Taiwan in one year!"

The head of the air forces marches up and bellows, "With 10,000 new planes and 100 million yuan, we could liberate Taiwan in six months!"

Finally, the little old woman sweeping the floor at the back of the hall couldn't stand it anymore. She runs up to the front, crying out, "We don't need to do all of that! Just send over 10,000 of our cadres! Within one month, their society will have collapsed from the corruption. Meanwhile, we'll save 100 million yuan in bribes alone!"

Given that many of China's political leaders and bureaucratic functionaries were popularly considered to be hopelessly corrupt, exploitative, and incompetent, how could the ruling regime retain its political authority? It was clear to any visitor to Harbin in the late 1990s that its residents felt free to complain about the government. Even with my tape recorder running, people voiced their criticisms with relish. Nor was this pastime confined to Harbin (Chen et al. 1997:51; Li 1997:26). Chinese urbanites were also willing to take their dissatisfaction to the streets. In the summer of 1997 in Harbin, angry retirees gathered in front of the provincial government headquarters every morning to express their fury at losing their pensions, not leaving until the police would come and gently shoo them away. For any observer of China's post-Tiananmen suppression, it was difficult to decide what was more astounding: the actual protest against the state, the subdued response of the authorities, or that such an event could be repeated daily. The residents of Harbin seemed to find these protests both mundane and amazing. In April 1998, I conducted an interview in an office which overlooked the provincial Communist Party headquarters, where over two hundred peasants had gathered, some driving tractors, angry that they had lost their land. Although my interviewee explained that they had been protesting for a couple of months already and that nothing was going to happen, he and the others in the office stopped to stare broodingly out the window whenever their tasks permitted.

Ironically, though, despite these protests, despite the criticisms of cadre corruption, and despite the devaluation of political capital, my interviewees were generally quite optimistic about the government. This was especially surprising to me because in 1994, during my first visit to the city, many Harbiners were predicting that the CCP was doomed to collapse from corruption. Yet a few years later, those who were pessimistic about the government were outnumbered five to one by their more hopeful counterparts. And in 1997–98, at the height of anxiety about xia gang, the vast majority of Harbiners told me the reforms brought more good than bad, and not one person claimed that the reforms had brought more problems than benefits. A retired professor offered blunt criticisms of the regime, but added, "Conditions in China are improving. It's a fact. Things are much better than ten years ago, when Deng began to put in effect the policies of reform." On the other side of the social spectrum, a young peddler told me: "The way I see it, if Chinese society continues down this path, it will be really good. A good future." Survey data from Beijing taken in 1995 and 1997 reveal similar views. Eighty-four percent of those surveyed said they believed China would not experience major sociopolitical turmoil in the next ten years, and ninety percent were confident that China would become a world-class economic power in the twenty-first century (Zhong et al. 1998:778). Like the people in Harbin, these Beijingers believed that the CCP, despite its flaws, would lead China to future wealth and power.

On the one hand, people were optimistic about the current political regime and its ability to lead China in the right direction. On the other hand, they claimed that their cadres were incompetent and corrupt. How can these two sides be reconciled? Part of the answer seemed to lie in the genuine faith that many Harbiners had in "good" cadres, especially in Zhu Rongji, who became premier in 1998, replacing the despised Li Peng. A fifty-four-year-old woman with a stall in the Russian Market expressed her hope: "You just look at our China and you'll see. It will definitely be different in three years. Didn't Zhu Rongji say so? 'One path, three reforms, five turnings.' So he'll solve these big enterprises losing money, solve the xia gang people's situations. Didn't he say, in these three years? And we hope it will be like this. Don't we common people all hope for this? We just want to live and work in peace and contentment." Indeed, three years later in 2001, Harbin's economy was doing better and the panic about xia gang had subsided.

Underlying this faith was a widely shared belief that the reforms were a good thing, and that most of the policies of the post-Mao government were generally correct. They did not have a problem with the overall direction of the party-state, but were instead concerned about the competence and morality of the people designated to implement it. Moreover, most Harbiners seemed to conclude, although corrupt and unqualified cadres were harming society, they were not actually derailing China's progress under market socialism. In the words of the forty-three-year-old head of the Disability Agency:

Of course [the reforms] are good! Are you saying that if it weren't for the reform, I wouldn't have to [worry about] xia gang? But you have to look at the overall situation—and the overall situation includes my life as an example, too—from Chinese society's progress to the rise in the overall standard of living. There's a saying among Chinese common people: "Short-term pain is better than long-term pain." After going through this short time of pain, things can get better. But if everyone just eats out of that big pot of rice, nothing ever gets better, everyone stays poor, that's long-term pain. . . . In the past in our work units, it would be like this. Have you heard the phrase, "eating from the big pot of rice"? There would be this huge pot full of rice gruel, getting thinner and more watery every time, and everyone's still scooping it up to eat.

In other words, even with corruption and xia gang and all the other troubles of the reform era, life was better than it was before. This, of course, was exactly the message that the party-state wanted people to believe, the one it was propagating through the narratives of economic management. These narratives argued that the goal of the government was not socialist paternalism, but instead to create conditions for its citizens to find their own economic success. Rather than being the ideological vanguard or the ever-caring parent, the ideal state was one which faded into the background. These narratives' themes emerged in some of my respondents' comments. A thirty-six-year-old professor turned entrepreneur explained:

Now whatever you're thinking of, you're thinking of how to make yourself wealthier, not caring about what the policies are. And this includes those who are supposed to be policy makers. Like if you ask people now, what is the policy about this or that, even if you ask professors at [the university], they'll say, I don't care. It's none of my business. My deal is to figure out how to make a little more money.

A forty-four-year-old cadre at a state foreign trade company told me: "People don't respect officials as much as before, but this is a kind of progress. We're all people, and we should be equal. Doesn't matter what your profession or position, you should deserve respect only if you do your job well." A twenty-nine-year-old office manager offered her view: "Common people think of cadres as corrupt. But what I personally think is that they can do whatever they want to do, as long as they run the economy. As long as common people can make a living, that's okay." A twenty-six year old who worked in a multinational firm, asked, "Who's really interested in politics and all that? What does Jiang Zemin have to do with me? As long as they run the government and keep the economy going, that's all that matters."

In 1994, I hardly heard anyone use these types of economic management narratives. By 1998, they were more common, though not nearly as prevalent as the narratives of paternalistic care and corruption. When I returned to the city last, in the spring of 2004, they were increasingly popular.

Despite the fact that economic management narratives came out of state discourse—and served the state by diffusing the corruption crisis—they continued the trend of undermining political capital and cadre status. They offered a vision of cadres as mere technocrats, chosen according to human capital, whose purpose was to facilitate the pursuit of economic capital. In this story, political capital, once so dominant in Chinese society, had faded away.

Chapter 5

**CONSTRUCTING ENTREPRENEURSHIP:
THE MORAL MEANING OF MONEY**

In the early post-socialist period, narratives were not only used to reconstruct existing occupations, such as that of cadres or intellectuals. They were also the tool used to engineer new professions, most notably that of self-employed entrepreneurs. Entrepreneurship has generated a great deal of attention in the literature on post-socialist transitions. Even though entrepreneurship and the "entrepreneurial spirit" are often considered to be vital components of a successful market economy, many assume that the Marxist socialist system crushes this entrepreneurial spirit, despite some research to the contrary (Yurchak 2002). Therefore, entrepreneurship (measured usually as self-employment) is often taken as a proxy measure for the success of marketization. In an effort to understand why entrepreneurship does or does not flourish in various post-socialist societies, scholars analyze the institutional conditions supporting or constraining small businesses (Barkhatova 2000; Barkhatova et al. 2001; Bonnell and Gold 2002).

Yet China in the early post-socialist period offers an anomalous case. Its institutions were certainly inadequate and unsupportive; aspiring entrepreneurs faced bribe-seeking officials (Wu 2001), lacked adequate legal safeguards (Chen 1999), suffered harassment (Ikels 1996:181), and found it impossible to get loans from banks (Tsai 2002). Even so, entrepreneurship flourished in China. By 1994, 5.6 percent of the working population (6.7 percent in urban areas) was self-employed. By 1998, this had risen to 8.7 percent for the nation, and 10.9 percent in urban areas (State Statistical Bureau 1999). In contrast, between 1991 and 1996, the percentage of the self-employed in Russia's labor force actually dropped from 1.7 to 1.4 percent (Gerber and Hout 1998:15). In 1990s Russia, entrepreneurship was confined to those with high levels of social and human capital, the offspring of managers and professionals (Gerber 2002), while in China self-employment initially attracted those from the lower strata of the socialist economy, although it eventually expanded to others as well.

These discrepancies reveal that entrepreneurship in the early post-socialist period was a qualitatively different occupation in China than it was in Russia. Or, as this chapter demonstrates, it was a set of qualitatively different *occupations*. Sociologists interested in post-socialist stratification have debated whether entrepreneurs were gaining status at the expense of cadres (Nee 1989, 1996; Nee and Lian 1994) or whether entrepreneurs were former cadres converting political power to economic might (Rona-Tas 1994; Lin 1995). Both sides seem to take entrepreneurs as the embodiment of market forces, so that the underlying issue behind the debate is whether market forces will conquer the power of state socialism (embodied in the form of cadres) or be co-opted by it. Neither side takes into consideration that entrepreneurs are narratively constructed and therefore a product of the local context and specific history. Despite their role in the capitalist economic system, they are not simply the generic invention of the market. Nor were they created by state policies. Instead, they were locally constructed through the collective narratives and actions of multiple groups of actors. These included state elites and global capitalists, but they also included the ordinary citizens whose lived experiences embodied the stratified occupations of the early post-socialist era.

My research reveals that, in the 1980s and 1990s, the ordinary residents of Harbin shaped the entrepreneurial occupation(s) through their talk and through their actions. To make sense of the new opportunity to start private businesses, they drew upon state legal policies, official speeches and publications, Confucian moral philosophy, political dissidence, and even paperback bestsellers to narratively create three separate entrepreneurial occupations: Some people I considered to be entrepreneurs were seen as "cadres," and judged by their ability to provide socialist benefits for their employees, rather than their success at generating profits. Most were considered to be *getihu*, which in Harbin connoted a vulgar, morally suspect, money-grubbing peddler. Yet those who were educated or who ran supposedly "high-tech" businesses were never categorized as getihu. These fortunate few were labeled with the neutral term "businessperson" (*shangren*) or "entrepreneur" (*qiyejia*) and seen in a positive light.

Harbiners also turned to their narrative resources to construct the *practice* of entrepreneurship and private business, one which could flourish in spite of the inadequate and hostile institutional environment. To do this, they adapted the narratives and practices associated with *guanxi*, which used the language of friendship and favors to generate sufficient trust to create trustworthy, expansive business networks in the absence of adequate legal guarantees—a type of capitalism without contracts.

Who Are Entrepreneurs? The Narrative Construction of the Occupation(s)

State Narratives and Policies

When socialist states began experimenting with "reform communism" and "market socialism" in the 1960s and 1970s, permitting some degree of entrepreneurship was a common policy. In some states, such as China, Hungary, and Poland, individuals were allowed to start small, private businesses under restricted circumstances. In most, cadres were also permitted a greater degree of entrepreneurial freedom in their state organizations (Yurchak 2002). How could communist leaders justify permitting, even supporting, private business ventures? We can understand not only why these policies came into being, but also their specific local form and content, by analyzing the narratives that created them.

Part of the appeal of Marxist socialism is that it promises "backward" societies a supposedly sure-fire method of catching up with (and surpassing) the "developed" nations of the world. For the reformers frustrated with the traumas inflicted by the leftist excesses of Stalinism (in Europe) or the Cultural Revolution (in China), this seemed like the most attractive message of Marxism, one which had been neglected but deserved priority. In Deng Xiaoping's narratives, economic progress was the core of the socialist project, and the measure of that progress was calculated not through steel production or life expectancy or literacy rates, but in the universal currency of money. In 1984, Deng announced that his regime's "political objective" was to achieve an annual GNP of one trillion U.S. dollars and a per capita GNP of US$800 by the year 2000. He explained that "with that achievement as a foundation we can strive to approach the level of the developed countries within 30–50 years" (Deng 1994 [1984]-a:85). To offer an image of this glorious future, Deng praised the city of Suzhou, which had reached that US$800 per capita level:

First, people in Suzhou don't want to leave for Shanghai or Beijing. . . . Second, the average living space exceeds 20 square meters per person. Third, everyone has received primary and secondary education, because the people have more money to spend on schools. Fourth, the people have no more problems with food or clothing, and many of them own television sets, household appliances and whatnot. Fifth, there has been a tremendous change in people's ethical standards, and crime and violations of discipline have declined significantly. There are other improvements that I can't recall now. But the ones that I have cited are impressive enough! (Deng 1994 [1984]-b:95).

According to Deng's narrative, when nation, city, or community gains more economic capital, its social problems begin to disappear, and each and every person experiences a higher standard of living. Needless to say, this tale glosses over a host of complicating factors, like the possibility of inequitable distribution. Instead, it offers up economic capital as a perfect measure for social progress.

This still left open the question of how to achieve these economic goals, and the answer depended on how one framed the problem. Deng Xiaoping offered several narratives to explain why economic growth had been stifled under the previous regime, though he was careful not to criticize Mao Zedong directly. Instead, he laid the blame at the feet of Lin Biao and the Gang of Four, who led China into the wasted "ten dark years" of the Cultural Revolution (1966–76). According to Deng's tale, these villains undermined the true socialist project of economic development by leading China into fanatical chaos. Among their crimes, they sabotaged the economy by keeping people from doing their jobs with the politicized turmoil.

One solution, then, was to de-politicize the workplace and allow productivity, rather than politics, to be the main motivating factor. Deng argued that enterprises should be given more autonomy. According to his stories, overbureaucratization was strangling economic progress:

When something has to be done, an enterprise currently has to submit its plan to the authorities of the province, the ministry, and the State

Planning Commission for approval. This process is too slow. Some of our comrades listen only to what higher authorities dictate and are afraid to use their own minds. We should, as Chairman Mao put it, "put down our mental burdens and use our own minds." . . . In the future, we should give cadres at enterprises both the power to make their own decisions and the authority to assess the efficiency of their own work (Deng 1984 [1978]-d:140).

By narratively connecting politicized workplaces with the deposed Gang of Four, Deng Xiaoping was able to make an argument for loosening the grip of the command economy and allowing cadres increased entrepreneurial activity. Through his managerial responsibility policy, Deng proposed giving the top managerial cadre in each firm much more autonomous power, even to the point where he or she could become its *chengbaoren*—the person who holds full legal responsibility for the firm, or its entrepreneur. These policies, initially proposed in the early 1980s, met with strong resistance from local cadres and were implemented inconsistently even in the late 1990s. Yet in at least some cases, large state enterprises were converted to stock-holding firms, while some small firms (or branches of larger firms) became quasi-private companies. State organizations were also encouraged to start for-profit ventures, like the University Technology Business Group. Ironically, these policies can be seen as a mirror-image reversal of the 1950s policies which reduced capitalists to state-paid managers.

In a related narrative, Deng Xiaoping claimed that the Cultural Revolution villains derailed China's economy by isolating it from foreign developments, most pertinently advances in science and technology:

Due to the interference of Lin Biao and the Gang of Four, China's development was held up for ten years. In the early 1960's, we were behind the developed countries in science and technology, but the gap was not so wide. However, over the past dozen years, the gap has widened because the world has been developing with tremendous speed. Compared with developed countries, China's economy has fallen behind at least ten years, perhaps 20, 30, or even 50 years in some areas. . . . Therefore, to achieve the four modernizations, we must be adept at learning from other countries and we must obtain a great deal of foreign assistance (Deng 1984 [1978]-e:143).

Through this narrative, Deng Xiaoping blamed China's isolationist policies on the deposed and discredited Cultural Revolution radicals, and was therefore able to justify opening China not only to foreign science and technology, but also to foreign direct investment and foreign companies—in order to learn foreign management techniques, of course. This exposed Chinese citizens to another group of entrepreneurs, ones who arrived with their capitalist cultural repertoires. As we shall see, the Chinese found these foreign entrepreneurs quite fascinating, and biographies of famous capitalists became immensely popular.

Ironically, Deng Xiaoping did not offer a grand narrative vision to justify the legalization of urban household businesses, or getihu, even though these became the most popular and visible form of entrepreneurship in China. (The term getihu refers to both the proprietor of the business, and to the firm itself.) For Deng, permitting small private businesses was a pragmatic move. They would help to ameliorate the problems of urban unemployment and to fill in some of the gaps left by the redistributive economy, offering a few goods and services to increase the quality of urban life. Yet it is clear from his narratives that they were expected to play a secondary role, operating in the crevices of the "real" economy, not to become a significant player in China's economic development:

> The individual economy (*geti jingji*) . . . operating within certain prescribed limits and under state control, is a necessary complement to the public sector of the economy. Experience has proved that this helps to make up for the inadequacies of the state and collective economies, creates more job opportunities, and revitalizes socio-economic life. But the state will not permit any activities in the individual sector of the economy to undermine the socialist economy" (Deng 1984:94).

Following this narrative, the first regulations legalizing getihu stipulated that they could have no more than seven non-family employees, and were limited to certain sectors of the economy. Yet in reality, some *geti* (individual) businesses grew larger than the purported limit, and no one was certain whether this was permissible or not. Deng deliberately withheld comment, as he admitted himself a few years later: "At that time, many people were uncomfortable—said this guy's made a million—and advocated intervention. I said, don't intervene, if you intervene people will say the policy's changed and the benefits are not worth the costs"(quoted in Naughton 1995:99). However, Deng also refrained from defending getihu, and instead sat back to see how the situation would play out, even if it developed in ways he himself had not foreseen.

With no clear messages from above, the Chinese media generated a confusing and contradictory set of public narratives about private business. In April 1980, a long piece in *Red Flag* explicitly invoked the Five-Anti Campaign and bluntly criticized the evils of "bourgeois ideology" as an ever-present danger in Chinese society. It warned that some people were "socialists in their words but capitalists in their deeds" ("*Hongqi* on Struggle between Bourgeois and Proletarian Ideologies" 1980:L14). These narratives reminded people of all the reasons why market practices had been condemned and vilified in decades past. However, less than one month later, a *Beijing Ribao* (*Beijing Daily*) article supported some types of geti business by attempting to explain the difference between "good" market practices and "bad" market practices. According to the author, "socialist commerce" served the people by meeting their needs. In contrast, "the sole aim of capitalists in running a business was to make money" ("Beijing *Ribao* Discusses Shrewd Business Sense" 1980:L8). In June 1980, Heilongjiang's governor explained that the non-exploitative individual economy served the country by providing jobs for unemployed youths and by supplementing the "main" state economy ("Heilongjiang's Chen Lei Speaks on Individual Economy" 1980:51). Although this narrative praised self-employment, it also implied that it was a second-rate option for those who were not able to get a "real" job in the "main" economy.

In sum, in the first six months of 1980, Chinese citizens were given state narratives which explained that private business practices were a) dangerous, b) evil, c) acceptable in some forms but not others, or d) useful for society, though only appropriate for marginalized people. The contradictory voices reflected factional disagreements in the central government about the market reforms. These mixed messages continued for the next two decades, until the 2001 tussle between President Jiang Zemin and other CCP elders over whether "capitalists" should be permitted to become Party members. Eventually, however, the sectoral restrictions were dropped, and in 1988, *siying* (private) firms with no size limit were legally recognized. Legally, the owners of these businesses were not getihu, but generic shangren (businesspeople).

Cadres, Getihu, and Real Businesspeople: Local Definitions

To some extent, formal policies explain the origin of the three categories of entrepreneurs (*chengbao* cadres, petty capitalist getihu, and generic shangren/qiyejia). Yet their definitions on the ground level deviated substantially from their legal content. Formally, if a cadre became a chengbaoren of a privatized enterprise, he or she was an entrepreneur. However, Harbiners considered the leader of any firm which was associated with the state a cadre, and not a businessperson at all.

For example, the founder and leader of the University Business Group was a former cadre whom I will call Mr. Fu. Although the state had no hand in funding or managing the Business Group, Mr. Fu was never considered an "entrepreneur" or a "businessperson" by anyone outside the top floors of his Administration Building. Instead, they called him a "cadre," as though he was a government-appointed bureaucrat at a state factory, and treated him as though he were running a state firm. Nor was Mr. Fu the only entrepreneur who was labeled a "cadre." Harbiners referred to the heads of joint venture firms and privatized state enterprises, as well as market ventures like the University Business Group, as though they were unambiguously state actors.

A twenty-year-old waiter at the Pizza Parlor explained why he would rather work in private firms than the state sector. In state organizations, he argued, connections mattered more than ability:

Because I've seen it happen. I have a friend. His father is a . . . cadre. He's a pretty good friend. . . . After he graduated, he looked for a job at an ordinary company. That company was some kind of joint venture. . . . He was an ordinary office worker, but he got caught in the middle of some unpleasant office politics. At that time, his dad still wasn't anything big, and couldn't do anything. His dad didn't say anything about it, but it was because of that incident—Anyway, three years later, his dad had risen up to a high position. And when he did, he used his position to fire thirty people, over thirty people from the director on down, those people who had wronged his son. This is a true story. Because he told me himself. So from that time, he climbed up to the position of general manager. And he's only 29. . . . Sometimes I think: why isn't my dad a big shot? [Laughs]

Although my interviewee used this story to highlight problems with state workplaces, the firm in question was actually a joint venture. He described his friend's ethically challenged father as a "cadre," even though he had a high position in a privatized, legally autonomous firm.

Because these "cadres" were still considered servants of the state, rather than market actors, popular opinion judged them by their ability to provide socialist benefits to their workers, not by their talent at making money, serving their customers, or expanding their businesses. In the eyes of Harbiners, the worst crime a cadre-entrepreneur could commit would be to lay off workers. Those who did were condemned with narratives of corruption for "eating and drinking people's salaries" through their decadent lifestyles. Unfortunately, many cadre-entrepreneurs inherited state firms which suffered from a surfeit of employees, a legacy from the communist commitment to full employment. Even firms which were new, such as the University Business Group, were pressured to hire and retain more employees than they wanted.

According to the legal definition, the difference between a getihu and a generic businessperson is the size of the business: a firm with less than seven nonfamily employees is a getihu rather than a siying business. Yet in Harbin discourse, firm size was not the deciding factor. Getihu had low levels of human capital, and they ran petty businesses. "Real" businesspeople, in contrast, had "modern" business and were of high "quality" (*suzhi*). At the University Business Group, I interviewed a high-ranking administrator and member of the board of directors, one of the few people in Harbin who considered Mr. Fu an entrepreneur. At one point I asked him whether he admired businesspeople or entrepreneurs. He immediately drew a distinction between "real entrepreneurs" like his employer, and the run-of-the-mill getihu:

[I admire entrepreneurs.] But out there, there are a lot of people who can't be called entrepreneurs (qiyejia). They're just small, small getihu. . . . Getihu and entrepreneurs aren't the same thing. I look down on those getihu. People will ask me, what will you do after you retire? I say, even after I retire, I'm not going to become one of those getihu, selling some clothes or vegetables or whatever to make a little cash. I'll stay home and baby-sit instead. I can't respect them, those getihu.

Like this administrator, many of my respondents made a clear distinction between genuine entrepreneurs and low-status getihu. When Harbiners talked about getihu, they were depicted as peddlers "standing on the corner with a cart of clothes," while entrepreneurs or businesspeople were seen as people with offices and briefcases. After meeting our neighbors, my roommate (an employee at a European multinational firm) smirked at the man's cheap suit and the woman's garish make-up: "You can tell that they're getihu. So hick (*tu*)!" She would never put these people in the same category as the head of her international telecommunications corporation. Several years after my initial research was finished, I gave a talk back in the United States about this distinction between getihu and respectable businesspeople. A fellow social scientist, who had grown up in Harbin and had returned there many times, caught only the tail end of the presentation. Unaware of my central argument, he inadvertently confirmed it by exclaiming, "But getihu are not entrepreneurs! They're not real businesspeople. They're just small—they're just peddlers!"

The distinction between "real" businesspeople and getihu was evident in marital choice. "Real" entrepreneurs were considered to be Harbin's most attractive eligible bachelors, yet getihu had low status in the marriage market. At the Russian Market, a fifty-four-year-old vendor bragged that none of her children had gone into business, but instead had all obtained "proper" jobs in the state sector. Later in the interview, she lowered her voice conspiratorially:

> You look at the getihu here, the men. A lot of them can't find girlfriends. But my sons had no problems. When looking for a spouse, you want someone who has education, someone in government. Not some getihu with money. So my son married a girl who graduated from [Heilongjiang University], Russian major. And a girl who's not bad-looking, either. Even when we're just here talking, chatting, about finding someone for someone, it's always "find one who works for the government, who has an education, knowledge." Rarely does someone say, "Okay, just find someone with money."

The low status of getihu on the marriage market was confirmed by a young man, whom I will call Mr. Ge, who also worked in the Russian Market. Good looking and well spoken, he had developed his small business to the point where he made hundreds of thousands of yuan a year, and even had several branches in other cities—all by the age of twenty-six. But all of these accomplishments failed to impress the parents of marriageable young ladies. He explained ruefully:

Every time someone's tried to introduce a girl to me, every one of those girls' families has looked down on me. . . . They think their daughter should marry someone with a proper (*zhengshi*). . . . They want their daughters to marry a college graduate, who works in a good work unit. Someone with a proper job, not one that may have its salary stopped or its workers laid off. With a stable income. That's the kind they all like. That's how all the parents, the fathers and the mothers think. They all look down on me and think I'm not good enough for their daughters.

Indeed, my one attempt at matchmaking in Harbin failed miserably because of my ignorance of the distinction between respectable businesspeople and getihu. A friend of mine had a younger sister who had reached the ripe age of twenty-six without getting married. Desperate to ameliorate this terrible situation, my friend was constantly asking for everyone's help in finding a suitable young man for her. One day, I suggested introducing her to Mr. Ge, who had made a good impression on me. The matchmaking brother was so appalled at the idea of his college-educated sister together with a lowly getihu that he was almost driven speechless. Yet he was thrilled when his sister eventually married an engineer who was working at a computer-related start-up, even though neither the firm nor the groom had as much economic capital as the businessman I had recommended.

Clearly, the three categories of entrepreneurs were somewhat contested in 1990s Harbin; people wanted to be labeled as a "good businessperson" or "real entrepreneur" and to avoid being seen as either a "cadre" or getihu. Moreover, the categories were changing over time. At the beginning of the decade, most entrepreneurs were considered suspect in Harbin and stigmatized with the characteristics eventually attributed only to getihu. By the turn of the century, more and more attention was being focused on "good businesspeople"—entrepreneurs with high status. However, overall, the divisions between these three categories operated along two different axes. First, there was a boundary drawn between firms "inside" the state sector and "outside" in the market: cadres worked "inside," while getihu and businesspeople worked on the "outside." Second, there was a boundary drawn along the axis of human capital, or suzhi (quality). Those who were considered "intellectuals" or to have "high-tech" firms were always seen as "businesspeople," never getihu.

Collective Narratives: "Inside" Versus "Outside"

Narratives of "inside" and "outside," which I discussed in chapter 1, were common in Harbin throughout the 1990s, though their popularity began to wane at the turn of the century. These stories divided all jobs into two mutually exclusive categories: those "inside" the state sector versus those "outside" in the market. In local rhetoric, people were either "staying inside the work unit" (*liu zai danwei limian*) with their "iron rice bowls" (*tie fanwan*) or they had "jumped into the sea" (*xia hai*) of the market, going "out into society" (*waimian de shehui*). These settings were relics of socialist narratives, where the obedient and skilled were rewarded by the state for their contribution to society with paternalistic care "inside" state work units. Conversely, those who were unable or unwilling to serve society were cast "outside" into "society" to fend for themselves. The safety of the state sector was summed up in the symbol of the "iron rice bowl." To leave that security was to "jump into the sea," an image of the risk and wild danger of the market.

In 1990s Harbin, "inside" or "outside" status determined the way that an entrepreneur would be labeled. The owners of "outside" businesses were usually seen as getihu, but the head of an "inside" firm must be a cadre. Indeed, for many of the Harbiners I talked to in 1997–98, "going outside" was starting a getihu business. Like the administrator at the University Business Group quoted above, my interviewees during those years would frequently respond to my questions about entrepreneurs with answers about getihu. Unconsciously, they assumed that any question about life "outside" must be a question about getihu, just as they assumed that getihu must be peddlers working literally "outside" in the streets.

Although Harbiners acted as though "inside" and "outside" were clear-cut categories, in reality there were many workplaces which fell between the two ideal types of the state socialist enterprise and the street stall. For most of them, though, a large firm associated, however obliquely, with the state and managed by a Party member with cadre experience must be an "inside" organization, not an "outside" one. Although Mr. Fu, at the University Business Group, considered himself an entrepreneur who had "jumped into the sea" of the market, only his closest cronies agreed with him. From the perspective of the average Harbiner (and his own employees), he had little in common with unproductive, petty getihu, so he was a cadre and not a businessman.

The World "Outside," Where Economic Capital Reigns

In 1990s Harbin narratives, the world "outside" was the realm of economic capital. Therefore, their assessment of "outside" businesspeople, such as getihu, was highly influenced by their narratives about economic capital. In their stories, Harbiners treated wealth very differently whether they were discussing a community or an individual. It was unequivocally good for a nation or a province or a city to be rich. Like their political leaders, Harbiners believed in the narrative of national economic development, where history is seen as a linear path of progress, but nation-states compete to move faster or slower along that road. People in Harbin (and elsewhere in China) would ask me how many years their nation was "behind" the United States, as though I would be able to confirm that the PRC in 1997 would be the exact equivalent of America in, say, 1972. At a dinner party in 1998, one of the guests told the following joke:

> Bill Clinton, Boris Yeltsin, and Jiang Zemin were permitted to go to heaven to ask God one question each.
>
> Clinton asked God, "When will the U.S. finally achieve development?" God replied, "In fifty years." Then Clinton wept, because he would not live to see it.
>
> Yeltsin asked God, "When will Russia finally achieve development?" God replied, "In one hundred years." Then Yeltsin wept, because he would not live to see it.
>
> Jiang Zemin asked God, "When will China finally achieve development?" There was a long pause . . . and then God wept.

At that dinner party, many people had been sharing jokes, but this one was the hit of the evening. The Chinese there roared with laughter, then spent the next ten minutes wiping their eyes and repeating, "And then God wept!"

Indeed, one of the major problems with businesspeople was that their work did not contribute to this national economic development, at least according to Harbin narratives. Socialist narratives validated agricultural labor, industrial production, and ideological service to the state as "true labor." Their status as genuine work was confirmed by their status "inside" the state sector. Private business, in contrast, was relegated "outside" to the margins of the economy precisely because it was not really productive. I heard a number of people snipe that businesspeople did not do "proper work," but instead they just made money by "moving goods from here to there." Harbiners, accustomed to state-controlled prices, thought it was immoral when businesspeople charged a higher price on a product just because someone was willing to pay that price. The idea that the private sector "created jobs" was completely alien to them.

Although wealth was good for the nation, it was personal wealth which was the driving force of the world "outside" and its occupations, according to 1990s Harbin narratives. Habiners told tales about all the money that the world "outside" offered. In 1998, one fifty-four-year-old woman described befriending two getihu in 1990, when she was a low-ranking cadre:

> They said to me, "You go to work and make how much?" At that time we thought getting 300 yuan salary [each month] was pretty good. They said, "We make that in a day." I would go over to visit and chat with them. Even in the winter they would be eating "fine" vegetables. Do you know what I mean by "fine" vegetables? Eggplant and cucumbers and tomatoes, in the winter! Their standard of living was a lot higher than it was for us working folk.

Inspired by this display of wealth, she retired early and became a getihu at the age of forty-six. Several years later, she had made enough money from her little stall selling ruffled aprons and embroidered towels in the Russian Market to spend the equivalent of over US$15,000 to buy her son an automobile. Those who observed her rise to wealth could now tell rags to riches tales praising the world "outside" and the opportunities offered by entrepreneurship.

Yet the world "outside" and the money it offered were also associated with immorality and waste. In Harbin narratives, at least until the late 1990s, rich people who wore designer clothes, drove their own personal cars, and flaunted the latest miniature cell phones were assumed to be either corrupt cadres or cheating businesspeople, even when there was no evidence of illegal or suspicious activity. These stories drew upon the logic built into the socialist narratives of asceticism, and the dissident narratives of corruption popularized by the Tiananmen Square Protests. According to those narratives, those who were morally upright lived simply and served others, ergo those who used their money to live decadently rather than help other people must be immoral. The underlying assumption in these tales was that personal wealth, "outside" wealth, was gained at the expense of national wealth, and that money wasted on consumption was money not used to serve and develop China. Wealthy individuals must be immoral, and therefore they must have used improper means to gain their wealth.

A forty-two-year-old low-level cadre at the Disability Agency insisted:

In China's current social situation, if you follow the laws in doing business, you won't profit. You have to bend the law to have success. It's not about really using ability, fairly competing in business. So if I see someone who's successful in business, I assume they used illegal methods. . . . If I saw an American or Japanese or European businessperson, I would assume they were okay, but if I see a Chinese business person, I'm suspicious. That's the way it is. In China, we have a saying, "Businesspeople all cheat (*pian*)."

A forty-three-year-old worker from the Agricultural Machine Factory told me, "Some people envy [businesspeople]. Others think that they make money from other people's misery. Some struggled hard to make their money, but others are different. So people say they get rich from tricking (pian) people. It's envy that people feel towards them, not respect."

A sixty-two-year-old retired professor explained:

At a time of transition, regulations were insufficient. At transition time, the policies were not complete. So some people with guts made money in ways that are now considered illegal, but the laws are incomplete. Loopholes like tax evasion, false goods, fake brand names. . . . You could get rich real fast. This development is not unique even in China. So maybe problems of the 90s in Harbin were the problems of the South in the 80s. Our new government is trying to deal with these problems. Also, they are learning from foreign countries how to manage the market, how to deal with corruption, illegal economics. Like copyright violation in software—dirty money.

In 1997, Heilongjiang residents in the private sector made 35 percent more on average than those in the state sector, and 160 percent more than those in collectives, and their earnings were increasing at a much faster rate (State Statistical Bureau 1998: table 5–23). Yet, by using narratives of "inside" versus "outside," many Harbiners could conclude during the 1990s that the extra cash was an insufficient incentive for leaving the state sector, at least to become a getihu. According to these stories, economic capital might be gaining value in Chinese society, but there were still limits to the usefulness of money. For example, the head of the Disability Agency admitted that even getihu often earned more money than she did, but insisted that the comparison was spurious: "Maybe our salary doesn't look high. But we also get benefits, like the shuttle bus to work, medical care, 100 yuan a month of free telephone calls, and housing at highly subsidized prices. So our lives are better than a peddler (*xiaofan*) who may make more money." Young people (and their parents) complained that "outside" jobs could not help a person obtain a *hukou* (urban registration permit) or housing. Life "outside" may offer more money and offer a taste of cosmopolitan glamour, but it was also unstable, insecure, undignified, and risky — the world of getihu and their shady deals.

Collective Narratives: Suzhi *and "Good Businesspeople"*

The scholarly literature reveals that the discourse of "inside" versus "outside" and its attendant prejudices against entrepreneurship existed in other cities in China, especially in the 1980s (Gold 1990; Jankowiak 1993; Ikels 1996; Lu and Perry 1997). That Harbiners apparently clung to these views longer and more intensely, as I heard them expressed well into the late 1990s, should not be surprising, given the city's strong investment in the ideology and institutions of state socialism, and its relatively shallow experience with capitalist business.

Yet even in Harbin, wholesale prejudice against businesspeople eventually began to fade in the late 1990s as the private sector expanded and the city's state sector was hit hard by xia gang. In the early years of the new millennium, the discourse of "inside" and "outside" was increasingly replaced by a new conceptualization of occupational status based on the rhetoric of suzhi. A number of anthropologists have noted the rise of suzhi discourse in the PRC (Yan 2003; Anagnost 2004; Kipnis 2004). As noted above, the Chinese term suzhi is usually translated into the English word "quality." In essence, suzhi discourse claims that people of "quality" or "high quality" deserve more status (more power, higher pay, better conditions, and so on) than those without "quality" or with "low quality."

Despite its ubiquity in popular discourse, when confronted by Western social scientists, Chinese respondents were universally unable to define suzhi, or to clearly explain how one determined whether an individual possessed suzhi or not (Anagnost 2004:197). Indeed, even at a 1987 national conference specifically about suzhi, scholars found themselves unable to define the term. However, the conference participants were able to agree that "*suzhi* [however defined] is for the most part higher in the city than in the countryside, higher in Han areas than in minority areas, higher in economically advanced areas than in backward areas." Moreover, it was higher in first world than third world countries, and overall, the level of suzhi in China's population was too low (Yan 2003:496).

According to Harbiners, getihu did not have suzhi, categorically. A twenty-year-old waiter explained:

> People respect those with quality (suzhi), like college graduates. It doesn't matter if they have skills or not, they have culture (*wenhua*), quality (suzhi). Even from the way they talk, not like ordinary people, not like me. When I talk with college students, it's different; it's at a different level. Now in China, it's those with knowledge who are respected, even if they don't make as much as a getihu. Getihu may make money, but they don't have real friends. What I admire is when intellectuals get together and talk.

The view that petty capitalists and cultured, high-quality people are two mutually exclusive groups has deep roots in Chinese history. Hill Gates points out that although petty capitalism flourished in pre-modern China for centuries, high social status was reserved for the literati, the educated and cultured men who passed the civil service examination and gained positions in the government bureaucracy. Business success, though admired, did not elicit respect because businesspeople served themselves (and their families), while the Confucian literati served society (Gates 1996).

By 2001, the attitude toward getihu in Harbin strongly echoed this pre-modern view. The strongest prejudices against getihu had faded. For example, I no longer heard anyone conflate getihu with ex-felons anymore, and it was less common for residents to insist that they were inherently dishonest or immoral. Instead, getihu were considered to be the ordinary people or *laobaixing* of the city, regular folk looking out for the welfare of their families. However, if getihu were less denigrated than before, it was still obvious to Harbiners that these petty entrepreneurs were not among those special citizens who truly served China in its quest for development, the contemporary version of the Confucian literati. Over and over again, when I asked my interviewees if businesspeople (shangren) were respected, they answered that getihu could be admired or envied, but they could not be respected because they did not have suzhi.

However, some people who went into business clearly did not fit the stereotype of the low-quality getihu. In the 1990s, China's emerging book market offered one model of hero-entrepreneurs through biographies of famous Western capitalists, such as Lee Iacocca (Chrysler), Bill Gates (Microsoft), Andy Grove (Intel), and Jack Welch (General Electric). These books were wildly popular in Harbin, to the point that these American entrepreneurs were household names. For Harbiners, the salient difference between getihu and the famous Western capitalists in the popular biographies was not so much their financial success, but their education and the technological nature of their business ventures. The capitalist-heroes were "intellectual" entrepreneurs with college degrees. They made money through their "knowledge" (*zhishi*), rather than by cheating and exploitation, in what Harbiners considered to be "high-technology" (*gao keji*) industries: computing, software, and automobiles. Furthermore, in contrast to self-centered getihu, their businesses did serve society and the greater good. Although their victories were measured in profits and growth, their success contributed to the wealth and economic dominance of the United States, the preeminent nation of the world. These were entrepreneurs with suzhi.

The capitalist biographies offered an alternative model for businesspeople in China. Entrepreneurs with college degrees, high culture, and "scientific and technological" businesses must be of "high quality," and therefore they must not be getihu. Unlike both getihu and cadre-entrepreneurs, these "real entrepreneurs" and "good businesspeople" were seen as the embodiment of suzhi. While cadres drained China's resources through their corruption and incompetence, and getihu focused narrowly on their own gain, "real entrepreneurs" contributed to China's national progress to modernity through their work. In the words of a twenty-five-year-old waitress at a fashionable pizza parlor:

> There is a portion of young entrepreneurs who used education to develop. Of course people respect them. But other kinds of businesspeople, well, [their views are different]. I know of one who left a high position at a state enterprise contributing to society to go back to school. This person got a master's degree at the Harbin Institute of Technology, and then went to Beijing to "jump into the sea." That's the kind of person I admire.

In addition to being connected with formal educational credentials, suzhi was also associated with "science and technology." A thirty-one-year-old graduate student, who had just started a computer repair firm, noted: "It is not that businesspeople are not respected, but it's qualitatively different than [the respect for] intellectuals. And it depends on the kind of entrepreneur— like the president of Legend Computers, he's respected. But not the guys who make money off of nightclubs, because these guys don't have culture. And also, they're not contributing to social development." When asked what kind of people he respected, a thirty-nine-year-old social science professor replied, "people with culture who are entrepreneurs, like those making high-tech products. Like Bill Gates, or the head of Intel."[1]

Suzhi was also associated with high culture. In the winter of 1998, I interviewed a successful and gregarious forty-four-year-old getihu at an open market. Although this former waitress with a middle-school degree was running a thriving business, she still insisted that high levels of education were necessary for business success:

> This is just an example—if someday the wind blows over a piece of paper with classical Chinese written on it, they can bring it to that kid and they'll understand it. If you don't know the words, then it's just scrap paper. If you can understand classical Chinese, you can gain all kinds of knowledge. It's not to say you can't make it without knowledge; you can. You can depend on yourself and make a little money. Money is good, it can do anything. But if your kid can really have an education, can have it in their hands, can get some good experience, then they can open a big company, one that spans the seas. Won't they make money? And without knowledge, they wouldn't be able to do this well. I still think the best is if a kid can learn to speak the languages of all kinds of countries. But you need education for that, right? Without education, how are you going to learn that?

Although she mentioned the usefulness of language skills for negotiating in international business, the greater portion of her narrative focuses on a far less practical skill. Understanding classical Chinese, which was used for written documents prior to the twentieth century, is comparable to a Western scholar knowing Latin. Even most academics rarely use it in daily life, but it is a marker of high culture and learnedness. And yet she claimed that there is a connection between knowledge of classical Chinese and the ability to succeed on the global market, to found a company that "spans the seas."

Harbiners were convinced that "good businesspeople" with suzhi, like the

Confucian literati of the imperial past, were infused with morality and concern for serving society. To quote a thirty-five-year-old government cadre: "You can divide [businesspeople] into two groups. There are those entrepreneurs who make money, but they take the money to contribute to society. Where there's suffering, they'll help—build a hospital, help the disabled. They'll take their money out. These people get respect. But some aren't like this: those who indulge themselves in wine, women, and song, and go out and play, go traveling."

Through the discourse of suzhi, a new model of entrepreneur appeared, in opposition to the corrupt cadre and the mundane getihu: the educated, cultured, "scientific," and moral businessperson who served China's national interest through his or her success on the global market.

Rewriting History: Suzhi and the Evolution of Chinese Business

Given the relationship between formal schooling, suzhi, and status as a respectable "real entrepreneur" in turn-of-the century Harbin, it is hardly surprising that educational credentials correlated with business success. Harbiners were aware of this trend and constructed a historical narrative to make sense of it. In 1998, I interviewed a thirty-six-year-old professor who had started a profitable chemical-analysis company. He offered me this rather self-serving history of private business in Harbin:

> In the early years of reform in Harbin, the first group to get rich was rascals. These were people without culture (wenhua). . . . Now they're all in jail. At that time, people weren't very clear about the market. And nobody had courage. Like the people in the university all thought, "Doing business is wrong; it's uncultured." People looked down on it. From 1985 to about 1990, at that time there were those who relied on power to make money. . . . Now, this kind of thing, it happens somewhat less than before. Now you can say that few people are using these kinds of methods. . . . Now we say that China is entering the period of the "scholar-businessperson" (rushang). That is to say now there are some scholars, or some scientists, or those who do scientific work, who are doing business. Like me. People who use their own technology, their own knowledge, or their own ideas.

A forty-three-year-old physics professor from the same university agreed:

At that time it was a seller's market. Now it's a buyer's market, a completely different situation. Now, the situation is different. In these past few years, the ones who are rich are the people who start companies. For example, you can buy computers cheaply in the South and sell them here for more. This is making money from information, and so now you need knowledge, and opportunity. Now it's becoming more knowledge based. There are teachers, professors, going into business.

In the late 1990s, I only heard this kind of story from professors. By 2001, it was more prevalent, and by the time I returned to Harbin in 2004, this narrative had become widely popular and was common among getihu, professionals, and cadres. In a visit to a getihu friend and his wife (a low-ranking cadre), I heard each of them tell the following story, though at different times during my trip: [Paraphrase] *Business is different now than it was before, much more competitive than it used to be. In the past, no one but the desperate would go into business, so it was people like former criminals who had just gotten out of prison. So of course it was easy to make money. But now, everyone's going into business, so culture (wenhua) matters. Now that educated people are in business, all those uncultured getihu without suzhi cannot compete. Many who had made fortunes before have nothing now.*

By the time the wife told me this narrative, I had heard variations of this story so many times that I could not resist asking, "What does book learning have to do with running a business? Why would anything you learn in school matter for entrepreneurship?" She was genuinely taken aback by my question, since it seemed self-evident to her that of course education mattered. After some thought, she responded with an example: an acquaintance of theirs had a son who went to a good college and studied computers. He graduated and started up a technology company, which now had over fifty people. "And he makes more than a little money!" she assured me.

In reality, technology start-ups have a notoriously high rate of failure because they require high levels of capitalization and rely on timely technical innovation for profits (Florida and Kenney 1990). But my friend was clearly unaware how rare such an example must be (assuming that it was accurate). For her, his story was proof that suzhi, developed through formal education, was necessary for business success. Moreover, as more and more people believed this was true, the more true it became, as social actors favored market actors blessed with educational credentials and other markers of suzhi. This, in turn, motivated more people to invest in formal schooling and to choose to start firms that would be considered "scientific" and "technological" by others.

Gender and Private Business

The narratives of the "high quality good businessperson" had implications for gender and entrepreneurship, shifting it from a relatively female-dominated activity to an increasingly male-dominated one. In general, Harbiners did not consider private business a gendered activity. When I asked female entrepreneurs what it was like to be a woman in business, they would stare at me blankly as though they had never considered their gender an issue. Harbiners seemed to tell the same sorts of stories about male and female businesspeople, though I should note that since spoken Chinese is less gendered than spoken English, it was not always obvious to the listener if the subject of their story was a woman or a man.

Research from other parts of China seems to indicate that getihu business was a male-dominated activity in some cities (Greenhalgh 1994), but this was not the case in Harbin, where women seemed to be in the majority through most of the 1990s. In this, we can see how local narratives affected the gender make-up of the emergent business class. In southern China, where getihu quickly lost their stigma, private business's fat profits made it an appealing profession, and it was soon controlled largely by men. In contrast, Harbiners coveted state sector positions and denigrated work "outside" for years after the private sector became an acceptable option in the PRC's coastal cities. As a result, entrepreneurship, for most of the 1990s, was relegated to those who had little to lose by leaving the state sector. Due to institutionalized sexism in the state sector, women were less likely than men to have high-status state positions they were unwilling to relinquish. Furthermore, gendered state regulations, like the fact that women retired five years earlier than men, also swelled the population of female entrepreneurs.

In the early and middle part of the decade, entrepreneurship allowed at least some women to raise their social positions and transform the power dynamics within their families. In the years before xia gang, starting a private business was still a voluntary activity. Many of the women who pursued this activity came from the lowest reaches of the socialist state hierarchy, such as the despised service sector. Some even had no "real" jobs at all, and were "just" housewives. Thanks to the relative scarcity of consumer products and the fact that most Harbiners still eschewed the private sector, it was not difficult to make considerable amounts of money in private business. A number of women made small fortunes, and their economic capital shifted the balance of power in their households.

For example, one of my interviewees was a former peasant with only three years of formal education. She was only allowed to move to Harbin because she managed to marry a city boy, but was unable to secure any kind of formal employment. Completely dependent on her husband, she had no choice but to become a housewife, raising the two children her minority status as a Korean allowed her to have. When geti business was legalized in the late 1980s, she was one of the few people willing to take advantage of the new policy—which in her case meant standing on a street corner selling pickled vegetables and enduring harassment from the local police. From this inauspicious beginning, she moved onto larger and larger business ventures. Ten years later, at the time of our interview, she was running a flourishing foreign trade company. Dressed in a tasteful business suit, she smiled and informed me that it was no longer worthwhile for her husband to keep his state sector job, since it earned so little money. So he stayed home to do the housework.

In the late 1990s, getihu business remained a female-dominated activity in Harbin, though for different reasons and with different results. State-sector managers, forced to lay off huge numbers of workers, targeted middle-aged women—in part because these women tended to have weaker qualifications than men, and in part because managers believed that males were family bread-winners, while women could always be supported by their husbands. Unlike the entrepreneurs who voluntarily chose to leave state work units five years earlier, these women were pushed out into the private sector against their will, often with no desire to do or aptitude for business. To make things worse, the pleasant sellers' market of the early 1990s had vanished, replaced by a cutthroat buyers' market. By 1998, the crowds of middle-aged female getihu, huddled on the street with their pathetic displays of cheap goods, had become a recurring narrative element in Harbin stories. These middle-aged female entrepreneurs were symbolic victims, representing the failure of the paternalistic state and the perfidious corruption of state officials.

At the same time, collective narratives of suzhi were creating a new category of entrepreneur: the "good businessperson" who was cultured, moral, and re-spectable. Although some female entrepreneurs certainly benefited from this new label, the way the category was constructed favored men. In contrast to the getihu of the early 1990s, "good businesspeople" tended to come from high positions in the state hierarchy, positions which were dominated by males. The single most salient qualification for a "good businessperson" was human capital, and men had higher levels of education than women. Furthermore, Harbiners popularly believed that males are "naturally" better at math and science than females, an obstacle for women who want to work in the prestigious fields of science and technology. (On the other hand, Harbiners were also convinced that females were "naturally" better at foreign languages, an important asset in private business.)

By the time I conducted my fieldwork at the turn of the twenty-first century, Harbin's markets were clearly dominated by female getihu, but among white-collar "good businesspeople" there seemed to be more men. Meanwhile, cadre-entrepreneurs were almost always male, reflecting the gender biases built into the state sector. For a brief period of time in the 1990s, entrepreneurship offered a strategy for some women in Harbin to destabilize the androcentric and patriarchal dynamics of power in the city's markets and homes. This moment was short lived, however, and the tripartite division of entrepreneurial occupations between getihu, "good businesspeople," and cadre-entrepreneurs reasserted male dominance in private business by turning to existing gendered institutions (such as the educational system) to determine status among entrepreneurs.

How to Build a Business? The Narrative
Construction of Business Practices

Harbiners used narratives not only to construct the different categories of entrepreneurs, they used them also to create the practices necessary for conducting business. In many ways, the obstacles facing aspiring entrepreneurs in the early post-socialist era seemed insurmountable. First, businesspeople lacked formal institutional support: the legal system was insufficient for enforcing contracts, the banking system refused to lend capital, and fees and bribes raised transaction costs. Second, the trust that is an essential prerequisite for market transactions was largely absent, as the majority of the self-employed were considered untrustworthy. Third, Chinese citizens had spent decades developing cultural repertoires to negotiate state socialist institutions, not to start their own businesses. For Harbin entrepreneurs to be successful, they needed collectively to construct entrepreneurial practices adapted from their existing cultural resources, ones which could generate the trust necessary for market transactions in a way that was not dependent on formal legal or economic institutions. They succeeded in doing so by utilizing the narratives of *guanxi*.

Guanxi and Marketization

As I discussed in chapter 2, the practice of guanxi is based on Confucian narratives of relationships and reciprocity, in which emotional feeling (*renqing*) must be manifest through gift exchange. Because post-imperial guanxi practice was constructed through narratives of friendship, each transaction had to be seen as part of an ongoing process rather than as an isolated event. Consequently, exchanges must be unequal. I give you a gift, and you respond with a gift of greater value, setting up the conditions of debt which allow me to respond in turn. In guanxi narratives, people who fail to maintain their guanxi relationships through the exchange of gifts and favors have failed to act like civilized human beings. They have no face (*meiyou mianzi*), and deserve to be shunned from guanxi networks.

Under Mao Zedong, Chinese people adapted guanxi narratives and practice to negotiate the scarcities and irrationalities generated by the socialist redistributive economy. In pre-revolutionary times, guanxi narratives and practice were based on kinship relationships, but under communist rule, they became "modularized" and transferred to friendship networks (Lo and Otis 2003). Guanxi practice and favor exchange became methods for expanding networks by starting new relationships. By offering gifts and favors, or asking for them, one could transform strangers (*shengren*) into friends (*shouren*). In the market socialist era, Chinese citizens no longer needed to turn to guanxi practice to obtain daily necessities. However, guanxi practice became an integral part of doing business. By using the language of guanxi narratives, social actors could exchange goods, services, and information through the rhetoric of "favors." They could expand their network of business contacts rapidly by using the mechanisms built into guanxi for acquiring friends.

Scholars of China have been aware of the importance of guanxi practice in post-socialist society, but they have been divided in their assessment of it effects on marketization. One school insists that guanxi impedes the development of market institutions and practices by encouraging corruption or impeding people's ability to make genuinely rational, market-based decisions.

According to this narrative, guanxi practice encourages the combination of the public with the private, and of business with gifts, easily devolving into rent-seeking and bribery (Wu 2001). Guanxi practice may lead Chinese proprietors to hire according to personalistic considerations, rather than seeking out the best possible candidate (Hui and Graen 1997). Potential employees may also avoid working for strangers. Hobbled by guanxi, managers may select their suppliers and clients on the basis of reciprocity, rather than on rational economic criteria (Guthrie 1999:181).

Although there is a grain of truth in all these contentions, the arguments embedded in this narrative are flawed by inaccurate understandings of guanxi practice. On one hand, it is true that corruption became a serious problem in early post-socialist China, and in many ways guanxi practice did facilitate it. The free flow of gifts and favors made it easier to offer and accept bribes. However, guanxi narratives actually condemn corruption as a violation of moral guanxi practice, and clearly distinguish between a guanxi transaction and a bribe. A bribe violates the central tenets of guanxi: it is an isolated, discrete transaction in which the desire for instrumental gain undermines the possibility of an emotionally close relationship (Smart 1993:289; Yang 1994:202; Lo and Otis 2003:144).

These guanxi-impedes-marketization scholarly narratives also espouse a very idealistic view of capitalism—as though Polanyi's ideal type of market transactions is how real market economies work, and individuals in market societies really are rational, autonomous beings selling to all and buying from all. Guthrie argues that guanxi practice is merely a response to scarcity and irrational institutions, and when rational economic institutions develop, the practice of guanxi will fade away (Guthrie 1998, 1999, 2002). Yet real markets are plagued with problems, such as free riders, incomplete information, and irrational decision makers. Regardless of how wonderful a society's formal institutions are, there will always be a scarcity of good jobs, talented employees, timely information, wealthy investors, inexpensive supplies, good business partners, and interested customers. Even if guanxi operates only in areas of scarcity, there will still always be areas of the economy that it can colonize (Yang 2002).

There are two main versions of the guanxi-impedes-marketization narrative. In one, guanxi practice dooms China's quest for modernity, preventing it from ever achieving the level of industrial capitalism enjoyed by less-encumbered societies (Fukuyama 1995). The other emplots the story of China's triumph over guanxi: as social actors learn how to build rational market institutions and participate in competitive market practices, they will abandon the inefficient and irrational practices of guanxi (Guthrie 1998; Guthrie 1999; Guthrie 2002). Neither of these narratives can explain why capitalism has flourished in societies rife with guanxi practice, including the PRC, Hong Kong, Taiwan, Singapore, and other destinations of the Chinese diaspora. If one were to generate a short list of all the states that have managed to move from so-called third world to first world economic conditions in the latter half of the twentieth century, a significant number would be societies in which significant populations practice some form of Chinese guanxi.

There is a substantial scholarship on Chinese societies outside the PRC which argues that guanxi practice, far from impeding capitalist development, instead has enabled the development of an alternative form of capitalism that may be just as viable as the bureaucratic, rationalized capitalism of the West (Redding 1990, 2000; Tong and Yong 1998; Hamilton 2000; Yeung and Olds 2000a, 2000b). Unfortunately, this literature tends to present a narrative based on cultural essentialism: Chinese culture is based on Confucianism and centered on family-centrism and personalistic guanxi ties. Confucian culture, in turn, has created "Confucian capitalism," built on family businesses organized according to the structure of the patriarchal clan. In "Confucian capitalism," transactions are predicated on *xinyong*, or guanxi-based trust, rather than written contracts. This narrative assumes that all Chinese people, regardless of where they have been scattered in the diaspora, are similarly rooted in Confucian culture and practice Confucian capitalism.

These Confucian capitalism narratives ignore the variation in both guanxi and business practices across supposedly "Chinese" communities. For example, in 1990s Harbin, family businesses were not the norm. In fact, Harbiners avoided going into business with their kin. Of the twenty-four small business owners I interviewed, in only two cases did the owner's spouse work for the firm. Even in businesses worth hundreds of thousands of yuan, the founder's wife or husband usually kept her or his job as a doctor, engineer, or factory manager. Instead, Harbin narratives of "inside" versus "outside" taught them that a small business was much too dangerous a place to risk the whole family. Guanxi practice, modularized and untethered from the patriarchal clan, allowed Harbiners to build their businesses with "friends" and keep their kin safe in the state sector. The prejudice against family business was hardly common through the rest of China, but it reflects the flexibility of guanxi practice to adapt to local conditions.

Yet Harbiners, like many people in other places, found guanxi narratives useful for constructing locally appropriate practices for doing business. In the 1990s, Harbiners used guanxi practice to secure transactions and generate trust, in lieu of legally unenforceable contracts. Guanxi practice was also used to bypass inadequate financial institutions. Whether one was raising capital, securing a permit or job, working out a possible business partnership, or obtaining a shipment of products, everything was negotiated in the language of friendship and favors, banquet and gifts, rather than legal contracts and paperwork. I met only one entrepreneur who was able to secure a loan from a bank, and he had strong guanxi ties with the bank officer. Most aspiring business owners in Harbin and elsewhere relied on an array of informal financial practices based on guanxi practice (Tsai 2002). The entrepreneurs I interviewed were willing to turn to formal institutions to hire lower-level employees (such as receptionists, janitors, or unskilled factory workers), but the more important the position, the more they relied on guanxi ties. It may have been easy to find an adequate cashier, but a good accountant or talented high-level engineer was a much scarcer resource. Also, entrepreneurs wanted trustworthy, loyal people to fill key positions in their firms, and those characteristics were inherently embedded in guanxi relationships.

In the early-post-socialist era, the practice of guanxi also offered benefits which were not provided by formal institutions even in Western capitalist societies. For example, in the West, new and young employees tend to have low organizational commitment and high turnover rates. In China, thanks to guanxi ties, neither youth nor job tenure significantly affected organizational commitment, so firms can invest more reliably in their new employees (Chen and Francesco 2000). There is evidence that guanxi practice sometimes helped protect social actors from exploitation and rent-seeking. Chinese migrants workers used guanxi narratives to assert their rights against harassment (Zhang 2001). The explicit purpose of guanxi was to build a long-term relationship, rather than one which lasted only the duration of an interaction or a contract. This encouraged both parties to follow social norms and to be moderate in their requests.

What markets require is not legal contracts per se but a relatively high level of security for transactions, an adequate degree of predictability, and some assurance that one has some recourse if the other party fails to follow through on their end of the deal. Legal contracts, and the system of formal and rational law which support them, may not be the only way to create these conditions (Chen 1999:110). Guanxi narratives and guanxi practice, in essence, allow capitalism without contracts. Through ever-expanding networks of "friends," aspiring business owners could raise capital, form partnerships, seek suppliers, gather information, and conduct relatively secure transactions. It was common practice in Harbin, for guanxi "friends" not only to lend each other money and share news, but to offer each other retail space and introduce potential clients. Thus it was possible for a person with very few resources, except "friends," to start and sustain a small business.

Narratives in Comparison: Chinese Guanxi versus Russian Blat

To highlight the role of guanxi narratives in producing entrepreneurial practices in China, it is helpful to draw a comparison with Russian *blat*. Like guanxi, blat was a practice that was used to negotiate the irrationalities and scarcities of the socialist redistributive economy. Like guanxi, blat involved the exchange of favors and was conducted in the language of friendship. Yet, in the post-socialist era, Russians did not develop a "capitalism without contracts" based on blat to bypass their inadequate formal institutions. Instead, blat devolved into elite corruption and rapacious exploitation, and faded in importance for ordinary citizens. Concomitantly, entrepreneurship failed to thrive in Russia. In the 1990s, the percentage of the self-employed in the Russian workforce never rose above 2 percent, less than a fifth of what it was in China. In 1997, Russia had fewer than 850,000 registered small businesses[2] (Barkhatova 2000:657). Furthermore, entrepreneurship was confined to the upper classes in Russia (Gerber 2002). Why did two such similar practices under socialism yield such dissimilar results in post-socialism?

The answer lies in the narratives which undergird the two practices. Although socialist-era blat was practiced much like Chinese guanxi, it was based on a very different set of stories. Guanxi narratives associated the practice with being both civilized and truly Chinese. It was rooted in Confucian narratives which argued that moral behavior was manifested through relationships, in which one acted out one's role as a wife, daughter, mother, sister, subject, or friend by giving and receiving gifts of material resources or services. Post-imperial Chinese also understood guanxi practice as a profoundly Chinese activity. From Sun Yat-sen to Mao Zedong to current-day social scientists, leaders and intellectuals have generated narratives which lauded or blamed Confucianism and guanxi practice for China's uniqueness. For Harbiners to participate in guanxi practice was to play a part in a shared story which defined their people historically and nationally.

In contrast, Russians understood the story of blat through a Soviet-era narrative. The term itself can be traced back to pre-communist criminal jargon, but most Russians were unaware of this, and instead assumed that the word appeared only after the Soviet system made the practice necessary (Ledeneva 1998:9–11). Even after blat entered the popular vernacular, it still carried some of its old shameful taint; it was a slang term avoided by Soviet state discourse and eschewed in polite conversation (Ledeneva 1998:13; Fitzpatrick 1999:63). In the Soviet era, few people admitted to participating in blat. In their narratives, they attributed this "antisocial" behavior to others, who were willing to "cheat the system" for personal gain (Ledeneva 2003:9, 12). (From a Chinese perspective, it is impossible to imagine guanxi practice characterized as "antisocial.") When people did participate in blat practice, they misrecognized their actions through narratives of friendship (Ledeneva 2003:12). A forty-year-old worker insisted: "It is purely human relations. If I like a person I will do my best to help, if not—then no. This is not *blat*. In my understanding classical *blat* is calculative—when you ask somebody and that person assesses what he or she can get out of you." His wife contradicted him: "To tell you the truth, he did do it. As a valued specialist he got me a part-time job at his lab. I am not educated. . . . You say this is nothing but influence, but still, one can say you arranged it by *blat*" (Ledeneva 1998:61).

Because blat narratives were less explicitly linked to a moral system than guanxi narratives, blat practice evolved in a different direction than guanxi practice in the post-socialist era. For example, Russians found it natural to begin using money in blat transactions, since cash became the most important scarce resource to obtain. Guanxi narratives already offered rules and mores about the proper exchange of cash in gift transactions. It also differentiated between a gift and a bribe: the former was an expression of friendship, while the latter was obviously exploitation. Without these constraints, blat could become more thoroughly moneterized, which made it harder to misrecognize blat transactions as anything but bribery and corruption. As one Russian said,

"In the new distribution system, where land, raw materials, and finance can be distributed in the same manner as sausages, cars, and apartments, the effect of connections is a hundred times stronger" (Ledeneva 1998:180). During privatization, elite actors used blat to purchase access to state property, including the opportunity to buy it at a fraction of its value. The Soviet natural gas monopoly, Gazprom, was privatized for only $20 billion, although its assets were worth $120 billion (Murray 2000:27).

Meanwhile, ordinary Russian citizens who had no get-rich opportunities to share with their friends, found it difficult to imagine a moral use for blat in the post-socialist era. After the advent of marketization, it was no longer necessary to use blat to obtain the necessities of daily life, like foodstuffs or train tickets. Instead, cash replaced connections as the most important form of capital. As blat's raison d'être for ordinary citizens disappeared, the practice no longer had any use. By the mid-1990s, young Russians considered the very term "blat" out-of-date, and the word *blatnoi* had regained its pre-Soviet definition of criminality (Ledeneva 2003:15).

Russians did use blat-like practices for doing business in the early-post-socialist era. To understand why it was less successful than guanxi-based "capitalism without contracts" in China, we need to analyze the different ways that friendship was framed in blat versus guanxi narratives. In Russia, friendship was understood as an "affiliation with a particular circle of trusted people" (Ledeneva 2003:6). Soviet-era *blatmeisters* described engaging in blat transactions with two different groups of people: "friends" (*svoi lyudi*, or "people of the circle") and "useful people" (*nuzhnye lyudi*) (Ledeneva 1998:121). Svoi lyudi were people with whom one had close personal relationships and a history of warm affection. Blat was easier to practice with "friends," while setting up blat transactions with "useful people" took more effort. In the words of one Russian: "if you are in the circle, everything happens by itself" (Ledeneva 1998:123). Friendship circles were generally understood to be relatively closed, although one could use blat with "good friends" of "good friends."

In Chinese narratives, by contrast, friendship was imagined in the language of networks or webs (*wang*) of dyadic relationships, which were constantly expanding. Anybody connected to you through the long chain of relationships, no matter how many degrees of separation lay between you, was considered a "friend." Nor did they admit distinctions between true "friends" and "useful people." In reality, of course Chinese people were emotionally closer to some "friends" than others, but guanxi narratives misrecognized the distinction, insisting that all friendship ties were animated by "human sentiment" (renqing). Guanxi participants were also confined to doing business with "friends," but the "modularized" nature of post-socialist guanxi practice meant that Chinese friendship networks were open to expansion and easily grew extremely large very quickly. This is not to say that Russians were incapable of making new friends, but that they were much less likely to add new *svoim* to their friendship networks as rapidly or as promiscuously as Chinese added shouren to theirs.

Unfortunately, smaller networks had negative implications for entrepreneurship. Like Chinese entrepreneurs, Russian businesspeople in the early-postsocialist period found that formal institutions provided insufficient means for enforcing contracts. Like their Chinese counterparts, they concluded that it would be safer to deal with "friends" rather than with "strangers," with whom they had no basis of trust. One entrepreneur explained: "We give goods on credit only to permanent clients. We would never give it to others. . . . If you are making purchases you should deal with your own acquaintances. Otherwise, you have no guarantees. They will sell distorted goods to you"(Radaev 2002:200). In Russia, however, this often meant confining business interactions to a relatively small and static population: the circle of personal friends, plus their friends' friends (Radaev 2002; Vinogradova 2005).

This practice made it difficult for newcomers to break into the market because they had no access to useful friends. In Russia, during the early-postsocialist period, entrepreneurship was confined to those with high levels of social and cultural capital, the offspring of managers and professionals (Gerber 2002). In China, by contrast, self-employment was especially popular for those in the lower strata of society, who had less to lose by leaving wage labor. Nonelite Russians, on the contrary, believed that it was safer to maintain a job, even one with intermittent wages and an uncertain future, than to start a business. Instead of turning outward, like Chinese entrepreneurs, they fell back on defensive strategies based on the household, with family members surviving by sharing their minuscule wages, the harvest of their dacha, and their government benefits (Burawoy et al. 2000).

Russian "Worms" versus Chinese "Caterpillars"

In his study of the small-business sector in the Czech Republic, Hungary, and Slovakia, Rona-Tas argued that there are two fundamentally different types of self-employment. Some self-employed are "caterpillars," infused with the entrepreneurial spirit and potentially capable of growing into full-fledged businesses ("butterflies"), while most are "worms," which have no potential for growth (Rona-Tas 2002).

"Worms" are often counted as small businesses, but they contribute much less to the economy. In contrast to genuinely entrepreneurial firms, "worms" are household businesses, started by people with lower status who were pushed into the market, and who often only run their "business" part time. Their goal is not expansion, but consumption—to increase the household's standard of living. Therefore, "worms" rarely seek credit or hire employees from the open market, confining themselves to friends and kin. They rely on local suppliers and clients, and profits come from exploiting personal skills and labor, rather than from discovering and exploiting market opportunities. "Caterpillars," by contrast, are growth oriented and geographically unconfined; they seek and follow business opportunities, they hire employees based on ability rather than connections, and they plow their profits into expanding their business. "Caterpillars," not "worms," are the engine for economic development because "worms" can never grow into larger businesses.

Of course "caterpillars" and "worms" are ideal types, and many self-employed share characteristics of both. In 1990s Russia, blat and related narratives encouraged the self-employed to act like "worms," even (to some extent) when they were running larger businesses. Nonelites fell back onto the household as their base of operations, while elites confined themselves to circles of trustworthy "friends." Blat narratives had taught Russians to seek out opportunities for predatory behavior, to value consumption over entrepreneurial investment and expansion. Even the leaders of Russia's most profitable firms often treated their own businesses not as opportunities for investment, but as cash cows to be milked in order to raise their family's standard of living to astronomical heights. This helps to explain the bizarre finding that in Russia, those who owned smaller businesses had higher incomes than those with more employees (Domanski 2000:78).

In contrast, guanxi narratives encouraged Chinese self-employed, even in the smallest of household businesses, to take on some "caterpillar"-like characteristics even when they should have been "worms." Many of the businesses I studied in Harbin were minuscule, involving between one and six people. Most of these tiny firms were started by people with high-school degrees, who had been "pushed" out into the market by lousy jobs or even unemployment. Thus, in many ways, they looked like stereotypical "worms." Yet, with very few exceptions (such as the self-employed grandmother who bought her son a car), these small businesses were growth oriented and focused on market opportunities.

Harbin's self-employed were certainly not geographically limited to the local economy. Instead, they followed market opportunities not only beyond the city, but beyond China's borders to Russia, Korea, and beyond. In one open market, the stall owners jokingly assured me that they all ran "multinational corporations" because they sold Korean goods to Russian customers. Some Harbiners set up travel agencies in China and Russia to facilitate the border trade, while others opened Chinese restaurants (in Russia) and "Western" restaurants (in Harbin) to serve the homesick. They made "friends" with every foreigner who came to town, eager to learn of international opportunities. One self-employed man asked me to teach him the intricacies of eBay, certain that online auctions could provide the perfect method for reaching an international customer base without raising much capital. Although they were interested in raising their family's standard of living, Harbiners also regularly reinvested their capital in their own firms, or in other business deals. They also lent their capital to relatives and "friends" with their own entrepreneurial aspirations. It is true that these self-employed were "confined" to seeking capital, personnel, and partners through relatives and "friends," but thanks to the expansive nature of guanxi friendship, this was not much of a limit.

Of course, not all of China's self-employed had the potential to evolve into "butterflies," and those labeled "real businesspeople" had a distinct advantage over those considered getihu. Many self-employed flitted from one business opportunity to another, perhaps traveling the world, but never managing to create a firm with any continuity—classic "worm" behavior (Rona-Tas 2002:43). But these were the results of failure, not of an aversion to growth per se. Even these self-employed contributed to China's economy by boosting productivity, encouraging exports, and relieving unemployment pressures. The narratives and practice of guanxi offered Harbiners the tools to create a local version of the entrepreneurial spirit, while the narratives of blat had failed to do the same in Russia.

The Value of Economic Capital and the Moral Meaning of Money

Marxist regimes deliberately set out to reduce the value of economic capital, and Mao Zedong's policies were no exception. In their own narratives, Western scholars often emplot market reforms as a return to a more "natural" (i.e., capitalist) relationship with money. Without the political baggage of socialism, they imply, money can return to its neutral role as the base form of capital underlying all transactions and as the central motivator for all actors. Entrepreneurs supposedly epitomize this new relationship with money. Breaking the shackles of socialist dependence, they pursue profits by converting everything into the universal currency of money. Entrepreneurship is read as a symbol of marketization, and as a measure of the degree to which post-socialist societies like China are capitulating to the logic of capitalism.

By examining the narratives through which market socialist practices were constructed, however, we find that economic capital was considered neither natural nor neutral in 1990s Harbin. Instead, the meaning of money was morally fraught, and negotiated through the language of contribution, development, culture, and nationalism. Harbiners considered economic capital morally suspect and dangerous unless it was leavened with contribution to the national project of modernization. Entrepreneurs were not simply the embodiment of market forces. Instead, through the narratives of "inside" and "outside" and suzhi, different types of entrepreneurs represented different facets of marketization. "Cadres" symbolized the uneasy introduction of market practices into the state sector. "Getihu" represented the petty, exploitative downside of capitalism. Their type of entrepreneurship was not "modern" but "backward," hearkening back to China's pre-revolutionary, "feudal" past. "Real businesspeople," in contrast, offered a glimpse of the potential future China, resplendent with wealth and power and wonderful technology.

The morality of money also played into the practice of doing business. Entrepreneurship flourished in early-post-socialist China, but not because the Chinese had shaken off the bonds of socialist thinking to become rational capitalist individuals who were focused solely on money. Instead, Chinese urbanites developed their own way of doing business by focusing on the currency of relationships. Through the narratives of guanxi practice, aspiring entrepreneurs parlayed their skill at utilizing social capital into business acumen. Instead of rational actors dependent on legal sanctions and contracts, businesspeople in China were moral actors dependent on the social sanctions of guanxi practice to undergird their market transactions.

Chapter 6   **TRUST IN KNOWLEDGE: HUMAN CAPITAL AND THE EMERGING *SUZHI* HIERARCHY**

> In the 1980s, intellect was seen as useless. But now, the respect level is up again. Now you need quality, knowledge, science and technology, economics, just to open a company, to go into business. To do anything big, you need knowledge. So all parents hope that the next generation has knowledge, to make good progress.
>
> —Middle-aged professor

After 1989, former state technocrats and dissident intellectuals became the new political elite in east central Europe, while those who had political capital, but little human capital, experienced a decline in status and power (Eyal et al. 1998). Evidence from Harbin reveals seemingly similar trends: Harbiners insisted that intellectuals were the most highly respected people in China, and intellectual occupations carried the highest prestige.[1] Moreover, my informants saw human capital as the only safe investment in a world where political capital was in precipitous decline and economic capital still seemed risky. They put their words into action by investing enormous amounts of energy and resources to obtain human capital for themselves and their children.

Yet in contrast to east central Europe, China's intellectuals lost their great battle of 1989 when the tanks rolled into Tiananmen Square. In the last two decades of the twentieth century,

China's intellectuals went from being Deng Xiaoping's greatest supporters to his most passionate critics, as evidenced by the tumultuous 1989 protests which spread to every major city in the PRC, including Harbin. After the violent suppression of the movement, many China scholars (and scholars in China) expected intellectuals to lead a democratic opposition against the autocratic state (Fang 1990; Link 1992; Goldman 1994; Miller 1996). Others argued that a combination of state suppression and consumer capitalist "money fever" would degrade the position and status of intellectuals in Chinese society to the point where they were irrelevant and ignored (Zhang 1994). However, a decade after Tiananmen, neither of these predictions had been borne out in Harbin.

Given the traumatic experiences of intellectuals in the 1980s and early 1990s, why would human capital experience a resurgence in value at the end of the century? And why did most scholarship on Chinese intellectuals fail to predict this? Most of that work focuses on the intellectuals' own assessment of their role in Chinese society, as well as their own perception of the value of human capital (Goldman 1981, 2000; Link 1992; Miller 1996). Although this is a valuable approach, it is also necessarily constrained. Intellectuals were not the only actors in society who constructed narratives interpreting the value of human capital. Harbiners, by the end of the twentieth century, had been exposed to narratives about human capital from multiple sources, ranging from traditionalist Confucian folk tales to state propaganda to capitalist advertising. In dialogue with these sources, they constructed collective narratives which argued that human capital was valuable, not because intellectuals deserved political power, but because this form of capital symbolized traditional Chinese morals and virtues, indicated socialist contribution, and was globally accepted as a marker of modernity and progress. Indeed, human capital provided a foundation for a new conceptualization of status based on the narratives of *suzhi* (quality), at a moment when the narratives based on the socialist framework were finally losing their explanatory power in Harbin.

Narrative Sources

Reform Narratives: Human Capital as the Key to China's Development

"One of the great ironies of the Deng era has been that scientific dissidence arose in political opposition to a regime that from the beginning attached a high priority to science and technology, worked actively to rebuild China's civilian science community, and sought persistently to enhance the standing of scientists as a social group" (Miller 1996: 69).

Late imperial China had been ruled by a meritocratic bureaucracy. Supported by narratives which associated education with culture, morality, and contribution, human capital was the key to political power and the basis of the stratification system. When the Marxist revolutionaries, led by Mao Zedong, established the People's Republic of China in 1949, they believed it was necessary to undermine the power of human capital. Yet they also needed the expertise of educated personnel to set up and manage the institutions of the socialist system. Unable to fully "tame" intellectuals, who had not forgotten the narratives of culture, morality, and contribution, the Maoist state vacillated between meritocracy and virtuocracy, between empowering the educated for the sake of economic progress, and attacking intellectuals in political campaigns for tainting communist truth with their bourgeois falsehoods. Indeed, the Maoist era ended with the Cultural Revolution (1966–76), which was such a thorough assault on human capital that China's educational institutions essentially stopped functioning for several years and were seriously impaired for quite some time afterward.

After the Cultural Revolution, the moderate leaders who survived returned to power, most notably Deng Xiaoping. From Deng's point of view, Mao Zedong's periodic attacks on human capital were a terrible mistake that did nothing but derail the socialist project of economic development. As a result, Deng Xiaoping and his followers deliberately set out to revive the prestige of intellectuals and to raise the value of human capital, propagating public narratives intentionally designed to replace Maoist views. The fundamental concept of Deng Xiaoping's political philosophy was the Four Modernizations—of agriculture, industry, national defense, and science and technology,[2] with science and technology as the linchpin.

The Four Modernizations narrative, which was taught to citizens throughout the country, revealed a new argument about the nature of economic growth in China. During the first three decades of CCP rule in China, the assumption was that economic growth came from raising production capacity and from increasing economies of scale. Even before he came to power, Deng was certain that this strategy had been played out, and that in the future, economic expansion had to come primarily from technological breakthroughs. In 1978, Deng gave the following speech at the National Conference on Science:

The key to the four modernizations is the modernization of science and technology. Without modern science and technology, it is impossible to build modern agriculture, modern industry or modern national defense. Without the rapid development of science and technology, there can be no rapid development of the economy. . . . With the same manpower and the same number of man-hours, people can turn out scores or hundreds of times more products than before. What has brought about the tremendous advances in the productive forces and the vast increase in labor productivity? Mainly the power of science, the power of technology (Deng 1984 [1978]-c:99–100).

Deng Xiaoping was willing to compare China to capitalist nations in terms of science and technology, and to find it sadly wanting. In a 1977 talk, Deng complained: "Now it appears that China is fully 20 years behind the developed countries in science, technology, and education. So far as scientific research personnel are concerned, the United States has 1,200,000 and the Soviet Union has 900,000, while we only have 200,000. . . ." (Deng 1984 [1977]:53).

Deng not only praised capitalist nations for their high level of technological and economic development, his narratives echoed contemporary narratives from those societies. In the twentieth century, especially in the United States, economic growth and social progress became increasingly associated with science and technology (Rosenberg 1997; Zachary 1997). Narratives linking development to science ranged from science fiction images of a technology-laden future to business magazines promising economic miracles with every technological "revolution," from automobiles to electronics to the Internet. In the bureaucratic West, educational systems were also believed to be meritocracies, and human capital in the form of academic credentials was taken as a reliable indicator of ability.

In addition, Deng Xiaoping's philosophy of economic growth reflected an ongoing and (as of yet) incomplete shift in the global market from the Keynesian and Fordist mode of capitalism, based on economies of scale and domestic markets, to the global and flexible accumulation mode, which relies on new technology, speed, and worldwide markets. As David Harvey points out, while the Fordist mode requires skilled laborers making decent wages, the new mode bifurcates the workforce into a small minority of highly paid, highly educated experts, and a large majority of poorly paid unskilled workers (Harvey 1990). Like Deng Xiaoping, Western scholars predicted that economic growth in the age of globalization would depend on having a critical mass of creative, highly trained intellectuals (Harvey 1990; Storper 1990, 1992).

Despite the similarities between Deng's narratives and capitalist narratives, Deng Xiaoping was not a capitalist. Instead, he had to make meritocracy and modernity narratives about human capital corroborate with socialist narratives, including those insisting on the superiority of the socialist system. In the 1977 National Science Conference, he explained that in capitalist societies, intellectuals' minds are "filled with bourgeois prejudices" and their work is "exploited by capitalists," but in a socialist society, the "overwhelming majority" of intellectuals serve the working class (Deng 1984 [1978]-c:101). As a result, Deng repeatedly argued against the Cultural Revolution concept of a "class division" between intellectuals and workers, insisting instead that intellectuals were members of the working class. In a direct attack upon the virtuocracy, Deng asserted that apolitical intellectual labor contributed more to society than "political factionalism" which prevents other people's productivity (Deng 1984 [1975]:45).

As we would expect, when Deng Xiaoping and his followers came into power in 1978, they revived and even expanded academic and research institutions. Students began again to compete for positions in key schools, and now they also had to take entrance examinations to get into good secondary schools (Rosen 1984). The national college entrance examination was reinstalled, centralized, and standardized. Elite academic and research organizations, like the Chinese Academy of Sciences, were reestablished or newly created, and intellectuals were given greater power and autonomy over these organizations and schools (Miller 1996:88–92). Also, educational credentials became important for Party membership and cadre rank, displacing class background, political obedience, and ideological enthusiasm as the primary criteria.

High Expectations, Unintended Consequences, and Disappointments

After the abusive oppression of the Cultural Revolution, it is no wonder that Chinese intellectuals at the beginning of the 1980s were euphorically optimistic, as well as enthusiastic supporters of Deng Xiaoping and his reforms. Given the re-valuation of academic credentials, intellectuals expected the stratification system to become reoriented to human capital rather than political capital, so that they would experience a gratifying rise in both their social status and their standard of living. Furthermore, drawing upon Confucian narratives of culture and state service, intellectuals assumed that they were regaining their position as political advisors and the state's moral conscience (Wang 1996:113). After all, Deng Xiaoping had coined the slogan, "Stress knowledge, stress talent"—what else could he possibly have meant?

Rather than focusing on academic work, narrowly defined, Chinese intellectuals in the 1980s acted as though they were responsible for China's fate. They analyzed "socialist alienation," offered political elites their advice on policies, and even dissected Marxist ideology, all in an effort to create better guiding principles for China's development (Link 1992: chapter 6; Miller 1996: chapter 4; Wang 1996: chapter 2). For example, although Fang Lizhi was an astrophysicist, he became famous worldwide in the 1980s for his political critiques of the Deng regime, the CCP, and Marxism in general—and for his advocacy of "complete Westernization." He even encouraged students to form protest movements, as long as they thought clearly about the real causes of their discontent (Fang 1990 [1985]:114). In December 1986, tens of thousands of students took to the streets.

Unfortunately, Deng Xiaoping and other political leaders had been envisioning China's intellectuals as a tame force for economic progress, not as political advisors, co-rulers, or fomenters of dissent. They found the intellectual ferment of the 1980s quite disturbing. Once again, the party-state had to struggle with the old tension concerning intellectuals between the state's desire for economic development and its need for political control. One month after the 1986 student protests, Fang Lizhi was ousted from his university, and the following year he was denounced by Deng Xiaoping by name in the official press. Throughout the decade of the 1980s, the state see-sawed between granting intellectuals unprecedented autonomy and reverting to periods of suppression, such as the rather vague and confusing campaigns against "spiritual pollution" and "bourgeois liberalization."

The reforms provided other reasons for China's intellectuals to feel dissatisfied. When Deng Xiaoping "opened up" the PRC to foreign connections, narratives lauding scientific progress and meritocratic human capital were not the only stories that streamed in from the outside world. Through advertisements, magazines, movies, and television, capitalist narratives came flooding in, promising happiness, fulfillment, and "modernity" through consumer products. China's intellectuals had naively assumed that Chinese citizens would use the relative freedom of the reform era to embrace knowledge and learning, but instead the populace seemed more interested in embracing shopping. In the way of dour academics everywhere, Chinese intellectuals were appalled, and they pathologized the phenomenon as "money fever."

In the late 1980s, intellectuals entertained each other with horror-story narratives about people who abandoned the quest for knowledge for the sake of crass material gain: *Twenty-five percent of China's primary age students have dropped out of school, mostly to "make money"! Shanghai high school students are intentionally scoring low on the college entrance exam to avoid going to college and risking a job assignment outside the city! Graduate students in Beijing are being shunned on the marriage market!* (Link 1992:74). One scientist grumbled, "Professors are not respected. We were poor during the Guomindang years, but the common people always respected a professor. You might still find that respect among older people today. But not the young. It's been destroyed" (Link 1992:74). Although intellectuals favored these woeful tales, these narratives were contradicted by my other interviewees, who insisted that educated people were always respected in urban China, except for the anomalous period at the height of the Cultural Revolution. Yet it is clear that intellectuals themselves felt that they had lost status and prestige in the 1980s.

Though intellectuals castigated "money fever" for seducing people from the pursuit of knowledge, this did not stop them from being displeased with their own perceived poverty. They relished quoting the insulting popular sayings, such as, "The doctor earns less than the old woman selling baked potatoes at the entrance to the hospital, and the barber who cuts a person's hair earns more than the surgeon who operates on the brain beneath it" (Calhoun 1994:264), and "Today, all things have gone up in price except two—professors and trash" (Miller 1996:122). In reality, the reforms raised most intellectuals' standards of living, which had been quite low under Maoist socialism. However, under Mao, Chinese intellectuals, like everyone else, had been taught to construct narratives of utility which compared their current (better) circumstances with their former (worse) conditions. In contrast, during Deng Xiaoping's regime, intellectuals learned to construct narratives of utility where they contrasted their lives with those of their counterparts in the first world, or—worse yet—with the uneducated nouveau riche of their own country.

In the 1980s, Chinese urban residents could strike it rich in three ways: by selling state goods at market prices as "entrepratchiks," by "jumping into the sea" as getihu, or by working for a foreign or joint-venture firm, usually in the service sector at the high-end hotels. Watching crass cadres, lowly peddlers, and hotel girls flaunt their new money, China's intellectuals suffered from a bad case of "red eye disease" (jealousy). Because of virtuocratic policies under Mao, Chinese intellectuals were rarely in a position to allocate state goods for private gain. Nor, by and large, did they take advantage of opportunities as entrepreneurs or *sanzi* employees. Their narratives of culture and money fever framed the realm of knowledge as antithetical to the world of commerce and commodification, both in terms of vulgar petty trade, and decadent foreign luxuries. To go "outside" to start a business was tantamount to admitting that human capital was worthless. By framing intellectual integrity in stark opposition to market commodification, these stories made it difficult for intellectuals to think of ways to use their skills and credentials as profitable assets.

Instead, their narratives taught them that the proper place for an intellectual was serving the state, and enjoying the state's generous recompense for their noble contributions. Unfortunately, intellectuals felt that the state's compensation was increasingly inadequate, especially when double-digit inflation eroded fixed state salaries in the late 1980s. In order to shrink the size of the government, Deng's regime froze the budgets of many major universities during the 1980s and encouraged university presidents to find alternative sources of funding (Link 1992:75). In the early 1990s, I saw university professors standing on Harbin's sidewalks amidst getihu, holding up signs which listed their academic qualifications and offering their services as tutors. Too proud to peddle merchandise, they were reduced to peddling themselves.

Dissident Narratives and the Tiananmen Protests

Throughout the 1980s, Chinese intellectuals emplotted narratives that painted an increasingly dismal view of the Chinese state and society, a story in which they were constrained from using their gifts and talents to serve the people and were themselves subject to insult and injustice. Meanwhile, other groups of Chinese urbanites also felt discontent over the effects of market socialism. This may seem counterintuitive, since the average urban resident's real income doubled between 1978 and 1987, living space had increased by 60 percent, and city-dwellers were enjoying a greater array of consumer goods and services than ever before (Hartford 1990:69). However, intellectuals were not the only group to be stung by rising rates of inflation; state workers, once touted as the core of the revolution, now found their buying power steadily eroding. By 1988, the bottom third of urban households had experienced a drop in real income (Hartford 1990:72). Nor were intellectuals the only residents who felt bewildered and offended by the topsy-turvy economic inequality of the first decade of reforms, or the shocking displays of consumerism by the nouveau riche.

Disgruntled intellectuals turned to narratives of corruption to emplot these new circumstances. During the imperial era, corruption narratives provided an oft-used explanatory framework for writers of Chinese political history. According to the plot, Chinese rulers who fail to listen to the Confucian literati who advise them are led astray, usually by the luxuries of imperial life. Without proper moral example or supervision, their officials indulge in corrupt behavior and exploit their subjects. Sometimes the scholar-advisors are able to call the regime back to its duties. Otherwise the regime decays to the point that the entire empire suffers, and the dynasty loses the Mandate of Heaven to rule and is overthrown. In 1978, Liu Binyan showed through "People or Monsters?" that the corruption narrative could be adapted to criticize the party-state (Liu 1983). In the 1980s, malcontent Chinese intellectuals used corruption narratives to argue that the social problems of the reform era were due to cadre corruption—and to the state's failure to listen to intellectuals, who could provide the true and righteous path for China's future. Taken to their logical conclusion, these narratives could be used to advocate the overthrow of the CCP in favor of a new regime run (or significantly influenced) by intellectuals. The power and resonance of these corruption narratives became exhilaratingly evident in 1989, when Chinese cities became engulfed in the Tiananmen Protests.

Beijing's students initially marched into Tiananmen Square because they wanted to be able to form their own organizations, and they also carried placards demanding "democracy," "freedom," and "free speech." But their most popular cause, in terms of attracting other Chinese urbanites into the movement, was their protest against corruption. When asked to describe the purpose of the movement, both the student protesters themselves and the non-students who joined them chose "an end to corruption" as their top response (Calhoun 1994:246–48). Dissident corruption narratives taught people to read China's social problems, including inflation and inequality, as signs of official immorality, neglect, and exploitation. Yet the Tiananmen narratives did more than blame China's social problems on a corrupt regime; they also asserted that Chinese intellectuals would make better rulers. In other words, corruption narratives offered a way for dissidents to argue that human capital, rather than political capital, was the proper prerequisite for political power.

The Deng regime's own attacks on virtuocracy had already supplied a repertoire of narratives questioning the competence of the cadre corps. Intellectual dissidents built on this by telling stories that blamed cadres' low levels of human capital for their incompetence and immorality. One student argued:

> Due to historical reasons, China's proletariat had the following inadequacies from the beginning: its members were few, youthful in age, and their level of education was low. . . . Only under historical conditions posing a threat to the Chinese nation did workers, peasants, students, merchants, and soldiers come together to form a greater force which pushed the proletariat onto China's historical stage. Once the revolution succeeded, these deficiencies of quality gradually became obvious (Han 1990:38).

A poster at People's University complained that the state "has not put the strongest men and the most outstanding minds to work on creating material wealth for society, but instead has diverted them into endless internal struggles in which they are preoccupied with criticizing others as well as defending themselves from attack" (Han 1990:160). Student protestors and other malcontent intellectuals insinuated that with the correct knowledge, the transition to modernity would be smooth and rapid, without the terrible social dislocations China was experiencing.

Ironically, the intellectual dissident movement was largely reactionary in its appeal, tapping into the discontent of those people who felt that they were being left behind by market socialism and who demanded a return to the economic stability of the iron rice bowl and simple, idealistic leadership. However, the intellectual dissident movement failed to attract support from China's rural majority, who were more satisfied with the reforms at that time. Furthermore, the intellectual dissidents offered few concrete solutions to China's economic challenges. The party-state's most devastating answer to the intellectual dissident threat was the narratives of economic management, which claimed that the true role of the state was to deliver economic opportunities (Hsu 2001). These narratives persuasively argued that the CCP, no matter how morally bankrupt, was the only power able to deliver what the Chinese people really wanted: social stability and continuously rising standards of living. Human capital may lead to morality and idealism, the narratives implied, but, unfortunately, intellectuals were not pragmatic enough to deliver the economic goods.

Despite its startling success for a few months in 1989, the intellectual dissident movement largely failed to accomplish its goals. After the state violently suppressed the student protests, Chinese intellectuals and China scholars in the West expected one of two outcomes. The first possibility was that the CCP was too corrupt and illegitimate to survive for long, and China would eventually follow the example of eastern Europe. Alternatively, the state would survive by reverting to pre-reform authoritarianism, repudiating the market reforms, crushing intellectuals, and reducing their status—and indeed that is what happened in the immediate aftermath of the protests. However, in the longer term, neither of these two visions materialized in the decade after Tiananmen.

These two predictions were flawed in that they were built on the same assumption: that the only possible role for intellectuals in New China was as China's new political vanguard. Instead, in the economic-centered market socialism constructed by the state, an alternative, depoliticized role for intellectuals and for human capital emerged, constructed in part by collective narratives from the populace.

Collective Narratives

The Intellectual Meritocracy

Intellectual dissidents focused on the contradictions between state narratives and their own vision of their role in society. In contrast, ordinary people developed collective narratives which were rooted in the areas where the multiple narrative strands converged. For example, everyone seemed to agree that educational credentials were a more accurate measure of worth than political capital. Deng Xiaoping and his followers propagated these narratives because they wanted to attack the Maoist virtuocracy and also to jump-start a technology-based economy. Intellectual dissidents sought to undermine the regime and argue for their own political credentials. Foreign capitalists found political capital incomprehensible and threatening, a symbol of all that they feared in "communist" China. They wanted Chinese society to move toward "international standards" (i.e., the standards of the global market), which included the currency of human capital. Despite their different agendas, all of these narratives agreed that human capital, in contrast to political capital, was the prize of honest competition and a transparent reflection of suzhi (quality). Virtuocratic local cadres may have disagreed with this assessment, but they had less control over communications media than these other groups, and their narratives were drowned out.

In reality, there were circumstances which could have been emplotted to question the competitive purity of intellectual institutions in China's cities. For example, some schools lowered their standards for those who could pay more money, although this practice was abandoned in the late 1990s, according to my interviewees who were professors. Baccalaureate institutes would offer vocational degree programs for those who could not test into their bachelor's programs. Those who gained these vocational degrees would sometimes pass themselves off as "real" graduates of their name-brand alma mater, never disclosing that they were in a lesser program. Moreover, there was evidence of illicit practices, such as the buying and selling of college admissions, or even degrees. One wealthy entrepreneur asked me point blank how much money would have to change hands for his son to get into Harvard. The head of one of Harbin's biggest state business groups was granted a master's degree at one of the city's most prestigious universities, although he never attended a single class. (I was given this information by the entrepreneur's supposed professor, who had never heard of this erstwhile student until he saw his name on the list of degree recipients.)

A handful of my interviewees emplotted narratives highlighting these unfair practices, but these stories were not common. Instead, in their narratives, Harbiners usually described intellectual institutions as above reproach, operating untouched by either the cash nexus or guanxi practice. The head of the Disability Agency stated, "And you can't just say, 'I have money so I can go to college.' You have to test in. It's something you can't purchase with money. . . . In China, there are some parents with money, but their children just have fun all the time and don't study. Some of these parents say, 'Well, we have all this money, can't we use this?' They want to send them to the schools they can't even get into." According to a forty-three-year-old physics professor, "There are government offices where the people are of low quality (suzhi). There, people with connections get the jobs. People without connections can't get in, regardless of ability. But to get into college, it's still fair. Anyone can take the entrance test and get in."

Harbin narratives focused on the fact that college or graduate school education was limited to a chosen few, and these were selected through a nationwide examination. These examinations were notoriously difficult, and the examiners went to elaborate lengths to ensure that the results were not tainted, to the point that the teachers were literally locked up for days on end while they graded the exams.

Borrowing the Legitimacy of Human Capital

Multiple narrative strands, from the state, dissidents, global capitalism, and ordinary people, converged at the shared idea that educational credentials were the reliable product of meritocracy. Consequently, by the late 1990s, the most efficient way for any occupation to gain credibility among multiple constituencies was to link it to human capital. As academic degrees became the salient criterion in more and more occupations, their value necessarily increased. Because almost everyone agreed on the meritocracy of intellectual institutions, human capital became the one form of currency recognized almost everywhere in society. In contrast to political capital, which was meaningless outside of the state sector, and economic capital, which could only be used illicitly in most state organizations, human capital was a useful asset in most occupations both "inside" and "outside."

For instance, one of the goals of Deng Xiaoping's reforms was to make China a competitive player on the global market. In 1978, when he began to reform the cadre corps so it would be more capable of accomplishing this task, he was well aware that human capital was internationally recognized, while political capital was not. Instead of trying to convince the world that Chinese cadres and Party members were sufficiently excellent because of their political credentials, Deng raised the academic requirements for cadre position and Party membership. By making a college degree a prerequisite for cadre position, the state increased the worth of that degree. Furthermore, when state enterprise and government xia gang hit Harbin, managers borrowed the narratives about human capital to decide which workers and cadres would be retained and which would be cut loose. Although educational level was far from the only factor, these narratives offered one way for managers to make (and justify) difficult decisions about layoffs.

Similarly, in the 1990s when Harbin's rising private business class was confronted with the stereotypes of greedy and amoral getihu, those who had higher levels of human capital responded by highlighting their educational credentials, thereby creating the new image of the cultured, modern, "good businessperson." As narratives dividing the business class between cheating, vulgar getihu and respectable, trustworthy entrepreneurs became part of the collective repertoire, businesspeople with human capital gained vital advantages in the marketplace, while their less-educated counterparts fought uphill battles against discrimination and prejudice. During the same years, foreign, private, and joint venture (sanzi) companies were proliferating in Harbin. The first sanzi firms were hotels and restaurants looking for young and good-looking employees, but by the late 1990s, the sanzi sector had diversified considerably, ranging from clothing boutiques to car dealerships to computer companies. Foreign managers, acting according to their own narratives about human capital, sought educated employees, especially those with technical or language skills. Those who were chosen were often offered impressive market-based salaries.

Chinese managers, wanting to impress both their foreign colleagues and their local customers with the "quality" (suzhi) of their establishments, also relied on academic criteria. The owner of a flourishing private restaurant admitted that, when examining potential employees, he never bothered asking about Party membership. But he insisted that educational credentials were important, even for hiring waiters and waitresses. He explained, "A college degree is a basic requirement. There is a qualitative difference between college graduates and other people." As cadres and businesspeople invested more deeply in human capital for their own reasons, they had every incentive to reiterate and reinforce the repertoire of positive narratives supporting academic credentials. In order to look meritocratic, companies borrowed practices from academic institutions. For example, at the University Business Group and most other large state or hybrid firms, job candidates were subjected to written examinations, even if they were applying to become factory workers. If an "assistant engineer" at one of the Group's factories wanted to rise to the level of "full engineer," he or she (usually he) would have to pass an examination. For promotion to "high-level engineer," it would be necessary to publish original research, just like a professor at a university. Rank was based on academic qualifications, not job performance.

Despite the reluctance of intellectuals to commodify their knowledge, by the end of the century, human capital was a hot commodity everywhere, at least according to Harbin narratives. Although a few of my respondents (including, not surprisingly, several professors) groused that intellectuals were underpaid, the majority assured me that human capital was the most useful investment a person could make in market socialist China if one wanted economic capital. The janitor at the University Business Group explained: "To find a job, the first requirement is a degree. Of course you need money to live on, but you can't see that as too important. If you have knowledge, naturally you will get money. If you meet certain requirements, there are regulations saying how much you must get paid." The head of the Disability Agency pointed out: "Education is much more important than before. You can't get a good job without it. For example, if you didn't go to college, you can't become a provincial level cadre."

A twenty-three-year-old worker had recently started his job at one of the University Business Group's factories (after passing the requisite examination). He dreamed of "developing himself" and eventually starting his own firm, but his parents insisted that he take this "safe" job. Despite the generational conflict, one thing they could agree upon was the value of education. He told me that if he had the opportunity, he would go back to school, but lamented that fact that he did not have time to pursue more education at the moment: "When you're looking for work, education is very important. It's like an entrance ticket. When enterprises are looking for people, they'll say what they require. If you don't have the education, you can't even sign up." The word he used, "enterprises," is generic. It could refer either to a state enterprise, like the ones his parents favored, or a sanzi company, such as the ones he longed to join.

Putting Words into Action: Pursuing Human Capital

Chinese urban citizens, attempting to negotiate a confusing and rapidly changing social world, clung to the fact that human capital would be valuable no matter what happened in the PRC, short of the increasingly unlikely return to the ideological obsession of the Cultural Revolution. Their narratives, in turn, shaped their actions, inspiring them to invest heavily in human capital for themselves and their children. In Harbin, the children of workers and peddlers, as well as the offspring of cadres, professionals, and businesspeople, had their evenings and weekends packed with tutoring sessions, special classes in English, math, or computers, plus lessons in music, painting, or calligraphy.

While doing research, I soon found that one of the best ways to put an interviewee at ease, if he or she were a parent, was to ask them about their child's studies. Regardless of whether their offspring were toddlers or teen-

agers, Harbin parents would pour out their concerns to me. At the Agricultural Factory, I interviewed a forty-three-year-old worker in May 1998. He
answered my questions thoughtfully but briefly, until we began to discuss his
teenage son. Suddenly, he couldn't stop talking:

> This year he's going to test into high school.[3] His studies are pretty good.
> . . . . He says, "I'd like to become a doctor." So I say, then you have to
> study well. He's really interested in it. I asked him what he wants to
> do—be a soldier? Then what—be a worker? "No way!" Then what? "Be
> a doctor. As doctor, you cure people's illnesses and [*unclear*]."
>
> [*I ask: To be a doctor, you have to go to college, right?*]
>
> Right now, he's still young, just testing into high school. Right now,
> he's working hard to test into high school. Here we have what we call
> key schools; he's hoping to test into a key school. The dates of the test are
> June 19, 20, 21.
>
> [*I laugh and tease him about having the dates memorized so clearly.*]
>
> Of course! This is a big deal! . . . There are the provincial key high
> schools, then the municipal key high schools, and then the regular high
> schools. In your application, you can list one provincial key school, one
> municipal key school. If you don't test in, you can choose an occupa-
> tional high school, an ordinary high school. You can list those.
>
> [*I congratulated him on having a child who was so serious about his
> studies. He sighs.*]
>
> Studying is studying. Who knows if he'll test high enough? You do
> everything you can. I give him topics and questions. If he learns it or
> not, that's up to him.

He estimated that 60 percent of their family income went to their son, mostly
for his studies. Although he and his wife earned less than 900 yuan a month
combined, "We pay 20 yuan an hour for tutoring classes and a language tutor.
My wife says we'll sell the house out from under ourselves to support his
schooling. Most people are like this, now that we only have single children.
You make money for your kids." This level of investment was common for
families in Harbin and elsewhere (Li 1997).

Despite the stubborn stereotypes that "boys are better at math and science"
and "girls are better at foreign languages," parents seemed willing to invest just
as much emotionally and materially in their daughters' education as in their
sons.' After all, given the One-Child Policy, most urban families had only one

child to invest in at all. One thirty-four-year-old oil refinery worker, a middle-school graduate, told me she was using all her money to buy her thirteen-year-old daughter a good education. "You need to get tutors and so on. Outside of school, she's taking piano, learning English. I do this because my own generation was too low in culture for this country to develop."

A forty-three-year-old getihu of Korean descent had only three years of formal education herself. Her lack of schooling did not prevent her from becoming a successful business woman, yet she still believed fervently in education. Able to have two children because of her minority status, she still invested most of her resources in their schooling:

> I do everything for them and for their studies. My son studies well and wants to study aeronautics. He's always begging me for computers and stuff. They make me work hard, but I'm willing to help them have what they want. My daughter wants to study in Russia for five years, and then study English for five years. As long as they want to study, I'll keep supporting them. If they study well, they will figure out what's best.

She explained: "The country is developing. Education is more and more important. To be like me, knowing nothing. . . . Maybe you won't be able to make it like I can now. Everything will be scientific and technical, and you'll need to understand it. I can support my kids through school, so they'll never be as poor as I was."

The more social actors invested in academic credentials, the more valuable and necessary those credentials became. The more that social actors constructed narratives that human capital contributed to business success, the more successful educated businesspeople became. The more that ordinary people told stories that said that human capital was the proper criteria for positions and promotions, the more cadres and managers felt justified in using those criteria. And when they needed new policies, they were more likely to adopt those which either depended upon or imitated academic practices, such as degree requirements or written examinations. By 2004, these practices were so well established that they had become taken for granted—they had become, in other words, institutionalized.

Human Capital and the Discourse of Suzhi

Although Harbiners certainly believed that educational credentials were useful for getting ahead, it was far from the only reason that they valued human capital. Instead, they insisted that human capital had intrinsic moral value, and that those who possessed human capital were inherently admirable. In my interviews, I asked respondents to name the most respected group in China. An overwhelming majority, sixty-two out of eighty-two people, replied "intellectuals," while thirteen indicated entrepreneurs, and eleven named cadres. When asked to explain why intellectuals were so admired, Harbiners often turned to narratives of suzhi. As a twenty-two-year-old waitress at the Pizza Parlor explained to me, if someone went to school, "even if they don't have money, they'll have quality (suzhi). Not like those people who dress in fancy clothes, but when they open their mouths, it's clear that they don't have culture." As her twenty-year-old coworker noted, "People respect those with quality (suzhi), like college graduates. It doesn't matter if they have skills or not, they have culture (*wenhua*), suzhi." As the owner of the high-end restaurant said when explaining why he hired only college graduates: "There is a qualitative difference [literally, a difference in suzhi] between college graduates and other people."

What did it mean to Harbiners to be a person with suzhi? For one thing, it meant that this person was able to contribute to society, to serve the collective good more effectively than people of lower quality. In the summer of 1998, I spent a day at the home of a music professor who taught piano to supplement her income, interviewing the parents as each waited for their child's lesson to begin. There I met a forty-six-year-old factory worker. Despite the fact that her middle-school education had not kept her from obtaining a stable and relatively well-paying job at an oil refinery, she hoped her thirteen-year-old daughter would go to college and graduate school: "I hope she becomes useful to society and has a path for development. So I'll use my money to buy her education, to get tutors and all that. Outside of school, she studies piano, English. Because my own generation's cultural level was too low for the country to develop. Knowledge and education are more and more important."

A thirty-five-year-old department store manager at the University Business Group had a vocational high school degree. He also expressed his hope that his daughter, then nine years old, would go to college and contribute to society:

[Some of us] are pursuing more [for our children]. Some of us are pursuing education. How do I say this? People come to the market to make a contribution to society. If they can't make a contribution, then they come in vain. Their parents bear them, and then let them come into society, but if they don't make a contribution, then why? You want to send your kids to college to let them gain a little knowledge. There's no limit to knowledge—the more the better.

Suzhi was associated with socialist and nationalist contribution. But to be a person of quality also meant to be a person of culture (*wenhua*), in the Confucian sense. A twenty-two-year-old *getihu* explained that he admired intellectuals not only because they "can make a lot of things which contribute to society," but also because "they can be self-controlled. They have courtesy." The word he used for "courtesy" (*li*) is a Confucian term referring originally to the rituals and behaviors necessary to assure smooth relationships in the religious and social world.

In 2004, perusing picture books for my own two year old in a Beijing bookstore, I was struck by the proliferation of high-culture products for children, such as calligraphy books, children's versions of famous works of fiction, and (most popularly) editions of Tang Dynasty poetry. I purchased my daughter a twelve-volume set of paperback picture books designed for pre-readers. In addition to the volume on fruits, animals, body parts, automobile models, and children's songs, there was the inevitable volume of Tang Dynasty poems. These poems are the Chinese equivalent of Shakespearean sonnets; they tend to be short, but are hardly easy to read. They are also markers of high culture and learnedness, and Chinese parents delight in teaching their young children to recite them, even if the youngsters had no idea what they were saying.[4] When my daughter proudly recited her ABC's to a Chinese playmate, the other little girl (also two years old) responded by quoting portions of the Three Character Classic (*Sanzi Jing*), the neo-Confucian primer that schoolboys recited in imperial times:

> If you do not study/How can you become a [true] human being . . .
>> Learn while young/When grown up put it to practice
>> Influence the ruler above/Benefit the people below.
>> (Wang 1999:807)

Yet suzhi was also associated with science and high technology, with the cutting-edge knowledge Deng discussed in the Four Modernizations. At the Disability Agency, a forty-eight-year-old low-ranking cadre evoked the Four Modernizations narrative quite directly.

Now intellectuals really have the respect of common people. They see them as "talent" and admire them. Because we all know that it's knowledge—that the state has developed to this certain level, but to go forward we'll need all kinds of knowledge, including agricultural development, high technology products. All these things require scientific content right? Like Heilongjiang province, with all of our grain crops. You can't just sell grain, you need to make a value-added product, then you can sell it on the global market and gain more income, right? Then you need science to accomplish this job. Without culture, knowledge, you just can't do it.

Other interviewees also associated suzhi with science and technology, but were less specific about why. For many, like the twenty-three-year-old technician and twenty-six-year-old engineer who argued that the members of China's Academy of Sciences were the most admirable people in the country, scientists were simply the embodiment of suzhi.

Indeed, Harbiners were often unable to describe exactly what kinds of contributions were being made by these "quality" people, beyond the fact that they were "scientific" and aided economic growth in some way. My respondents, especially those with lower levels of education, took it on faith that intellectuals were contributing in ways which were beyond their comprehension. Indeed, the very ambiguity about intellectual contribution made it easier for everyone to agree that great, though unspecified, contributions were happening. Thus, suzhi discourse allowed Harbiners to combine high culture and morality, socialist contribution, science and technology, and the nationalist project of capitalist economic development into one package, associated with human capital. Respondents would explain in the same breath that they respected intellectuals because they could read ancient texts in archaic Chinese and because they could run multinational companies, or because they understood scientific things and had refined speech and deeper, truer friendships than ordinary people.

Due to the ambiguous nature of intellectual contribution, and to the moral benefits associated with suzhi, Harbiners believed in the general principle that more education was better, regardless of the particular course of study. In 1990s China, most urban residents had only high school credentials, most cadres never went to college, and even professionals (doctors, teachers, engineers) had only vocational or bachelor's (benke) degrees. Under these circumstances, I expected parents to aspire for their children to attend college, either a three-year vocational (*zhuanye*) program, or a four-year benke program, since that was what would be useful on the job market. I was not prepared to hear parent after parent tell me that their dearest dream was for their child to attain the maximum amount of education available in the world: to attend graduate school for a doctorate. Over and over again, I heard the mantra: "a key high school, a famous college, and then go overseas for graduate school, master's, Ph.D., go all the way." (Some would also add: "And then get a post-doc," as though it was another, higher, type of degree.)

Most parents were well aware that their offspring would not reach this lofty goal, yet they planned to support their children's educational development as long as possible. At the Russian Market, I asked the forty-four-year-old getihu who admired those who could read classical Chinese what her hopes were for her sixteen-year-old son:

Hope? Of course I hope that he studies well, gets good grades, and gets into a good college. Of course you can hope, that's no problem. . . . Middle-aged people all would really like their kids—and it doesn't matter if they're boys or girls—to be devoted to their work, to progress in their studies, to get into college, and to go overseas and study abroad. That's the path of glory we all want, isn't it? [*She turns to the bystanders for confirmation, and they all nod and murmur their assent.*]

A middle-school graduate herself, she boasted that she knew someone who had achieved this "path of glory," as though knowing a graduate student was the equivalent of knowing a movie star.

To go overseas, to study abroad, that's even more impressive. There was a young person in my husband's work unit. Tried to get into college but failed the first time, so he [gender unclear[5]] ended up in my husband's factory. My husband took special care of him, didn't let him do the work that was too hard or tiring. And then he got into Qinghua University's Physics Department! And now he's in America, but he still calls us up on the telephone. Oh, we admire him so much! Really admire him, really look up to him. Yeah, now he's in some kind of graduate program— doctorate? Masters? I don't know. But he really does still telephone us. Really. My educational level is too low—no culture. You're really wasting your time talking to someone like me.

Conclusion: Intellectuals, Suzhi, and Global Capitalism

In 1978, Deng Xiaoping announced his Four Modernizations vision, which included a strategy to rehabilitate the status of intellectuals and enhance the value of human capital. In the 1980s, the regime and the intellectuals discovered that their respective narratives about human capital, which had initially seemed so compatible, were actually in violent conflict with one another. Even though the 1980s brought the unanticipated clash between the state and intellectuals, culminating in the massacre at Tiananmen Square, the 1990s offered the unexpected healing of that rift. Ordinary people created collective narratives that colonized the areas of convergence between state and dissident narratives. Through these narratives, they constructed a new intellectual, just as they had constructed cadres and entrepreneurs, and determined the practices and role of that occupation. Just as their collective narratives shaped the meaning and value of political and economic capital, they also defined human capital as the marker of "quality" (suzhi). On the one hand, this new collective conception was acceptable to the state because intellectuals were not politicized. On the other hand, the new collective conception was also acceptable to intellectuals, because they were seen as a distinct social group marked by wisdom and morality. Indeed, if anything, intellectuals were considered too high for the lowly world of politics, which was now viewed as the realm of expedient economic management and self-indulgent corruption.

However, this story that I just have emplotted is missing a crucial character: global capitalism. At every step, the relevant characters were reacting in part to narratives coming into China from the outside world. Deng Xiaoping's regime re-valued human capital because it wanted China to be a competitive player on the global market. Not only was human capital the form of currency which represented meritocracy and "quality" worldwide, but mainstream narratives in capitalist nations, especially after the 1970s, argued that economic growth depended on scientific and technological progress.

Although the intellectual dissidents invoked Confucian narratives about state scholars, they were also reacting to narratives from the capitalist West, though ones that owed more to Vannevar Bush than the *Wall Street Journal*. Bush, who launched the Manhattan Project and was instrumental in setting up the U.S. military-industrial complex, argued for a vision of highly trained scientists, given enormous amounts of resources and extensive freedom by the state, conducting research which would produce wonderful benefits for the nation (Zachary 1997). Dissidents also hearkened back to Western revolutionary thinkers, from Copernicus and Galileo to Bacon and Rousseau, who argued for truth in the face of opposition (Fang 1990 [1986]), or to Western revolutionaries, like the participants in the Paris Commune of 1871 (Calhoun 1994:239). Intellectual dissidents, especially during the Tiananmen Protests, were also savvy enough to play to the Western media, constructing a "Goddess of Democracy" patterned after the Statue of Liberty. Ironically, both regime and dissident narratives held up as role models for China the developed nations of the capitalist West, though they disagreed vehemently about which Western characteristics were the salient ones.

Ordinary Harbiners were also aware, through biographies of Western capitalists, advertisements about "scientific" and "technological" products, and the requirements listed in the job advertisements at foreign companies, that human capital was the necessary currency in their increasingly globalized world. Their narratives about human capital and intellectuals constantly referred to the world outside of China: The "path to glory" was to "go overseas to graduate school"; uneducated people could not go to foreign countries because they did not know English; and intellectuals could found firms that might "span the seas." Human capital was not only what individuals needed to raise their own level of suzhi, but it was also what China needed to develop its suzhi and to compete successfully against other nations in the global market. Therefore, human capital was the best investment because it served self and society equally well. As for intellectuals, Harbiners had learned from Western narratives (sometimes filtered through state and dissident discourse) to conflate "science" and "technology" with "progress" and "modernity." Scientists, who in Harbin were considered the ideal type of intellectuals, were therefore the epitome of the "developed," "modern," and "quality" person.

Yet we must not overstate the case and imagine that foreign stories, through the invasion of globalization, wiped out or replaced local repertoires. Instead, Harbiners combined the narrative elements linking human capital, science, and modernity with socialist narratives about collective service and Confucian stories about intellectual wisdom and morality. They redefined intellectual knowledge to be "science," and redefined intellectual contribution as "economic development," but that made neither the knowledge nor the contribution any less mysterious and wonderful to my interviewees. Through suzhi narratives, turn-of-the-century Harbiners could praise intellectuals for their "scientific contribution," their economic savvy, and their refined speech and cultured "courtesy" all in the same breath, and see no contradiction between the disparate characteristics. China's intellectuals may have lost their bid for political power per se, but through the development of collective narratives, they had been made into the representatives of both China's future "modernity" and its traditional "culture."

By drawing together multiple narrative strands, suzhi discourse offered a coherent ideology to make sense of status and meaning in post-socialist Harbin. At a time when the socialist foundations of stratification were clearly disintegrating, this ideology offered an alternative moral basis of hierarchy and stratification, with human capital at its center. Suzhi ideology increasingly shaped the actions of Harbin residents in their roles as parents, managers, business owners, clients, and cadres. In turn, their actions transformed the institutions of stratification. By the turn of the century, it was growing clear where different types of cadres, businesspeople, and intellectuals fit in the status and occupational hierarchies.

Chapter 7

THE NARRATIVE CONSTRUCTION OF CLASS
AND STATUS UNDER MARKET SOCIALISM:
THE EMERGING *SUZHI* HIERARCHY

Since Deng Xiaoping began instigating his reforms in 1978, China scholars have offered a great deal of evidence to doubt market socialism's chances for success. The PRC was hobbled by the legacy of Maoism as it struggled with post-socialist reforms. Among other things, it had to deal with an inadequate legal structure (Chen 1999), a primitive financial system (Tsai 2002), outmoded and uncompetitive state enterprises (You 1998), and an inappropriately organized bureaucracy staffed by inappropriately trained bureaucrats (Lu 2000). In addition, it had to address the culture of state dependence which had been fostered so deliberately by the Maoist regime, not to mention the pernicious practice of personalistic connections or guanxi (Yang 1994). Without the Western traditions of civil society, impersonal trust, individual rights, and a division between public and private realms, however, how could Chinese society deal with the brutal profit motives and cash nexus of capitalism without disintegrating into amoral exploitation and cynical distrust? The regime's obvious reluctance to address the traumatic moral contradictions between Maoist socialism and market capitalism appeared to be a recipe for a cultural crisis. When the late 1980s brought economic dislocations, "money fever," and the Tiananmen Protests, it seemed natural to assume that the Chinese state was incapable of accomplishing its experiment in market socialism.

Yet such a prediction of the failure of market socialism contains a blind spot: it focuses on preexisting categories. By definition, innovative and ad hoc solutions may have characteristics which are unusual and unexpected. For example, many analysts ignore the regime's claim that market socialism is truly a new system, a "third way" between market capitalism and state socialism. Consequently, they tended to judge market socialist practices as market institutions, and to measure them against the standards of capitalist economies. Using these criteria, many of the characteristics of Chinese economic practices were read as pathologies. The strong role of the Chinese state in the economic sphere and the prominence of personal relationships in business were seen as problems because analysts assume market institutions must be "free" from state intervention and require a clear separation between public and private spheres. These views underlie, for example, Doug Guthrie's influential work, *Dragon in a Three-Piece Suit* (1999).

Similarly, those seeking moral values in Chinese society arrived with predetermined categories. For example, a number of scholars sought evidence of emerging "Western" values. In wake of the fall of communism in eastern Europe, quite a few looked for the rise of civil society in post-Mao China, usually to be disappointed (Wasserstrom and Perry 1991; Brook and Frolic 1997). By focusing on a specific list of "necessary" values, they concluded that Chinese society lacked morality and was descending into unbridled money lust. Ironically, one could come to the same conclusion by searching for Maoist socialist values. My interviewees, especially the older ones, would complain that young people no longer knew anything about self-sacrifice, egalitarianism, or contribution. A search for "traditional" Chinese values would yield the same empty results; the flirtation with Confucianism and "new authoritarianism" in the 1980s was quite brief, and hopes for a political meritocracy were crushed under the tanks at Tiananmen Square. From any of these perspectives, Chinese society appeared to have lost its moral foundation.

Ordinary People and Ad Hoc Solutions

However, instead of looking for what is not there, the narrative approach allows us to seek what is actually present. First, it allows us to see an entirely different set of social actors participating in the construction of new economic practices and a morality to govern those practices. Through the narrative approach, we can see that political elites are not the only actors involved in the process of institutional change. Instead, institutions are created in multiple steps, from the central policy writers to the local policy implementers to the actual participants to outside observers (Stark 1989). With this in mind, we can see a whole array of actors from the center on out contributing their creativity and ingenuity to the process. In other words, even if the policy makers are flawed in their dictates, other people can help make the practices work by improvising collective ad hoc solutions which become institutionalized.

This kind of ad hoc improvisation is a well-documented aspect of institutions and work (Moe 1987; Stark 1989; Meyer and Rowan 1991; Henke 2000). Yet research on post-communist societies often focuses on the dysfunctional, rather than helpful, effects of these informal practices, especially for marketization and economic growth. In the most naive form, scholars castigate "culture" (as in "Chinese culture" or "Russian culture") for preventing a society from achieving "normal" forms of economic institutions. For instance, Francis Fukuyama argues that "Confucian culture" causes people spontaneously to organize within kinships groups, even while doing business, a practice which impedes the development of a more desirable Western- or Japanese-style "bureaucratic capitalism" (Fukuyama 1995). Other, more nuanced, research reveals how barter practices in the former Soviet Union (both before and after its dissolution) reduced economic efficiency by fostering semi-exclusive trading networks, price discrimination, distorted production incentives, and reduced innovation (Commander and Mummsen 2000; Ledeneva and Seabright 2000; Prendergast and Stole 2000). Researchers have examined the problematic legacies of favor-exchange practices similar to Chinese guanxi practices, such as blat in Russia (Ledeneva 1998) or the relational dynamics within the *srodowisko* in Poland (Wedel 1992). About blat, Ledeneva writes, "Pervasive bribery, corruption, the so-called 'nomenclatura businesses,' a criminal 'second' society and active interpenetration of big business with politics are all part of the criminalized legacy of the economy of favors" (Ledeneva 1998:212).

This study reveals the other side of the coin. Informal practices cannot only aid the formation of new economic institutions, but they can also be an integral part of the process. Narrative analysis reveals how those informal practices emerge and evolve and interact with formal policies. Moreover, they also provide social scientists with tools to understand why some informal practices may facilitate economic stability in one context, while similar practices impede it in another. Chinese guanxi and Russian blat are both favor-exchange practices, and under the oppressive, irrational pressure of similar socialist systems, they evolved notably similar characteristics. In the post-socialist era, however, the cash nexus transformed blat so that Russians felt that they could trust fewer and fewer people. Yet guanxi practice also facilitated economic growth, generating sufficient trust for overseas Chinese to invest generously in the PRC before adequate legal protections existed, creating informal institutions for raising capital when banks refused to give out loans, and providing a way for aspiring entrepreneurs to find partners, suppliers, employees, timely information, and clients (Smart 1993; Chen 1999; Tsai 2002; Lo and Otis 2003).

Suzhi Discourse and Neoliberalism

Without the insight that narrative analysis provides about the active role of ordinary people in social transformation, the rise of suzhi discourse can be interpreted as the disturbing creation of an authoritarian state acting in service of global capitalism. Indeed, by focusing only on the virtues that China appeared to lack (democracy; civil society; sufficient social movements; impersonal trust; adequate institutions for worker and consumer protection), it was not difficult to conclude that Chinese society was descending into neoliberal capitalism in its most brutal form. Several scholars have used this lens to interpret the rise of suzhi discourse (Yan 2003; Anagnost 2004).

The contemporary usage of the term suzhi first emerged in the early 1980s in official propaganda which claimed that the One-Child Policy was necessary to raise China's "population quality" (*renkou suzhi*) by reducing its quantity (Kipnis 2004:10–11). Therefore it is not inaccurate to claim that suzhi discourse was initially the product of the authoritarian state, and that it was created for rather oppressive purposes. By the end of the century, suzhi narratives had been co-opted and adapted by the general population, becoming the ubiquitous language of distinction in Chinese society. Suzhi discourse was used for everything from justifying educational reforms to selling nutritional supplements, from trumpeting real estate developments to denigrating litterbugs and short people:

> Human resource managers in both the public and private sectors justify recruitment and salary decisions in terms of *suzhi*. Rural cadres justify their own leadership positions in terms of their *suzhi* being higher than that of the peasants around them, and, of course, urbanites discriminate

against ruralites for their lack of *suzhi*. The language of *suzhi* has become the politically correct language of social snobbery, as well as everything else (Kipnis 2004:2).

Yan (2003) and Anagnost (2004) ignore the ways that suzhi discourse became a resource for ordinary citizens, as a tool in their cultural repertoires. Instead, they focus on the ways that suzhi discourse could be used to oppress ordinary citizens, brainwashing them into service to the global market by inculcating them with a "neoliberal subjectivity." Most scholars studying suzhi discourse have noted the inability of Chinese respondents to define the content of suzhi. When asked, they cannot explain how one determines whether a person has suzhi or not (Yan 2003:496; Anagnost 2004:197). Yan and Anagnost both take the essentially "empty" content of suzhi as evidence that it reduces the worth of human beings to their market value. Yan points out that, on the one hand, the Chinese argue that the level of suzhi must be raised (on an individual, community, regional, and national level) because that is the key to economic development. On the other hand, one's level of suzhi (on an individual, community, regional, or national level) is also measured by one's level of economic development (Yan 2003). This tautology makes "quality" essentially equivalent to "market value."

Therefore, according to these scholars, the "empty" discourse of suzhi is fundamentally about false consciousness, serving the purposes of neoliberal capitalism by orienting Chinese citizens, individually and collectively, to the global market. Suzhi discourse justifies the exploitation of rural migrants by claiming that working in the city will raise their suzhi (Yan 2003), while teaching middle-class urbanites to voluntarily invest in transforming themselves and their children into servants of the global marketplace (Anagnost 2004). In this scholarly narrative, the Chinese citizen is essentially a passive victim. After all, since the Chinese populace lacked any of the moral traits or social institutions which these scholars associated with resistance to neoliberal capitalism, what could it do besides comply meekly as it was fed into the insatiable maw of the global market?

Unfortunately, this interpretation of suzhi discourse must ignore the ways that these narratives are used by ordinary citizens to undermine and negotiate with state power, and to resist the reductive values of neoliberal capitalism. Kipnis (2004) points out when Yan and Anagnost see suzhi discourse as a tool of neoliberal domination, their arguments depend on a vague, undertheorized definition of "neoliberalism" which is so broad and encompasses such diverse phenomenon that it is no longer useful. When we pin down the specific ideological bases of neoliberalism, rather than just using the term to refer to every unpleasant side effect of capitalism, we find that they fundamentally contradict the worldview underlying suzhi discourse.

Drawing upon Nikolas Rose's analyses of liberal versus neoliberal governmentality, we find that, although suzhi ideology may possess some salient characteristics of the former, it shares very little of the latter (Rose 1993, 1996, 1999). According to Rose, liberalism is based on the concept of the free individual as the subject of rule. The role of the government is to develop "free" individuals capable, in a sense, of ruling themselves. It carries out this mission by drawing on expertise in the social and human sciences, and creating institutions (schools, asylums, prisons) that promise to take uncivilized members of society and make them into self-controlled individuals (Rose 1993:290–91). Suzhi ideology, which divides the populace between "high quality" people who pursue their own "development" and "low quality" people who must be "developed" through institutional intervention, clearly reflects the central logic of liberalism. As Rose puts it, liberal governments believe "the national objective of the good citizen" fuses with "the personal objective for the good life" (1993:291).

Although suzhi ideology may represent a form of liberalism, it resembles the welfare liberalism of mid-twentieth-century capitalist states much more than the neoliberalism of the last several decades. Rose terms neoliberalism "advanced liberalism" because he understands it as a subcategory of liberal governmentality. As such, neoliberal governments still rely on the expertise of social scientists. However, while welfare states rely on the "positive knowledges of human conduct" drawn from sociology and psychology, neoliberal governmentality depends on the economic sciences and statistics—the "calculative regimes of accounting and financial management" (Rose 1996:54). The central trope of the "free market," imagining citizens as "customers" with "free choice," leads to monetization; activities which were formerly considered noneconomic (educating a student, performing surgery, a social work visit) now must be justified in cash terms (Rose 1996:54). Although the cash nexus is certainly on the rise in China, the underlying logic of suzhi ideology is more rooted in humanistic philosophy than economic science, and there is little sign of the calculative regime of accounting and budget discipline.

Despite Anagnost's and Yan's claims, suzhi discourse does not reduce human worth to market-exchange value. Yes, overall, poverty was associated in general with a lack of suzhi. But, at least in Harbin, human capital rather than economic capital was the primary marker of "quality." Rich *getihu* did not have suzhi, no matter how fat their profit margins grew, while college graduates had high "quality," regardless of how lean their wallets were. For Harbiners, many indicators of wealth were considered antithetical to suzhi; consumerism was a sign of nouveau riche vulgarity and amoral money grubbing, not quality. People with suzhi were supposed to be above the temptations of material goods. If they inadvertently became wealthy, they would inoculate themselves against criticism by giving their money away, rather than spending it on the market.

According to Rose, neoliberalism also leads to the "de-governmentalization of the state" as the government seeks to distance itself from both experts and citizens through decentralization and privatization (Rose 1996:55). Although the last few decades have certainly witnessed the retreat of the state in China, if anything, suzhi ideology encourages state interference in the most private spheres of citizens' lives (after all, suzhi discourse started with the One-Child Policy). Under neoliberalism, citizens are "customers" who "fulfill their national obligations not through their relations of dependency and obligation to one another, but through seeking to *fulfill themselves* . . ." through consumption (Rose 1996:57). In contrast, the rhetoric of suzhi explicitly links individual development to the collective good and to national progress.

Neoliberalism posits that all individuals are competing on essentially equal terms; it is an ideology which ignores and erases the roles of class difference and social hierarchies (Kipnis 2004:17). Those who do poorly can only blame their own individual flaws, or (alternatively) their failures are seen as the result of individualized pathologies, such as a lack of self-esteem or entrepreneurial spirit (Rose 1996:59). As a result, neoliberal logic argues that these people must not be aided through social programs, which only encourage dependency and low self-confidence, but instead must be empowered with a better sense of self-worth and skills of self-promotion (Rose 1996:60). In contrast, suzhi discourse emphasizes the unevenness of the playing field by focusing on the structural causes of inequality. The central premise of suzhi narratives is that an individual's, community's, or nation's level of quality can be raised by improving institutions; suzhi is not inborn, nor primarily the product of individual hard work or discipline. Neoliberals believe that "welfare queens" live in squalid conditions because they lack morals; suzhi ideology claims that country bumpkins lack morals because they live in squalid conditions. Contrary to the neoliberal project, suzhi discourse "offers a way of speaking explicitly about class without using the word class" (Kipnis 2004:19). As such, suzhi discourse offers a language for denouncing unequal structural conditions and demanding institutional change.

Suzhi Discourse and Emerging Hierarchies of Class and Status

Yan and Anagnost are certainly partially correct when they claim that suzhi discourse serves global capitalism, both by sacralizing "development" and by convincing social actors to transform themselves (and their children) into the type of educated employees that the labor market demands. But suzhi rhetoric also serves as the language of resistance against neoliberalism, by emphasizing the importance of social structures and by positing a moral vision of status based on contribution and culture, rather than money. This moral vision is not simply a product of "traditional Chinese culture," although it certainly gestures back to traditional values and institutions. Nor is it particularly "Western" or "socialist," which is why it remained unnoticed for so long by scholars waiting to see if China would ever develop the "right" predetermined values.

Where did this resonant, powerful, morally charged discourse come from? Although the term suzhi had originated in birth control policy propaganda, by the late 1990s, suzhi rhetoric had evolved considerably beyond narrow party-state narratives, even to the point where it could be used to criticize the regime (in the form of corruption discourse). As narrative analysis reveals, suzhi discourse was not the product of either state elites or market forces, but of ordinary Chinese people telling stories to make sense of their changing world, drawing upon the narrative resources available to them. In doing so, they created an ideology based on the virtues of social contribution, which is rich and powerful enough to animate a complex system of social stratification right at a time when socialist narratives were finally losing their explanatory power.

Recall that a system of stratification consists of three sets of institutions: the first determines the value of different forms of capital; the second determines how valued forms of capital are allocated across occupations and positions;

and the third consists of the mechanisms which link individuals to different positions, thus generating unequal access to valued forms of capital. The ideology of suzhi shapes all three by sacralizing human capital as the central standard of worth determining the allocation of economic and political capital, and reifying the social inequalities which maintain unequal access to human capital.

Because suzhi narratives shaped actions, they also shaped institutions, transforming the landscape of power in post-socialist China. The valuing of human capital at the expense of political capital undermined the ideological role of cadres, and of the party-state itself. As a result, the purpose of the government changed from society's ideological vanguard to its economic manager, and its cadres were desacralized into mundane technocrats. In the private sector, suzhi discourse gave entrepreneurs with educational credentials an inherent advantage over their less-learned competitors. Indeed, party-state officials and cadres were being replaced by "scholar-entrepreneurs" (*rushang*) as China's new role models.

Meanwhile, suzhi discourse raised the status of intellectuals by labeling them the epitome of "quality": the embodiment simultaneously of China's traditional cultural morality, its socialist virtues, and its future progress into "modernity." Despite their elevated position in society, this was an essentially depoliticized role far from the visions of the intellectual protestors who flooded Tiananmen Square in 1989. In a way, suzhi ideology had given the party-state what it had always sought: tame intellectuals who worked hard for economic development but kept their noses out of politics. Ironically, it had achieved this goal mostly by devaluing political position and power.

I do not mean to elide the problematic aspects of suzhi ideology; like all ideologies underlying stratification systems, it serves to create and maintain social inequalities by justifying the unequal treatment of social actors. Suzhi ideology is particularly unappealing in its assertion that a person's overall "quality" can be determined by a few superficial "qualities" such as dress, speech, hometown, and educational credentials (Kipnis 2004:14–15). Even as it focuses on the structural causes of inequality, it encourages and rationalizes prejudice and discrimination against the victims of those unequal structures, especially rural residents. Meanwhile, urban children are subjected to anxious, intensive, and exhausting cultivation. My argument is not that suzhi ideology is something good, but that it is something new and different. And, as such, it reveals the role of ordinary, nonelite people in shaping the economic institutions of post-socialism.

Final Thoughts

The Chinese experiment in market socialism may not have been particularly well planned or implemented, and it may not succeed in the long run. Regardless, by the beginning of the twenty-first century, the People's Republic of China had managed, against expectations, to take market socialism further than any other society. One may quibble whether the emerging system is either "market" or "socialist," but it is clear that new economic practices are becoming institutionalized, that new class and status hierarchies are emerging. This offers the social scientist an excellent opportunity to study the process of institutional transformation.

I have argued that we cannot understand this process without taking into consideration the narratives and practices of nonelites—the ordinary people who are the cocreators of emergent institutions. By focusing solely on elites, one would see China's experiment in market socialism as an exercise in futility: an incompetent state betraying its people's culture and values against the backdrop of brutal, exploitative global capitalism. However, when we put the people back into the story as active participants, a whole new side of institutional development is revealed. We discover that China's urban citizens were much more proactive and flexible than anticipated. They constructed innovative ad hoc solutions to negotiate their changing society. Far from passively reacting to their circumstances, they creatively mobilized and synthesized narratives from their cultural repertoires in order to create a new moral order, based on the ideology of suzhi, for new market socialist institutions.

Post-socialist societies offer an unprecedented opportunity to study the rise of new forms of capitalism. These new forms do not conform to the categories and conceptualizations designed to explain the capitalist economies and societies of North America and Europe. Indeed, far from being a liability, this is what gives these research sites the potential for groundbreaking social science. Narrative analysis offers a valuable approach that allows us to see how social actors create those new categories and conceptualizations, as well as those new institutions, of these new capitalisms.

FIELDWORK SITES AND INTERVIEW SAMPLE AND QUESTIONS

List of Work Sites

Government Agencies

Disability Agency
Public Security Bureau
Railroad Bureau
Post and Telecommunications Office

Traditional State Enterprises or Organizations

Agricultural Machine Factory
Electronics Factory
University

Hybrid State Enterprises and State Companies

University Business Group, including
—Administration
—Food Products Factory
—Department Store
Foreign Trade Company 1
Foreign Trade Company 2

Foreign, Joint, or Private (**Sanzi**) *Firms*

Fast Food Franchise
Upscale Western Restaurant
Pizza Parlor
Japanese Electronics Joint Venture

Korean Electronics Branch
Advertising Company

Open Markets

Russian Market
Clothing Market

Formal Interviews

Total of eighty-two interviewees

Most of my informants consider themselves "ordinary people" (in Chinese, *laobaixing*), a vague and subjective term which can be used to refer to anyone outside the elite. Even so, many were heavily invested in political, economic, or human capital as cadres, businesspeople, and intellectuals. Because I assumed that these aspirations would have an effect not only on their experiences, but also their narratives, I made sure each group was well represented. I also made sure to interview a number of people who were not obviously aligned with any of these forms of capital.

List of Formal Interviews

Workplace	M/F	Age	Occupation	Party Member
1. Ag. Machine Factory	M	50	Sales	Yes
2. Ag. Machine Factory	M	43	Worker	Yes
3. Ag. Machine Factory	M	25	Worker	No, applying
4. Communist Party	M	42	Cadre—chuzhang	Yes
5. Data Comm. Bureau	M	44	Engineer—cadre/director	Yes
6. Data Comm. Bureau	F	27	Engineer—cadre	Yes
7. Data Comm. Bureau	M	25	Engineer—cadre	Yes
8. Disability Agency	F	48	Cadre—kezhang	Yes
9. Disability Agency	F	43	Cadre—tingzhang	Yes
10. Disability Agency	F	35	Cadre—kezhang	Yes
11. Disability Agency	M	42	Cadre—unknown rank	Yes
12. Electronics Factory	F	45	Cadre—kezhang	Yes
13. Electronics Factory	M	30	Worker	Yes
14. Electronics Factory	M	28	Engineer and manager	No, applying
15. Foreign Tech. Company	M	31	Manager	No
16. Foreign Trade. Company	M	44	Manager	Yes
17. Foreign Trade Company	M	39	Manager	No
18. KFC	M	34	Manager	?
19. Museum	M	55	Curator	No
20. Newspaper	M	41	Editor and reporter	No

Workplace	M/F	Age	Occupation	Party Member
21. Oil Refinery	F	46	Worker	No
22. Open Market	M	24	Salesperson	No
23. Own Business	M	59	Entrpr. and professor	Yes
24. Own Business	M	45	Entrpr.—trade	?
25. Own Business	M	42	Entrpr.—restaurant, etc.	former
26. Own Business	M	39	Entrpr., state firm manager	Yes
27. Own Business	M	38	Entrpr.—publishing	No
28. Own Business	M	38	Entrpr.—restaurant	Yes
29. Own Business	M	35	Entrpr.—restaurant	Yes
30. Own Business	M	35	Entrpr.—ad company	No
31. Own Business	M	31	Entrpr.—computers	No
32. Own Business	F	27	Entrpr.—ad company	Yes
33. Own Business	F	25	Entrpr.—retail	No
34. Own Business	F	23	Entrpr., state firm manager	No
35. Pizza Parlor	F	36	Entrpr.—restaurant	No
36. Pizza Parlor	F	25	Server	No
37. Pizza Parlor	F	23	Cashier	No
38. Pizza Parlor	F	22	Server	No
39. Pizza Parlor	M	21	Server	No
40. Pizza Parlor	M	20	Server	No
41. Post Office	M	48	Cadre—chuzhang	Yes
42. Provincial government	M	43	Cadre—tingzhang	Yes
43. Public Security	M	41	Party secretary	Yes
44. Russian Market	M	60	Salesman	No
45. Russian Market	F	54	Entrpr.—retail	No
46. Russian Market	F	50	Entrpr.—trade	No
47. Russian Market	F	44	Entrpr.—trade	No
48. Russian Market	F	43	Entrpr.—trade	No
49. Russian Market	F	43	Entrpr.—retail	No
50. Russian Market	M	40	Entrpr.	No
51. Russian Market	F	36	Entrpr.—retail	No
52. Russian Market	F	32	Entrpr.—trade	No
53. Russian Market	M	26	Entrpr.—retail	No
54. State company	M	22	Manager	Yes
55. Technology Park Admin.	M	58	Manager/cadre	Yes
56. Technology Park Admin.	F	46	Janitor	No
57. Technology Park Admin.	M	40	Economist and Administrator	Yes
58. Technology Dept. Store	F	42	Department manager	Yes
59. Technology Dept. Store	M	35	Department manager	No, applying
60. Technology Park Factory	M	60	Manager/cadre	Yes

Workplace	M/F	Age	Occupation	Party Member
61. Technology Park Factory	M	54	High-level engineer	No
62. Technology Park Factory	M	51	Engineer (mid-level)	No
63. Technology Park Factory	M	35	High-level engineer	No
64. Technology Park Factory	F	29	Secretary	No
65. Technology Park Factory	M	29	Worker	No
66. Technology Park Factory	M	26	Engineer (low level)	No
67. Technology Park Factory	M	25	Worker	No
68. Technology Park Factory	M	23	Technician	No
69. Technology Park Factory	M	23	Worker	No
70. Technology Park Factory	F	20	Worker	No
71. Telephone Bureau	F	34	Salesperson	No
72. Undecided	M	23	Undecided	No
73. University	M	73	Professor, retired	Yes
74. University	M	62	Professor, retired	No
75. University	F	58	Professor and Dept. chair	Yes
76. University	M	43	Professor	Yes
77. University	M	39	Professor	Yes
78. University	M	36	Professor	Yes
79. University	M	36	Entrepreneur and professor	No
80. University	M	27	Graduate student	Yes
81. University	M	24	Graduate student	Yes
82. University	M	24	Graduate student	Yes

Interview Questions

These questions were used as guidelines for conversation, rather than a strict description of the interrogation. Therefore, I often used several kinds of questions to get at a certain piece of information. With more talkative subjects, they would often provide answers to my questions before I asked them.

PRELIMINARY FORMAL QUESTIONS

1. Work unit and position
2. Salary
3. Gender
4. Age
5. Education
6. Income
7. Party membership

1. Parents' work unit and position (before retirement)
2. Spouse's work unit and position
3. Geographic background (where they grew up: village, town, city, etc.)
4. Child's age, education, and work unit and position (if applicable). Aspirations for children. I would often ask if they hoped that their children would follow in their footsteps, occupationally.
5. If the interviewee is young, ask what their parents aspired for them.

WORK HISTORY

1. How long have you worked at this position?
2. List previous jobs in reverse chronological order.
3. Starting with first job, describe why you chose each job and how you obtained the position. Also include in your explanation why you chose to leave the previous job.
4. Do you plan to stay in your current position, or do you hope to move on? Describe your ambitions.

OPINIONS

1. In Chinese society, in order to get a better position, what is most useful? Good connections, high educational degree, good political background, money . . .
   A. Which is pursued the most by ordinary people?
   B. Is this different than it was ten, fifteen, twenty years ago? In what way?
   Alternatively: Is money/education/connections/etc. important in Chinese society today? More or less important than it was in the past? What do you predict will become more important in the future?
2. Who do you think people respect the most in China—cadres, intellectuals, entrepreneurs? Why?
   A. Is this different than it was before the reforms?
   B. What do you predict for the future?
   Alternatively: What do common people think about cadres/intellectuals/entrepreneurs? Do they respect them?
3. Who do you respect the most? Why? Which group do you respect the least? Why?
4. Does your spouse share your opinions? Do your parents? Children?
5. Can you think of someone you know who has been very successful? How did they succeed?
6. Can you think of someone you know who has failed. Why did they fail?
7. Can you give me an example of someone in China who is successful, but doesn't deserve their success?
8. Can you give me an example of someone you think is worthy of admiration?
9. What are the most important social problems facing China today?

10. Overall, do you think the reforms have brought more good to Chinese society or more harm?

    A. Describe the benefits.

    B. Describe the downside to the reforms.

Additional Questions

1. What's the most important factor for succeeding in Chinese society today? For example, what's more important: political background, social connections, money, or educational level?
2. What do you think common people in China pursue? What do you think they want out of life?
3. How important is the generation gap? Do young people think differently than middle-aged people or older people?
4. Who do you think common people respect the most in China today?
5. Who do you respect the most?
6. In your opinion, is Chinese society fair as it is now? Is it changing? How is it changing? How should it change?

Appendix 2 **GLOSSARY OF CHINESE TERMS**

Beijing Ribao 北京日报: *Beijing Daily*

benke 本科: (n) a four-year college program or degree, equivalent to a bachelor's degree in the U.S. system

chengbaoren 承包人: (n) the person who holds full legal responsibility for a firm

chuang yi chuang 创一创: (v) take initiative, achieve something (for the first time)

chuangzao 创造: (v) to originate, found, or start something new

chuzhang 处长: (n) division-level cadre, above *kezhang* but below *tingzhang*

danwei 单位: (n) work unit

de 德: (n) virtue, morals

dingti 顶替: (v) to substitute, to take someone's position in the work unit. This practice allowed children to inherit their parents' position.

dongbei 东北: (n) or (adj) the Northeast, the common way to refer to Manchuria in Chinese

fazhan 发展: (v) develop, (n) development. *tfazhan ziji* 发展 自己: to develop oneself

fenpei 分配: (v) to assign a state sector job, or (n) the job assignment itself

fubai 腐败: (n) corruption, (adj) corrupt

gao keji 高科技: (n or adj) high technology

getihu 个体户: (n) "individual business," a small private business with fewer than eight employees, or the owner of such a business

geti jingji 个体经济: (n) "individual economy," the economic practices of individual or small-scale private businesses, legalized in the reform era

gongxian 贡献: (n) contribution

guanxi 关系: (n) connections or favors

hukou 户口: (n) urban registration permit, which allows a person to legally reside in a particular city

Jiefang Ribao 解放日报: *Liberation Daily*

kao ziji 靠自己: depend on oneself, be self-sufficient

keji 科技: (n) science and technology, or (adj) scientific and technological

kezhang 科长: (n) branch-level cadre, below the *chuzhang* level

laobaixing 老百姓: (n) ordinary or common people (literally, the "hundred surnames")

li 礼: (n) courtesy, manners; also ceremony or rites (as in Confucian rituals)

liu zai danwei limian 留在单位里面: remain in one's work unit, rather than leaving for the private sector

mianzi 面子: (n) face, (metaphorically: reputation); *meiyou mianzi* 没有面子: to lose face, or to have no face

neng 能: (n) ability, capability, (v) to be able to

pian 骗: (v) trick, deceive, hoodwink, or cheat someone

qiye 企业: (n) enterprise; *guoying qiye*: state-owned enterprise; *siying qiye*: private enterprise

qiyejia 企业家: (n) entrepreneur

Renmin Ribao 人民日报: *People's Daily*, the premier official newspaper in China

renqing 人情: (n) human sentiments, sympathy

rujia 儒家: (n) Confucianism (literally, "the school of the scholars")

rushang 儒商: (n) scholar-entrepreneur

sanzi 三资: (adj) a term which refers to foreign, joint venture, and private firms (literally, "three [types of] capital"

Sanzi Jing 三字经: "Three Character Classic," a neo-Confucian text cited by schoolchildren in the late imperial era

shangren 商人: (n) businessperson

shehui 社会: (n) society; *chu qu shehui shang* 出去社会上: to go out into society

shengren 生人: (n) stranger

shige dangguan, jiu ge tan 十个当官，九个贪: "Out of ten officials, nine are taking bribes"

shouren 受人: (n) friend, acquaintance, familiar person

sibuxiang 四不像: (n) literally, "four-not-like," a mythical Chinese beast made up of the parts of four different animals, but "not like" any of them

siying 私营: (adj) privately owned [firm], in contrast to a state-owned firm

suzhi 素质: (n) quality

tanwu 贪污: (n) bribery, graft; often used in the phrase *tanwu fubai*: bribery and corruption

tie fanwan 铁饭碗: (n) iron rice bowl

tingzhang 庭长: (n) head of a department, the cadre rank above *chuzhang*

tu 土: (adj) rustic, hick, vulgar, local

waimian de shehui 外面的社会: (n) "out into society" or "the society outside"

wang 网: (n) net, network; *guanxiwang* 关系网: *guanxi* or relationship network

wenhua 文化: (n) culture, civilization, education

xia gang 下岗: (n or v) "to be called off duty," euphemism for state-sector layoffs

xia hai 下海: (v) literally, "to jump into the sea," slang for to leave the state sector for the private sector, or to leave a salaried position to start a business

xiao fan 小贩: (n) peddler

xinyong 信用: (n) trustworthiness

Xuexi 学习: *Study*, title of a Communist Party journal

zhengshi 正视: (adj) proper, formal, regular, as in *zhengshi de gongzuo* 正视的工作, a proper job

zhishi 知识: (n) intellect, knowledge

zhishi fenzi 知识分子: (n) intellectual

zhuanye 专业: (adj) vocational, as in vocational college degree. Vocational college programs are usually three years long in China, in contrast to the higher-status four-year *benke* college degree.

ziji de laoban 自己的老板: [to be] one's own boss

zou houmen 走后门: (v) to go through the back door, to use informal or illicit methods

NOTES

1. How Narratives Shape Institutional Change

1. The term "cadre" (*ganbu*) originally referred to the leaders of the revolution but eventually denoted any person on the state payroll who was not engaged directly in manual labor. The category contained both the political elite and bureaucratic functionaries. I will also use the term "official" sometimes to refer to cadres in the government.

2. Others, especially cadres, participated in some market activities without leaving their state sector positions, but this is a more complicated issue which will be discussed in chapter 5.

3. Two professors asked to be interviewed in English, for the rare pleasure of chatting with a native speaker. In both cases, their English was excellent, though we reverted to Chinese when I sought clarification.

4. I had one more potential source of *guanxi* which I was quite reluctant to use. My father is a highly placed executive in a transnational technology company with significant interests in the PRC. Initially, I ignored this connection: according to my cultural repertoire of ontological narratives, it would be a humiliating admission of weakness to have to ask my father for help with my job. However, my Chinese friends, once they realized the guanxi gold mine I was sitting on, vociferously urged me to exploit this relationship. I wrestled with the issue for several months, and eventually played this card with great reluctance. In the end it made no difference. The connections I had gained by my father's guanxi never helped me much in my research.

2. Narratives and Socialist Stratification

1. In referring to "Confucian" narratives, I run the risk of essentializing a complex and continuously evolving set of cultural practices. In no way am I implying that imperial China had the same "Confucian" culture

for centuries. Yet a politicized version of the Confucian meta-narrative was used as an official state philosophy in the late imperial era, and state narratives promoted Confucian-influenced understandings of contribution, high culture, social roles, and relationships which infiltrated the collective and ontological narratives of ordinary people.

2. "Intellectual" is a common Chinese term, and people seem to use it to label anyone who has more education than most of the population. By definition, then, as the average level of education in China has increased, the cut-off point for "intellectuals" has also risen. At the end of the twentieth century, it was common for Chinese urbanites to have finished senior high school, so to be considered an "intellectual" required at least a tertiary degree.

3. From Paris of the East to the Rust Belt

1. A brief note on geography from the perspective of the average Harbiner: The Northeast (*Dongbei*) refers to China north of the Great Wall and east of Inner Mongolia, including Heilongjiang, Jilin, and Liaoning provinces, and the major cities of Harbin, Changchun, Shenyang, and Dalian. In common parlance, the Chinese tend to divide their country into "The North" (*Beifang*) and "The South" (*Nanfang*), with the split located somewhere between the Yangtze and Yellow rivers. However, Harbiners, from their point of view in the far north, will sometimes use the term "Southerner" to refer to anywhere south of Dongbei, including, for example, Shandong province, which is considered "Northern" by everyone else in China.

2. In 1965, China was divided into twenty-two provinces, four "autonomous regions," and three independent municipalities: Beijing, Shanghai, and Tianjin. In the reform era, Hainan was added as a province. In the late 1990s, Chongqing was separated from Sichuan province as an independent municipality. I will use the generic term "region" to describe these administrative units. Hong Kong and Macao are not included in my statistics.

3. I should note that I was a bit suspicious that my interviewees here were handpicked in order to give me a good impression. They were all Party members and several were "model workers." This work unit was one of the few places where I obtained formal permission (rather than relying on informal guanxi ties) to conduct my research. On the other hand, the cadres in charge spoke to me with a great deal of candor about problems both at the work unit and in Chinese society in general. Given that 80 percent of their workforce had been laid off, it is quite possible that these model workers and Party members were all that were left.

4. Revising the Meaning of Political Capital

1. Although Deng Xiaoping was never president nor premier of China, and stepped down from all important positions in the party-state hierarchy by the late 1980s, he is widely accepted to be China's undisputed leader from his ascent in 1978 till his death in 1997. Jiang Zemin, his successor and protégé, became general secretary of the CCP in 1989, and president of China in 1993.

2. In 1978, it was still politically impossible to blame Mao for the debacle, so Deng and his supporters targeted the Gang of Four, the leaders of the CCP's radical faction.

3. Under the Maoist version of socialism, much of the urban housing stock was distributed through work units. Because housing was part of compensation, rents were extremely low. Under Deng Xiaoping and his successor, Jiang Zemin, work unit housing was replaced by a housing market. The late 1990s was the last gasp of the old system, and people were scrambling to obtain cheap work unit apartments to avoid paying market prices.

     During the 1990s, in order to have access to city services, most notably its schools, one had to have an urban registration card (*hukou*) for that city. Hukou were limited, and distributed primarily through the city's state-sector work units.

4. Fifty square meters is about 540 square feet.

5. In the PRC, urban apartments would come with little more than cement floors and bare walls. Therefore, "decorating" a new apartment often included installing everything from the stove to the toilet to even walls and doors, and it is a major financial burden.

6. Zhou Enlai was the PRC's premier from 1949 to 1976.

5. The Moral Meaning of Money

1. Bill Gates dropped out of college before earning his degree, but no one in China seemed to take much note of this fact. Because Chinese universities have extremely high graduation rates, students and their parents focus all their anxiety on getting into college and pay much less attention to graduation. Everyone seemed to know that Gates went to Harvard, and that was enough.

2. In Russia, a "small business" is officially defined as one with fewer than one hundred employees in construction or manufacturing, and fewer than fifty employees in trade or other industries. As scholars estimate that between 10–20 percent of these businesses are unregistered, the actual number may have been as high as one million in 1997.

6. Human Capital and the *Suzhi* Hierarchy

1. In China, "intellectuals" (*zhishi fenzi*) are seen as a distinct social group, although not as a class per se. The definition has changed over time, depending on the level of education available to the populace. Earlier in the twentieth century, anyone with any formal education could be considered an "intellectual," but in the 1990s, one had to have gone to college. It is important to note that this includes students, as well as graduates. In China, the meaningful point of competition is getting into college or graduate school, not graduating. Consequently, students tend to be treated with the equivalent status as someone who has received their degree.

2. In Chinese, "science and technology" is a single compound word (*kexue jishu*, shorted to *keji*) rather than two words in a list, as it is in English. Therefore, I will treat the term as a singular, rather than plural, noun, and beg the reader to forgive the awkward grammar in English.

3. During this period, Chinese children began school at age six or seven, attended six years of primary school, three years of middle school, and three years of high school. The first nine years of schooling were mandatory by law, and in urban areas it was normal to graduate from high school as well.

4. When my father saw the book, he snorted and said that it seemed a bit much to inflict upon little Chinese children. I pointed out that my mother had taught me to recite Tang Dynasty poems when I was a preschooler. He responded, "Yes, but your parents are intellectuals."

5. Spoken Chinese has fewer gender indicators than English ("he" and "she" are pronounced the same; young people are often referred to as "youths" rather than "guys" or "girls"). I do not know, from her account, whether the student was male or female. I chose to use the pronoun "he" because more Chinese males than females go overseas to study, and because it seems less likely that her husband would have become so close to a young female co-worker.

BIBLIOGRAPHY

Abbott, Andrew. 1992. "From Causes to Events: Notes on Narrative Positivism." *Sociological Methods and Research* 20:428–55.

Anagnost, Ann. 2004. "The Corporeal Politics of Quality (*Suzhi*)." *Public Culture* 16:189–208.

Anderson, Marston. 1990. *The Limits of Realism: Chinese Fiction in the Revolutionary Period*. Berkeley: University of California Press.

Aslund, Anders. 2002. *Building Capitalism: The Transformation of the Former Soviet Bloc*. Cambridge: Cambridge University Press.

Bai, Di. 2001. "My Wandering Years in the Cultural Revolution." 77–99. In *Some of Us: Chinese Women Growing Up in the Mao Era*, ed. by Xueping Zhong, Zheng Wang, and Di Bai. New Brunswick, N.J.: Rutgers University Press.

"The Ballad of Mulan." 1994. 474–76. In *The Columbia Anthology of Chinese Literature*, ed. by Victor Mair. New York: Columbia University Press.

Barkhatova, Nonna. 2000. "Russian Small Business, Authorities and the State." *Europe-Asia Studies* 52:657–76.

Barkhatova, Nonna, Peter McMylor, and Rosemary Mellor. 2001. "Family Business in Russia: The Path to the Middle Class?" *British Journal of Sociology* 52:249–69.

Barnett, A. Doak. 1964. *Communist China: The Early Years 1949–1955*. New York: F. A. Praeger.

"Beijing *Ribao* Discusses 'Shrewd Business Sense.'" 1980. "Beijing *Ribao* Discusses 'Shrewd Business Sense'" (text). *Beijing Ribao* in Chinese, 5 May 1980. Translation by Foreign Broadcast Information Service. FBIS *Daily Report—China*, 22 May 1980. PrEx 7.10: FBIS-CHI-HK160954, p. L8.

Bian, Yanjie. 1994. *Work and Inequality in Urban China*. New York: State University of New York Press.

Bian, Yanjie, and Zhanxin Zhang. 2002. "Marketization and Income Distribution in Urban China, 1988 and 1995." *Research in Social Stratification and Mobility* 19:377–415.

Bonnell, Victoria E., and Thomas B. Gold, eds. 2002. *The New Entrepreneurs of Europe and Asia*. Armonk, N.Y.: M. E. Sharpe.

"The Boot that Reveals the Culprit." 1996. 505–23, ed. by Y. W. Ma and Joseph S. M. Lau. Boston: Cheng and Tsui.

Bourdieu, Pierre, and Jean-Claude Passeron. 1979. *The Inheritors: French Students and Their Relation to Culture*. Chicago: University of Chicago Press.

Bourdieu, Pierre, and Loïc J. D. Wacquant. 1992. *An Invitation to Reflexive Sociology*. Chicago: University of Chicago Press.

Bray, David. 2005. *Social Space and Governance in Urban China: The Danwei System from Origins to Reform*. Stanford: Stanford University Press.

Briggs, Charles L., ed. 1996. *Disorderly Discourse: Narrative Conflict and Inequality*. New York: Oxford University Press.

Brook, Timothy, and B. Michael Frolic, eds. 1997. *Civil Society in China*. Armonk, N.Y.: M. E. Sharpe.

Burawoy, Michael, Pavel Krotov, and Tatyana Lytkina. 2000. "Involution and Destitution in Capitalist Russia." *Ethnography* 1:43–65.

Calhoun, Craig J. 1994. *Neither Gods nor Emperors: Students and the Struggle for Democracy in China*. Berkeley: University of California Press.

Carr, David. 1984. "*Temps et Recit*: Tome 1 (Book review)." *History and Theory* 23:357–70.

Chen, Albert H. Y. 1999. "Rational Law, Economic Development and the Case of China." *Social and Legal Studies* 8: 97–120.

Chen, Jie, Yang Zhong, Jan Hillard, and John M. Scheb. 1997. "Assessing Political Support in China: Citizens Evaluation of Governmental Effectiveness and Legitimacy." *Journal of Contemporary China* 6:551–66.

Chen, Zhen Xiong, and Anne Marie Francesco. 2000. "Employee Demography, Organizational Commitment, and Turnover Intentions in China." *Human Relations* 53:869–87.

Cheng, Chu-yuan. 1963. *Communist China's Economy 1949–1962*. South Orange, N.J.: Seton Hall University Press.

Chi, Yun (1724–1805). 1996. "The Shansi Merchant." 135–36. In *Traditional Chinese Stories*, ed. by Y. W. Ma and Joseph Lau. Boston: Cheng and Tsui.

Clausen, Soren, and Stig Thogersen. 1995. *The Making of a Chinese City: History and Historiography in Harbin*. New York: M. E. Sharpe.

Commander, Simon, and Christian Mummsen. 2000. "The Growth of Non-Monetary Transactions in Russia." 114–46. In *The Vanishing Rouble*, ed. by Paul Seabright. Cambridge: Cambridge University Press.

Confucius. 1998. *The Original Analects: Sayings of Confucius and His Successors*. New York: Columbia University Press.

Davis, Deborah S. 1990. "Urban Job Mobility." 85–108. In *Chinese Society on the Eve of Tiananmen*, ed. by Deborah Davis and Ezra Vogel. Cambridge, Mass.: Harvard University Press.

De Bary, William Theodore, and Richard Lufrano, eds. 2000. *Sources of Chinese Tradition.* New York: Columbia University Press.

Deng, Xiaoping. 1984. *Speeches and Writings.* Oxford: Pergamon Press.

———. 1984 [1975]. "Priority Should be Given to Scientific Research." 45–47. In *Selected Works of Deng Xiaoping.* Beijing: Foreign Languages Press.

———. 1984 [1977]. "Respect Knowledge, Respect Trained Personnel." 53–54. In *Selected Works of Deng Xiaoping.* Beijing: Foreign Languages Press.

———. 1984 [1978]-a. "Hold High the Banner of Mao Zedong Thought and Adhere to the Principle of Seeking Truth from Facts." 137–39. *In Selected Works of Deng Xiaoping.* Beijing: Foreign Language Press.

———. 1984 [1978]-b. "Realize the Four Modernizations and Never Seek Hegemony." 122–23. In *Selected Works of Deng Xiaoping.* Beijing: Foreign Language Press.

———. 1984 [1978]-c. "Speech at the Opening Ceremony of the National Conference on Science." 98–111. In *Selected Works of Deng Xiaoping.* Beijing: Foreign Language Press.

———. 1984 [1978]-d. "Update Enterprises with Advanced Technology and Managerial Expertise." 140–42. *In Selected Works of Deng Xiaoping.* Beijing: Foreign Language Press.

———. 1984 [1978]-e. "Carry Out the Policy of Opening to the Outside World and Learn Advanced Science and Technology from Other Countries." 143–44. In *Selected Works of Deng Xiaoping.* Beijing: Foreign Languages Press.

———. 1994 [1984]-a. "Our Magnificent Goal and Basic Principles." 85–87. *In Selected Works of Deng Xiaoping.* Beijing: Foreign Language Press.

———. 1994 [1984]-b. "Speech at the Third Plenary Session of the Central Advisory Commission of the Communist Party of China." 90–99. In *Selected Works of Deng Xiaoping.* Beijing: Foreign Languages Press.

Ding, X. L. 1994. *The Decline of Communism in China: Legitimacy Crisis, 1977–1989.* New York: Cambridge University Press.

Domanski, Henryk. 2000. *On the Verge of Convergence: Social Stratification in Eastern Europe.* Budapest: Central European University Press.

Eastman, Lloyd E. 1972. "Fascism in Kuomingtang China: The Blue Shirts." *China Quarterly* 49:11–29.

Eyal, Gil, Ivan Szelenyi, and Eleanor R. Townsley. 1998. *Making Capitalism without Capitalists: Class Formation and Elite Struggles in Post-Communist Central Europe.* London and New York: Verso.

Fang, Lizhi. 1990. *Bringing Down the Great Wall: Writings on Science, Culture, and Democracy in China,* ed. and trans. by James H. Williams. New York: W. W. Norton and Company.

———. 1990 [1985]. "Thoughts on Reform." 95–121. In Fang, *Bringing Down the Great Wall: Writings on Science, Culture, and Democracy in China.* New York: W. W. Norton and Company.

———. 1990 [1986]. "On Political Reform." 135–56. In Fang, *Bringing Down the Great Wall: Writings on Science, Culture, and Democracy in China.* New York: W. W. Norton.

Fitzpatrick, Sheila. 1999. *Everyday Stalinism: Ordinary Life in Extraordinary Times: Soviet Russia in the 1930s.* New York: Oxford University Press.

Florida, Richard L., and Martin Kenney. 1990. "Silicon Valley and Route 128 Won't Save Us." *California Management Review* 33:68–88.

Friedland, Roger, and Robert R. Alford. 1991. "Bringing Society Back In: Symbols, Practices, and Institutional Contradictions." 232–63. In *The New Institutionalism in Organizational Analysis*, ed. by Walter Powell and Paul DiMaggio. Chicago: University of Chicago Press.

Fukuyama, Francis. 1995. *Trust: The Social Virtues and the Creation of Prosperity*. New York: Free Press.

Gardner, John. 1969. "The *Wu-fan* Campaign in Shanghai." 477–539. In *Chinese Communist Politics in Action*, ed. by A. Doak Barnett. Seattle: University of Washington Press.

Gates, Hill. 1996. *China's Motor: A Thousand Years of Petty Capitalism*. Ithaca: Cornell University Press.

Gerber, Theodore P. 2002. "Joining the Winners: Self-Employment and Stratification in Post-Soviet Russia." 3–38. In *The New Entrepreneurs of Europe and Asia*, ed. by Victoria Bonnell and Thomas Gold. Armonk, N.Y.: M. E. Sharpe.

Gerber, Theodore P., and Michael Hout. 1998. "More Shock than Therapy: Market Transition, Employment, and Income in Russia, 1991–1995." *American Journal of Sociology* 104:1–50.

Giddens, Anthony. 1986. *Central Problems in Social Theory: Action, Structure, and Contradiction in Social Analysis*. Berkeley: University of California Press.

Gold, Thomas B. 1990. "Urban Private Business and Social Change." 157–78. In *Chinese Society on the Eve of Tiananmen*, ed. by Deborah Davis and Ezra F. Vogel. Cambridge, Mass.: Harvard University Press.

Goldman, Merle. 1981. *China's Intellectuals: Advise and Dissent*. Cambridge, Mass.: Harvard University Press.

———. 1994. *Sowing the Seeds of Democracy in China: Political Reform in the Deng Xiaoping Era*. Cambridge, Mass: Harvard University Press.

———. 2000. "The Potential for Instability among Alienated Intellectuals and Students in Post-Mao China." 125–42. In *Is China Unstable?*, ed. by David Shambaugh. Armonk, N.Y.: M. E. Sharpe.

Greenhalgh, Susan. 1994. "De-Orientalizing the Chinese Family Firm." *American Ethnologist* 21:746–75.

Grusky, David B. 2001. "The Past, Present, and Future of Social Inequality." 3–51. In *Social Stratification: Class, Race, and Gender in Sociological Perspective*, ed. by David B. Grusky. Boulder: Westview Press.

Guthrie, Doug. 1998. "The Declining Significance of Guanxi in China's Economic Transition." *China Quarterly* 154:254–82.

———. 1999. *Dragon in a Three-Piece Suit: The Emergence of Capitalism in China*. Princeton: Princeton University Press.

———. 2002. "Information Asymmetries and the Problem of Perception: The Significance of Structural Position in Assessing the Importance *of Guanxi* in China." 37–56. In *Social Connections in China*, ed. by Thomas Gold, Doug Guthrie and David Wank. Cambridge: Cambridge University Press.

Hamilton, Gary G. 2000. "Reciprocity and Control: The Organization of Chinese Family Owned Conglomerates." 55–74. In *Globalization of Chinese Business Firms*, ed. by Henry Wai-chung Yeung and Kris Olds. New York: St Martin's.

Han, Minzhu, ed. 1990. *Cries for Democracy: Writing and Speeches from the 1989 Chinese Democracy Movement*. Princeton: Princeton University Press.

Hartford, Kathleen. 1990. "The Political Economy behind Beijing Spring." 50–82. In *The Chinese People's Movement: Perspectives on Spring 1989*, ed. by Tony Saich. Armonk, N.Y.: M. E. Sharpe.

Harvey, David. 1990. *The Condition of Postmodernity*. Cambridge, Mass: Blackwell.

Hayhoe, Ruth. 1989. *China's Universities and the Open Door*. Armonk, N.Y.: M. E. Sharpe.

"Heilongjiang's Chen Lei Speaks on Individual Economy." 1980. "Heilongjiang's Chen Lei Speaks on Individual Economy" (text). Harbin Heilongjiang Provincial Service in Chinese, 19 June 1980. Translation by Foreign Broadcast Information Service. *FBIS Daily Report—China*, 20 June 1980. PrEx 7.10: FBIS-CHI-SK200717, p. S1.

Henke, Christopher R. 2000. "The Mechanics of Workplace Order: Toward a Sociology of Repair." *Berkeley Journal of Sociology* 44:55–81.

Henze, Jurgen. 1984. "Higher Education: The Tension between Quality and Equality." 93–153. In *Contemporary Chinese Education*, ed. by Ruth Hayhoe. London: Croom Helm.

"*Hongqi* on Struggle between Bourgeois, Proletarian Ideologies." 1980. "*Hongqi* on Struggle between Bourgeois, Proletarian Ideologies" (text). Beijing *Hongqi* in Chinese, 16 April 1980. Translation by Foreign Broadcast Information Service. *FBIS Daily Report—China*, 14 May 1980. PrEx 7.10: FBIS-CHI-HK081056, pp. L11–L16.

Hsu, Carolyn S. 2001. "Political Narratives and the Production of Legitimacy: The Case of Corruption in Post-Mao China." *Qualitative Sociology* 24:25–54.

Hsueh, Tien-tung, Qiang Li, and Shucheng Liu. 1993. *China's Provincial Statistics 1949–1989*. Boulder: Westview Press.

Hui, Chun, and George Graen. 1997. "Guanxi and Professional Leadership in Contemporary Sino-American Joint Ventures in Mainland China." *Leadership Quarterly* 8:451–66.

Hwang, Kwang-kuo. 1987. "Face and Favor: The Chinese Power Game." *American Journal of Sociology* 92:944–74.

Ikels, Charlotte. 1996. *The Return of the God of Wealth: The Transition to a Market Economy in Urban China*. Stanford: Stanford University Press.

Jankowiak, William R. 1993. *Sex, Death, and Hierarchy in a Chinese City: An Anthropological Account*. New York: Columbia University Press.

———. 2004a. "Introduction." *Urban Anthropology* 33:115–37.

———. 2004b. "Market Reform, Nationalism, and the Expansion of Urban China's Moral Horizon." *Urban Anthropology* 33:167–210.

Jepperson, Ronald L. 1991. "Institutions, Institutional Effects, and Institutionalism." 143–63. In *The New Institutionalism in Organizational Analysis*, ed. by Walter Powell and Paul DiMaggio. Chicago: University of Chicago Press.

Jia, Yi (201–169 BCE). 1994. "The Faults of the Qin." 228–31. In *Sources of Chinese Tradition*, ed. by William Theodore De Bary and Irene Bloom. New York: Columbia University Press.

Kau, Ying-Mao. 1969. "The Urban Bureaucratic Elite in Communist China." 216–67. In *Chinese Communist Politics in Action*, ed. by A. Barnett Doak. Seattle: University of Washington Press.

Kipnis, Andrew B. 1997. *Producing Guanxi: Sentiment, Self and Subculture in a North Chinese Village*. Durham: Duke University Press.

———. 2004. "Homo Hierarchicus or Homo Neo-Liberalis? *Suzhi* Discourse in the PRC." Paper presented at Society for East Asian Anthropology Conference at the University of California, Berkeley.

———. 2006 "*Suzhi*: A Keyword Approach." *China Quarterly* 186:295–313.

Kornai, Janos. 1992. *The Socialist System: The Political Economy of Communism*. Princeton: Princeton University Press.

Kraus, Richard Curt. 1981. *Class Conflict in Chinese Socialism*. New York: Columbia University Press.

Kuhn, Philip A. 1984. "Chinese Views of Social Stratification." 16–28. In *Class and Social Stratification in Post-Revolution China*, ed. by James L. Watson. Cambridge: Cambridge University Press.

Lattimore, Owen. 1932. *Manchuria: Cradle of Conflict*. New York: Macmillan.

Ledeneva, Alena V. 1998. *Russia's Economy of Favors*: Blat, *Networking and Informal Exchange*. Cambridge: Cambridge University Press.

———. 2003. "Informal Practices in Changing Societies: Comparing Chinese Guanxi and Russian Blat." 1–29. In *Working Paper No. 45*. London: School of Slavonic and East European Studies.

Ledeneva, Alena V., and Paul Seabright. 2000. "Barter in Post-Soviet Societies." 93–113. In *The Vanishing Rouble*, ed. by Paul Seabright. Cambridge: Cambridge University Press.

Lee, Hong Yung. 1991. *From Revolutionary Cadres to Party Technocrats in Socialist China*. Berkeley: University of California Press.

Lensen, George A. 1974. *The Damned Inheritance: The Soviet Union and the Manchurian Crises 1924–1935*. Tallahassee: Diplomatic Press.

Li, Bobai, and Andrew Walder. 2001. "Career Advancement as Party Patronage: Sponsored Mobility in the Chinese Administrative Elite, 1949–1996." *American Journal of Sociology* 106:1371–1408.

Li, Cheng. 1997. *Rediscovering China: Dynamics and Dilemmas of Reform*. New York: Rowan and Littlefield.

Li, Xifan (Hsi-fan). 1981 [1957]. "An Adverse Trend in Creative Activity Sparked by 'The Inside News of the Newspaper.'" 465–68. In *Literature of the Hundred Flowers*, Volume 2, ed. by Hualing Nieh. New York: Columbia University Press.

Lieberthal, Kenneth. 1995. *Governing China: From Revolution through Reform*. New York: W. W. Norton and Company.

Lin, Nan. 1995. "Local Market Socialism: Local Corporatism in Action in Rural China." *Theory and Society* 24:301–54.

Ling, Meng-ch'u. 1996 [1628]. "The Swindler Alchemists." 562–74. In *Traditional Chinese Stories*, ed. by Y. W. Ma and Joseph Lau. Boston: Cheng and Tsui.

Link, Perry E. 1992. *Evening Chats in Beijing: Probing China's Predicament*. New York: W. W. Norton and Company.

Liu, Binyan. 1983. "People or Monsters?" 11–68. In *People or Monsters? And Other Stories and Reportage from China after Mao*, ed. by Perry Link. Bloomington: Indiana University Press.

Liu, Binyan. 1981 [1956]. "The Inside News of the Newspaper." 411–64. In *Literature of the Hundred Flowers*, Volume 2, ed. by Hualing Nieh. New York: Columbia University Press.

Lo, Ming-cheng M., and Eileen M. Otis. 2003. "Guanxi Civility: Processes, Potentials, and Contingencies." *Politics and Society* 31:131–62.

Logan, John R., Fuqin Bian, and Yanjie Bian. 1999. "Housing Inequality in Urban China." *International Journal of Urban and Regional Research* 23:7–25.

Lu, Xiaobo. 2000. *Cadres and Corruption*. Stanford: Stanford University Press.

Lu, Xiaobo, and Elizabeth J. Perry, eds. 1997. *Danwei: The Changing Chinese Workplace in Historical and Comparative Perspective*. Armonk, N.Y.: M. E. Sharpe.

Lui, Adam. 1979. *Corruption in China During the early Ch'ing Period: 1644–1660*. Hong Kong: Centre of Asian Studies Occasional Papers and Monographs.

Lung, T'u Kung An, and Leon Comber. 1964. *The Strange Cases of Magistrate Pao*. Rutland, Vt: C. E. Turtle.

Maines, David. 1993. "Narrative's Moment and Sociology's Phenomena: Toward a Narrative Sociology." *Sociological Quarterly* 34:17–38.

Mao, Zedong (Tse-tung). 1954 [1926]. "Analysis of the Classes in Chinese Society." 13–20. In *Selected Works of Mao Tse-tung, Volume 1*. New York: International Publishers.

———. 1954 [1937]. "On Practice." 282–97. In *Selected Works of Mao Tse-tung, Volume 1*. New York: International Publishers.

———. 2001 [1957]. "On The Correct Handing of Contradictions among the People." 432–79. In *Selected Readings from the Works of Mao Tse-Tung 1926–1963*. Honolulu: University Press of the Pacific.

Massey, Doreen B., Paul Quintas, and David Wield. 1992a. *High-Tech Fantasies: Science Parks in Society, Science, and Space*. New York: Routledge.

———. 1992b. "Academy–Industry Links and Innovation: Questioning the Science Park Model." *Technovision* 12:161–75.

Mauss, Marcel. 1967. *The Gift: Forms and Functions of Exchange in Archaic Societies*. New York: W. W. Norton and Company.

Meyer, John W., and Brian Rowan. 1991. "Institutionalized Organizations: Formal Structure as Myth and Ceremony." 41–62. In *The New Institutionalism in Organizational Analysis*, ed. by Walter W. Powell and Paul J. DiMaggio. Chicago: University of Chicago Press.

Miller, H. Lyman. 1996. *Science and Dissent in Post-Mao China*. Seattle: University of Washington Press.

———. 2000. "How Do We Know if China is Unstable?" 18–25. In *Is China Unstable?*, ed. by David Shambaugh. Armonk, N.Y.: M. E. Sharpe.

Moe, Terry. 1987. "Interests, Institutions, and Positive Theory." *Studies in American Political Development* 2:236–99.

Murray, Brian. 2000. "Dollars and Sense: Foreign Investment in Russia and China." *Problems of Post-Communism* 47:24–33.

Naughton, Barry. 1995. "Deng Xiaoping: The Economist." 83–106. In *Deng Xiaoping: Portrait of a Chinese Statesman*, ed. by David Shambaugh. Oxford: Clarendon Press.

Nee, Victor. 1989. "A Theory of Market Transition: From Redistribution to Markets in State Socialism." *American Sociological Review* 54:663–81.

———. 1996. "The Emergence of a Market Society: Changing Mechanisms of Stratification in China." *American Journal of Sociology* 101:908–49.

Nee, Victor, and Peng Lian. 1994. "Sleeping with the Enemy: A Dynamic Model of Declining Political Commitment in State Socialism." *Theory and Society* 23:253–96.

Nee, Victor, and Rebecca Matthews. 1996. "Market Transition and Societal Transformation in Reforming State Socialism." *Annual Review of Sociology* 22:401–35.

Niu, Seng-ju. 1996 [Tang Dynasty]. "Scholar Ts'ui." 413–15. In *Traditional Chinese Stories*, ed. by Y. W. Ma and Joseph Lau. Boston: Cheng and Tsui.

Ochs, Elinor, Ruth C. Smith, and Carolyn E. Taylor. 1996. "Detective Stories at Dinnertime: Problem-Solving through Co-Narration." 95–113. In *Disorderly Discourse: Narrative Conflict, and Inequality*, ed. by Charles L. Briggs. New York: Oxford University Press.

Oi, Jean C. 1999. *Rural China Takes Off: Institutional Foundations of Economic Reform*. Berkeley: University of California Press.

"The Oil Peddler Courts the Courtesan." 1996. 177–208. In *Traditional Chinese Short Stories*, ed. by Y. W. Ma and Joseph Lau. Boston: Cheng and Tsui.

Oksenberg, Michel. 1969. "Local Leaders in Rural China, 1962–5." 155–215. In *Chinese Communist Politics in Action*, ed. by A. Doak Barnett. Seattle: University of Washington Press.

Pawlik, Wojciech. 1992. "Intimate Commerce." 73–94. In *The Unplanned Society*, ed. by Janine Wedel. New York: Columbia University Press.

"Policy of Promoting Intellectuals Examined." 1984. "Policy of Promoting Intellectuals Examined" (text). Beijing *Guangming Ribao* in Chinese, 20 November 1984. Translation by Foreign Broadcast Information Service. *FBIS Daily Report—China*, 28 November 1984. PrEx 7.10: FBIS-CHI-HK271600, pp. K14–K15.

Polkinghorne, Donald. 1988. *Narrative Knowing and the Human Sciences*. New York: State University of New York Press.

Prendergast, Candice, and Lars Stole. 2000. "Barter Relationship." 35–70. In *The Vanishing Rouble*, ed. by Paul Seabright. Cambridge: Cambridge University Press.

P'u, Sung-ling (1640–1715). 1996a [18th Century]. "The Lady Knight-Errant." 77–81. In *Traditional Chinese Short Stories*, ed. by Y. W. Ma and Joseph Lau. Boston: Cheng and Tsui.

———. 1996b [18th Century]. "Red Jade." 379–83. In *Traditional Chinese Stories*, ed. by Y. W. Ma and Joseph Lau. Boston: Cheng and Tsui.

Radaev, Vadim. 2002. "Entrepreneurial Strategies and the Structure of Transaction Costs in Russian Business." 191–213. In *The New Entrepreneurs of Europe and Asia*, ed. by Victoria Bonnell and Thomas B. Gold. Armonk, N.Y.: M. E. Sharpe.

Redding, S. Gordon. 1990. *The Spirit of Chinese Capitalism*. New York: Walter de Gruyter.

———. 2000. "What is Chinese about Chinese Family Business? And How Much is Family and How Much is Business?" 31–54. In *Globalization of Chinese Business*, ed. by Henry Wai-chung Yeung and Kris Olds. New York: St. Martin's.

"*Renmin Ribao* on Standard in Selecting Cadres." 1980. "*Renmin Ribao* on Standard in Selecting Cadres" (text). Beijing *Renmin Ribao* in Chinese, 16 December 1980. Translation by Foreign Broadcast Information Service. FBIS *Daily Report—China*, 29 December 1980. PrEx 7.10: FBIS-CHI-HK250712, pp. L23–L26.

"*Renmin Ribao* on Recruiting Intellectuals for the CPC." 1984. "*Renmin Ribao* on Recruiting Intellectuals for the CPC" (text). Beijing *Renmin Ribao* in Chinese, 20 November 1984. Translation by Foreign Broadcast Information Service. FBIS *Daily Report—China*, 23 November 1984. PrEx 7.10: FBIS-CHI-HK210824, pp. K6–K7.

Ricoeur, Paul. 1991. "Life in Quest of a Narrative." 20–33. In *On Paul Ricoeur*, ed. by David Wood. London: Routledge.

Ries, Nancy. 1997. *Russian Talk: Culture and Conversation during Perestroika*. Ithaca: Cornell University Press.

Rona-Tas, Akos. 1994. "The First Shall Be Last? Entrepreneurship and Communist Cadres in the Transition from Socialism." *American Journal of Sociology* 100:40–69.

———. 2002. "The Worm and the Caterpillar: The Small Private Sector in the Czech Republic, Hungary, and Slovakia." 39–65. In *The New Entrepreneurs of Europe and Asia*, ed. by Victoria Bonnell and Thomas Gold. Armonk, N.Y.: M. E. Sharpe.

Rose, Nikolas S. 1993. "Government, Authority, and Expertise in Advanced Liberalism." *Economy and Society* 22:283–99.

———. 1996. "Governing 'Advanced' Liberal Democracies." 37–64. In *Foucault and Political Reason*, ed. by Andrew Barry, Thomas Osborne, and Nikolas Rose. Chicago: University of Chicago Press.

———. 1999. *Powers of Freedom: Reframing Political Thought*. Cambridge: Cambridge University Press.

Rosemont, Henry. 2000. "China's New Economic Reforms: Replacing Iron Rice Bowls with Plastic Cups." 171–94 in *China beyond the Headlines*, ed. by Timothy Weston and Lionel Jensen. Lanham, Md.: Rowman and Littlefield.

Rosen, Stanley. 1984. "New Directions in Secondary Education." 65–92. In *Contemporary Chinese Education*, ed. by Ruth Hayhoe. London: Croom Helm.

Rosenberg, Charles E. 1997. *No Other Gods: On Science and American Social Thought*. Baltimore: Johns Hopkins University Press.

Schwartz, Benjamin I. 1964. *In Search of Wealth and Power: Yen Fu and the West*. Cambridge, Mass.: Harvard University Press.

ShanghaiMe. 2004. "Jiao Yulu (Movie Synopsis)." Shanghai Guide. Shanghai: Shanghai U.C. InfoTech Company.

Shirk, Susan L. 1982. *Competitive Comrades: Career Incentives and Student Strategies in China*. Berkeley: University of California Press.

———. 1984. "The Decline of Virtuocracy in China." 56–84. In *Class and Social Stratification in Post-Revolution China*, ed. by James L. Watson. Cambridge: Cambridge University Press.

Sima, Guang (1019–86). 1994. "History as a Mirror." 656–58. In *Sources of Chinese Tradition*, ed. by William Theodore De Bary and Irene Bloom. New York: Columbia University Press.

Smart, Alan. 1993. "Gifts, Bribes, and Guanxi: A Reconsideration of Bourdieu's Social Capital." *Cultural Anthropology* 8:388–408.

Somers, Margaret R. 1992. "Narrativity, Narrative Identity, and Social Action." *Social Science History* 16:591–630.

Somers, Margaret R., and Gloria Gibson. 1994. "Reclaiming the Epistemological 'Other': Narrative and the Social Constitution of Identity." 37–99. In *Social Theory and the Politics of Identity*, ed. by Craig Calhoun. Cambridge, Mass.: Blackwell.

Stark, David. 1989. "Coexisting Organizational Forms in Hungary's Emerging Mixed Economy." 137–68. In *Remaking the Economic Institutions of Socialism*, ed. by Victor Nee and David Stark. Stanford: Stanford University Press.

Stark, David, and Laszlo Bruszt. 2001. "One Way or Multiple Paths: For a Comparative Sociology of East European Capitalism." *American Journal of Sociology* 106:1129–37.

State Statistical Bureau, People's Republic of China. 1996. *China Statistical Yearbook.* 288–89, Table 9–12. Beijing: China Statistical Publishing House.

———. 1998. *China Statistical Yearbook.* Table 5–1. Beijing: State Statistical Bureau, People's Republic of China.

———. 1999. *China Statistical Yearbook.* Table 5–1. Beijing: State Statistical Bureau, People's Republic of China.

Steinmetz, George. 1992. "Reflections on the Role of Social Narratives in Working-Class Formation." *Social Science History* 16:489–516.

Storper, Michael. 1990. "Industrialization and the Regional Question in the Third World: Lessons of Post-Imperialism; Prospects of Post-Fordism." *International Journal of Urban and Regional Development* 14:423–44.

———. 1992. "Regional 'Worlds' of Production: Learning and Innovation in the Technology Districts of France, Italy, and the USA." *Regional Studies* 27:433–55.

Swidler, Ann. 1986. "Culture in Action: Symbols and Strategies." *American Sociological Review* 51:273–86.

Tong, Chee Kiong, and Pit Kee Yong. 1998. "Guanxi Bases, Xinyong and Chinese Business Networks." *British Journal of Sociology* 49:75–96.

Tsai, Kellee S. 2002. *Back-Alley Banking: Private Entrepreneurs in China.* Ithaca: Cornell University Press.

"Tu Tzu-Ch'un." 2000. 830–35. In *The Columbia Anthology of Traditional Chinese Literature*, ed. by Victor Mair. New York: Columbia University Press.

Verdery, Kamerine. 1996. *What Was Socialism, and What Comes Next?* Princeton: Princeton University Press.

Vinogradova, Elena. 2005. "The Big Issue of Small Businesses: Contract Enforcement in the New Russia." Ph.D. dissertation, Department of Sociology, University of Maryland.

Walder, Andrew G. 1994. "The Decline of Communist Power." *Theory and Society* 23:297–323.

———. 1995a. "Local Governments as Industrial Firms: An Organizational Analysis of China's Transitional Economy." *American Journal of Sociology* 101:263–301.

———. 1995b. "Career Mobility and the Communist Political Order." *American Sociological Review* 60:309–28.

———. 1996. "Market and Inequality in Transitional Economies." *American Journal of Sociology* 101:1060–73.

Walder, Andrew G., Bobai Li, and Donald J. Trieman. 2000. "Politics and Life Chances in a State Socialist Regime." *American Sociological Review* 65:191–209.

Wang, Jing. 1996. *High Culture Fever: Politics, Aesthetics, and Ideology in Deng's China*. Berkeley: University of California Press.

Wang, Lihua. 2001. "Gender Consciousness in My Teen Years." 120–31. In *Some of Us: Chinese Women Growing Up in the Mao Era*, ed. by Xueping Zhong, Zheng Wang, and Di Bai. New Brunswick, N.J.: Rutgers University Press.

Wang, Meng. 1981 [1956]. "A Young Man Arrives at the Organization Department." 473–510. In *Literature of the Hundred Flowers*, Volume 2, ed. by Hualing Nieh. New York: Columbia University Press.

Wang, Yinglin (1223–96). 1999. "The Three Character Classic (*Sanzi Jing*)." 804–7. In *Sources of Chinese Tradition*, ed. by William Theodore De Bary and Irene Bloom. New York: Columbia University Press.

Wang, Zheng. 2001. "Call Me 'Qingnian' But Not 'Funu.'" 27–52. In *Some of Us: Chinese Women Growing Up in the Mao Era*, ed. by Xueping Zhong, Zheng Wang, and Di Bai. New Brunswick, N.J.: Rutgers University Press.

Wasserstrom, Jeffrey N., and Elizabeth J. Perry, eds. 1991. *Political Protest and Popular Culture in Modern China: Learning from 1989*. Boulder: Westview.

Wedel, Janine R., ed. 1992. *The Unplanned Society: Poland during and after Communism*. New York: Columbia University Press.

Weston, Timothy B. 2000. "China's Labor Woes." 245–71. In *China beyond the Headlines*, ed. by Timothy Weston and Lionel M. Jensen. Lanham, Md.: Rowman and Littlefield.

White, Gordon. 1981. *Party and Professionals: The Political Role of Teachers in Contemporary China*. Armonk, N.Y.: M. E. Sharpe.

White, Lynn T. 1978. *Careers in Shanghi: The Social Guidance of Personal Energies in a Developing Chinese City, 1949–1966*. Berkeley: University of California Press.

Whyte, Martin K., and William L. Parish. 1984. *Urban Life in Contemporary China*. Chicago: University of Chicago Press.

World Bank. 1998. *World Development Indicators*. Washington, D.C.: World Bank. Report No. 4530-S64.

Wu, Jieh-Min. 2001. "State Policy and Guanxi Network Adaptation in China: Local Bureaucratic Rent-Seeking." *Issues and Studies* 37:20–48.

Wu, Xiaogang. 2002. "Work Units and Income Inequality: The Effect of Market Transition in Urban China." *Social Forces* 80:1069–99.

Wu, Xiaogang, and Yu Xie. 2003. "Does the Market Pay Off? Earnings Returns to Education in Urban China." *American Sociological Review* 68:425–42.

Yan, Hairong. 2003. "Neoliberal Governmentality and Neohumanism: Organizing Suzhi/Value Flow through Labor Recruitment Networks." *Cultural Anthropology* 18:493–523.

Yang, Mayfair Mei-hui. 1994. *Gifts, Favors, and Banquets*. Ithaca: Cornell University Press.

———. 2002. "The Resilience of *Guanxi* and its New Deployments: A Critique of Some New *Guanxi* Scholarship." *China Quarterly* 170:459–76.

Yang, Mayfair Mei-Hui. 1989. "The Gift Economy and State Power in China." *Comparative Studies in Society and History* 31:25–54.

Yeung, Henry Wai-chung, and Kris Olds, eds. 2000a. *Globalization of Chinese Business Firms*. New York: St Martin's.

———. 2000b. "Globalizing Chinese Business Firms." 1–30. In *Globalization of Chinese Business Firms*, ed. by Henry Wai-chung Yeung and Kris Olds. New York: St. Martin's.

You, Ji. 1998. *China's Enterprise Reform: Changing State Sector Relationships after Mao*. New York: Routledge.

Young, Louise. 1998. *Japan's Total Empire: Manchuria and the Culture of Wartime Imperialism*. Berkeley: University of California Press.

Yurchak, Alexei. 2002. "Entrepreneurial Governmentality in Postsocialist Russia." 278–324. In *The New Entrepreneurs of Europe and Asia*, ed. by Victoria Bonnell and Thomas Gold. Armonk, N.Y.: M. E. Sharpe.

Zachary, G. Pascal. 1997. *Endless Frontier: Vannevar Bush, Engineer of the American Century*. New York: Free Press.

Zang, Xiaowei. 2002. "Labor Market Segmentation and Income Inequality in Urban China." *Sociological Quarterly* 43:27–44.

Zhang, Li. 2001. "Migration and Privatization of Space and Power in Late Socialist China." *American Ethnologist* 28:179–205.

Zhang, Xinxin, and Ye Sang. 1987. *Chinese Lives: An Oral History of Contemporary China*. New York: Pantheon Books.

Zhang, Xudong. 1994. "On Some Motifs in the Chinese 'Cultural Fever' of the 1980s." *Social Text* 39:129–56.

Zhong, Yang, Jie Chen, and John Scheb. 1998. "Mass Political Culture in Beijing: Findings from Two Public Opinion Surveys." *Asian Survey* 38:763–83.

Zhou, Xueguang, Nancy Brandon Tuma, and Phyllis Moen. 1997. "Institutional Change and Job Shift Patterns in Urban China, 1949–1994." *American Sociological Review* 62:339–65.

Zhu, Weizheng. 1992. "Confucius and Traditional Chinese Education." 3–22. In *Education and Modernization: The Chinese Experience*, ed. by Ruth Hayhoe. New York: Pergamon Press.

INDEX

Note: Page numbers in italics refer to figures and tables.

cadres (*continued*)

100; perpetual class struggle and, 36–37; political capital and, 26; at Provincial Disability Services Agency, 62–65; responses to Deng's policies, 88–93. *See also* government sector; state enterprises

capital, forms of, 22–26. *See also* economic capital; human capital; political capital; social capital

capitalism: consumer narratives from, 162–63; economic comparisons to, 86, 160; global, 178–80; heroes from, 139; inapplicability of assumptions to socialist systems, 8–9; Keynesian vs. Fordist, 160; neoliberal, 184; "without contracts," 149–50

careers. *See* occupational status and career choice

"caterpillars" vs. "worms," 153–55

CCP. *See* Chinese Communist Party

Chen Xitong, 101–2

children, 171–73, 176–77, 184, 203 n. 3, 204 n. 4

Chinese Communist Party (CCP): academic requirements raised for membership in, 169; cadre careers and party membership, 63–64; Chinese context of narratives and, 35–38; civil war with Nationalist Party, 32; collective narratives on viability of, 116–21; decline in value of membership in, 98–99; Deng's unintended consequences on, 108; in Harbin, 55, 63; institution construction by, 32; Mr. Gong's description of entering, 13; views of gaining membership in, 38–39, 105–7

Chinese Lives (Zhang and Sang), 42–43, 47, 89

chuzhang (division level), 64

civil service bureaucracy, 44, 45. *See also* cadres

class and status hierarchies, *suzhi* discourse and, 188–90

class struggle: exploitation narratives, 40–41; paternalism vs., 84; perpetual, 36–37; unequal distribution of resources and, 34–35

collective narratives: creation of institutions through, 4–5; defined, 9–10, 15; emergence of, 16; public narratives vs., 16; repertoires of, 15–16

collectives, 35, *58*

Communist Party. *See* Chinese Communist Party (CCP)

competition narratives, 104–8

Confucian capitalism narratives, 148–49

Confucianism: complexity of, 201–2 n. 1; contribution narrative and, 37–38; corruption narrative and, 94; *guanxi* and, 49, 150–51; human capital and, 44–45, 48; *suzhi* and, 175

connection narratives. See *blat*; *guanxi*

consumerism, 162–63

contracts, capitalism without, 149–50

contribution (*gongxian*): collective or ontological narratives supporting, 38–39; Confucian roots of, 37; meaning and prestige narratives under marketization, 108–14; as occupational narrative, 14; shift to development, 22; *suzhi* and, 174–75, 176; wealth and, 134–36

convergence theory, 7

core knowledge, 45–46

corruption narratives: anti-corruption campaigns and, 96; cadre status and, 101–4, 107–8, 111–14; Confucian roots of, 94; entrepreneurship and, 135–36; *guanxi* narratives and, 147; *guanxi* practice and, 92–93; intellectuals and, 165; marketization dissidents and, 93–96; Party membership and, 98–99; political campaigns and, 90–91; in Russia, 151–52; social progress and, 119–20; state viability and, 117–18; *xia gang* and, 112–13

courtesy (*li*), 175

cultural narratives in imperial era, 44–45

Cultural Revolution: Deng narratives on, 84–85, 125–27, 161; ideology vs. expertise and, 47; political campaigns and, 38; political narrative, effects on, 82–85; reasons for, 83–84

"culture," scholarly castigation of, 183

danwei. See work units

Daqin Hotel, Harbin, 77

Deng Xiaoping and regime: cadre reform and, 22, 106, 109; cadre responses to, 88–93; economic progress narratives, 124–28; global market and, 169; housing under, 203 n. 3; human capital and, 159–61, 162, 167, 178; managerial-responsibility policy, 89–90; market mechanisms of, 91–92; narratives and policies of, 84–88; at National Conference on Science, 159–60; opinions of, 14; role in government, 202 n. 1; unintended results of policies of, 108. *See also* market socialism

development. *See* economic development narrative

dingti (substitution), 66

Disability Services Agency, Provincial, 62–65

dissidents: corruption narratives of, 93–96, 165; critical narratives and Tiananmen protests, 164–67; economic management narratives as answer to, 166; Fang Lizhi, 162; human capital and, 157–58; Western capitalist narratives and, 178–79. *See also* intellectuals

division level (*chuzhang*), 64

Dragon in a Three-Piece Suit (Guthrie), 182

Eastern Europe, 20–21, 83, 88

economic capital: assumptions about, 8; in Deng narratives, 125; entrepreneurship and moral meaning of money, 134–37, 155–56; *guanxi* and financing, 75, 184; human capital vs., 157; intellectual criticism of "money fever," 162–63; non-monetary benefits, 42–43; ordinary

people and narratives of, 42–43; overview of, 23; security valued over, 20; statistics by province, *60, 61*; within stratification systems, 5–6; *suzhi* and, 187; in traditional stories, 41; undermining of, 39–43

economic development narrative: Deng moderates and, 84–85; entrepreneurship and, 124–28; human capital and, 158–61; shift from contribution to, 22; as solution to corruption crisis, 96. *See also* market socialism

economic irrationalities in socialist system, 48

economic management narratives, 120–21, 166

economic reforms. *See* market socialism

education: as benefit, 101; cadre careers and, 64, 101; of children, 171–73, 176–77, 203 n. 3; collective narratives on value of, 167–74; Deng's policies and, 87, 161; entrepreneurship and, 139–40, 141, 142; examinations, 168–69, 170; expertise vs. ideology and, 46–47; gender and, 172–73; illicit practices in, 168; overseas study, 177, 179; *suzhi* and, 174. *See also* human capital; intellectuals

emplotment, 11

Enterprise Law (1988), 90

entrepreneurs: constructed history of business evolution, 141–43; economic capital and moral meaning of money, 134–37, 155–56; formal vs. local categories of, 129–32; gender and, 143–45; *guanxi* and marketization, 146–50; "inside" vs. "outside" and, 133–37; obstacles to in early post-socialist era, 145–46; overview of, 122–24; Pizza Parlor profile, 72–76, *73*; Russian Market profile, 76–80, *78*; in Russia vs. China, 150–55; state narratives and policies on, 124–28; *suzhi* and "real" businesspeople vs. *getihu,* 130–32, 137–41; "worms" vs. "caterpillars," 153–55. *See also*

entrepreneurs (*continued*)
  businesspeople (*shangren*); *getihu* (individual businesses or peddlers); private business
Europe, Eastern, 20–21, 83, 88
examinations, 168–69, 170
expertise vs. ideology, 46–47. *See also* education
exploitation narratives, 40–41

face, work unit as, 19
factories, 56–57, 65–67, 70. *See also* work units (*danwei*)
family business, Harbin prejudices against, 148–49
Fang Lizhi, 162
favor exchange practice, 48–49
films, 110–11
financing, personal connections for, 75
Five-Anti Campaign (1952), 40–41, 50–51, 128
folk tales, 41, 44–45
Four Modernizations, 22, 159–60, 175–76, 178
friendship, 146, 151, 152–53. See also *guanxi* (connections)
Fukuyama, Francis, 183

Gang of Four, 85, 125–26, 202 n. 2
Gates, Bill, 203 n. 1
Gates, Hill, 138
GDP by province, *60*
gender, 143–45, 172–73, 204 n. 5
generational conflict, 75–76, 171
getihu (individual businesses or peddlers):
  "good businesspeople" vs., 72, 78, 169; legal and local definitions of businessperson vs., 130–32; legalization of, 127–28; Russian Market (Harbin), 76–80, *78*; as stock narrative character, 20; *suzhi* and, 138–39
Giddens, Anthony, 15

gift exchange practice, 49–50, 103
globalization and human capital, 160–61, 178–80
gongxian. See contribution
government institutions. *See* state institutions
government sector, *58*, 62–65. *See also* cadres
guanxi (connections): author's experience with, 201 n. 4; *blat* vs., 150–53; "caterpillar" entrepreneurs and, 154–55; corruption narratives and, 92–93, 103, 107–8; effects of, on business practices, 149–50; for entrepreneurial financing, 75; marketization and, 92, 146–50, 184; overview of, 24; relational focus of, 49–50; scholarship on, 183. *See also* social capital
Guthrie, Doug, 182

habitus, 12
Han Xiaozu, 51–52
Harbin: Agricultural Machine Factory, 65–67; in historical context, 54–56; location of, 54, *56*; market reforms and economic status of, 56–62; Pizza Parlor, 72–76, *73*; Provincial Disability Services Agency, 62–65; Russian Market, 76–80, *78*, 112; University New and High Technology Park and Business Group, 67–72, *69*, 116, 129–30
Harvey, David, 160
"Hebei people" in Harbin, 55
Heilongjiang Province, 55–56, *56*, 57–59. *See also* Harbin
High Technology Park and Business Group, 67–72, *69*, 116, 129–30
hiring practices and *guanxi,* 149
hoarding, 48
household businesses. See *getihu* (individual businesses or peddlers)
household income, 59, *61*, 164–65. *See also* salaries
housing, 102–3, 203 n. 3, 203 n. 5

layoffs (*continued*)

    sector, 64–65; human capital narratives used in, 169; meaning of, 57; women and, 144

leaves of absence, 74–75

Ledeneva, Alena V., 183

liberalism vs. neoliberalism, 186

li (courtesy), 175

Lin, Nan, 7

Lin Biao, 125, 126

Link, Perry, 2

Li Peng, 116–17

Liu Binyan, 93–94, 106, 165

local state corporatism theory, 7

managerial-responsibility policy, 89–90

Manchukuo, 55

Maoism, 17, 19. *See also* socialist system

Mao Zedong, 31, 34, 83–84, 146. *See also* Cultural Revolution

Mao Zedong Thought, 36, 45–46

marital choice, 131–32

market socialism: cadre responses to, 88–93; competition narratives and, 104–8; contribution, meaning, and prestige narratives, 108–14; creation of collective narratives and, 17; Deng policies, 84–88; dissidents and corruption narratives, 93–96; economic management narratives, 120–21; effects of, on Harbin, 56–62; *guanxi* and, 146–50; "inside" vs. "outside" narrative and, 17–22; market mechanisms introduced, 91–92; party-state and political legitimacy and, 116–21; political capital utility narratives, 97–104; relationship with money under, 155–56; state–people relationship and, 114–16; success of, doubts about, 181–82. *See also* entrepreneurs

Marx, Karl, 5

Marxism-Leninism: common meta-narrative and local differences, 32–33; core knowl-edge and, 45–46; creation of stratification systems in, 31; human capital in, 43; key narratives in, 33–34; market reforms and human capital, 87. *See also* Mao Zedong Thought

meaningful work, 108–14

meritocracy: intellectual meritocracy narrative, 167–69; political vs. human capital and, 88; socialist system and, 161. *See also* human capital

Miller, H. Lyman, 158–59

mixed command-market economies, 91–92. *See also* market socialism

moderates, 84–85. *See also* Deng Xiaoping and regime

money. *See* economic capital

moonlighting, 74–75

moral logic, 6–7, 188

narrative approach, 11–16, 182–83. *See also* collective narratives

narrative theory, 11–15

National Conference on Science, 159–60

neo-institutional theory, 3–5

neoliberalism, 4, 184–88

networks, 146. See also *guanxi* (connections)

Northeast (*Dongbei*), 54, 202 n. 1

occupational status and career choice: contribution, prestige, and meaningful work narratives, 108–14; "inside" versus "outside" narrative, 16–22; narrative theory and, 13–15; sector statistics by province, *58*; socialist public narratives vs. post-socialist collective narratives of, 17, 18–19; stratification systems and, 6. *See also* entrepreneurs

One-Child Policy, 184

ontological narratives, 15

ordinary people (*laobaixing*): economic capital narratives and, 42–43; human capital narratives and, 46–48; narrative construction by, 9–15, 25; political capital narratives and, 38–39; role in creating institutions, 4–5

overseas study, 177, 179

"Paris of the East," Harbin as, 55, 59

Party membership: academic requirements raised for, 169; cadre careers and, 63–64; decline in value of, 98–99; views of gaining, 38–39, 105–7

party-state and implied contract with citizens, 34. *See also* Maoism; socialist system

paternalistic narrative: assessment of cadres based on, 109–11, 130; contradictions with, 82–83, 84; economic management vs., 120; socialist stratification system and, 33–34

peddlers. See *getihu*

"People or Monsters?" (Liu), 93–94, 106, 165

People's University, 166

petty capitalists. See *getihu*

Pizza Parlor (Harbin), 72–76, *73*

political campaigns: anti-corruption, 96; Anti-Rightist campaign, 47; creation of institution of, 36; Cultural Revolution and, 38; Deng's abandonment of, 85–86, 90–91; Five-Anti Campaign (1952), 40–41, 50–51, 128; rectification campaigns, 36–37, 51–52; social capital and, 51

political capital: cadre reform and human capital as replacement for, 87–88; cadre responses to reforms and, 89–90; Chinese context and, 35–38; competition narratives and, 107; Deng's reforms and, 87–88; dominance in Marxist socialist system, 33–35; human capital vs., 157, 167; ordinary people and narratives about, 38–39; overview of, 23; within stratification systems, 6; utility narratives, 97–104

political dissidents. See dissidents

post-socialism: *blat* and *guanxi* transformed by, 184; China's transition to, 3–5; emplotment in, 11; inapplicability of capitalist assumptions to, 7–9; instability of stratification systems in, 8; in Russia and Eastern Europe, 4, 20–21. *See also* market socialism

power conversion hypothesis, 7

prestige, social, 108–14

private business: Five-Anti Campaign and, 41–42; human capital narratives and, 169–70; narrative construction of, 14, 19–21; percent of employees by province, *58*; Pizza Parlor profile, 72–76, *73*; *sanzi* sector, proliferation of, 170; size limit restrictions dropped for, 128. *See also* businesspeople (*shangren*); entrepreneurs; *getihu*

progress and prosperity narrative, 33–34. *See also* economic development narrative

proletarians, urban, 35–36

protests against the state, 118, 162, 166. *See also* Tiananmen Protests (1989)

Provincial Disability Services Agency (Harbin), 62–65

public narratives, defined, 16

Public Security Bureau (PSB), 63

Qing imperial state and dynasty, 31–32, 44–46

quality. See *suzhi*

rectification campaigns, 36–37, 51–52

Red Guards, 84

redistributive economy, 33, 51

reforms, economic. *See* market socialism

renqing (human feeling), 51–52

repertoires of narratives, 12, 15–16, 51

Ricoeur, Paul, 11

River Elegy (TV), 94–95

Rona-Tas, Akos, 153–54

Rose, Nikolas, 186, 187

Russia and Soviet Union: economic shift, 83; entrepreneurs in, 123, 150–55; Harbin, control of, 54–55; post-socialism in, 4; "small business" in, 203 n. 2. See also *blat* (connections)

Russian Market (Harbin), 76–80, *78*, 112

Russian traders in Harbin, 77, 78

salaries: cadre criticism and, 113; complaints about, 100–101; in government sector, 63; of intellectuals, 163–64; at private firms, 75; at state enterprises, 65; at Technology Business Group, 71

Sanzi Jing (Three Character Classic), 45, 175

sanzi sector (foreign, private, or joint enterprises), proliferation of, 170

science and technology: Chinese term for, 203 n. 2; Deng on, 160; *suzhi* and, 139–40, 175–76; Western development narratives and, 160, 179

security, 20, 71

self-employment. See entrepreneurs; *getihu*

seniority, 37

sexism, 143–45

"Shandong people" in Harbin, 55

shangren. See businesspeople

shared narratives. See collective narratives

small business. See entrepreneurs; *getihu*; private business

social action, narrative theory of, 11

social capital: counter-narratives to, 50–51; market reforms and increases in, 91, 92; overview of, 24; in socialist system, 48–52; within stratification systems, 5–6

socialist system: contradictory narratives of, 82–83; debate over collapse of, 1–3; economic capital, devaluation of, 39–43; history of, 31–32; human capital and, 43–48, 159, 161; planned nature of, 31; political capital, dominance of, 33–39; social capital and, 48–52. See also post-socialism

"Soldiers, Look How Profiteering by Government Officials is Eating You Up" (handbill), 95–96

South Korean traders in Harbin, 77

Soviet Union. See Russia and Soviet Union

Stark, David, 4

state enterprises: hybrid, 67–72, *69*, 170; traditional, 65–67, 74–75, 170. See also cadres; work units (*danwei*)

state institutions, narratives criticizing, 22

state sector. See government sector

state viability and collective narratives, 116–21

stratification systems, 5–9, 31, 188–89

street markets, 76–80, *78*, 112

substitution (*dingti*), 66

suzhi (quality) discourse: academic criteria and, 170; constructed history of business evolution and, 141–43; emerging hierarchies of class and status and, 188–90; "empty," 185; gender and "good" businessperson category, 144–45; global capitalism and, 178–80; human capital and, 173–77, 187, 189; indefinability of, 137–38; "inside" vs. "outside" discourse replaced by, 21–22, 137; neoliberalism and, 184–88; "real" businesspeople vs. *getihu* and, 130–32, 137–41

Suzhou, China, 125

technological advances and economic progress, 86–87. See also science and technology

Technology Park and Business Group, 67–72, *69*, 116

Three Character Classic (*Sanzi Jing*), 45, 175

Tiananmen Protests (1989): corruption narratives and, 165; human capital and, 157–58; intellectual political movement and, 22; suppression of, 167

tie fanwan ("iron rice bowl"), 2, 18, 20, 133

traders, Russian and South Korean (in Harbin), 77, 78
trust, 146. See also *guanxi* (connections)

underemployment, 27
University New and High Technology Business Park and Business Group, 67–72, *69*, 116, 129–30
urban registration cards (*hukou*), 203 n. 3
utility narratives, 97–104, 163

virtuocracy: cadre responses to reforms and, 88–89; Deng on, 161; Maoist narratives and, 37; Marxist social systems and, 35, 43

Wang, Lihua, 48
Wang Shouxin, 93–94, 106
Wang Zheng, 34
wealth, personal, vs. communal, 134, 135–36. *See also* economic capital
women and entrepreneurship, 143–45
workplace profiles: Agricultural Machine Factory, 65–67; Pizza Parlor, 72–76, *73*; Provincial Disability Services Agency, 62–65; Russian Market, 76–80, *78*; University New and High Technology Park and Business Group, 67–72, *69*
work unit housing, 203 n. 3
work units (*danwei*): as face, 19; generational differences in expectations, 75–76; *getihu* and, 79–80; heavy industry units in Harbin, 56; as "inside," 17–22; openness of, to non-employees, 27; terminology of, 34; transformation of private firms into, 41–42. *See also* state enterprises
"worms" vs. "caterpillars," 153–55

xiagang. See layoffs
xia hai ("jumping into the sea"), 18, 23, 71–72, 133

Yan, Hairong, 185, 187, 188
Yi Zhongtian, 19

Zhou Enlai, 51–52, 112, 203 n. 6
Zhu Rongji, 116–17, 119

Carolyn Hsu is an associate professor of sociology at Colgate University.

Library of Congress Cataloging-in-Publication Data
Hsu, Carolyn L., 1969–
Creating market socialism : how ordinary people are shaping class and status in China /
Carolyn L. Hsu.
p. cm. — (Politics, history, and culture)
Includes bibliographical references and index.
ISBN-13: 978-0-8223-4017-1 (cloth : alk. paper)
ISBN-13: 978-0-8223-4036-2 (pbk. : alk. paper)
1. Social change—China—21st century. 2. China—Social conditions—21st century.
3. China—Economic policy—21st century. I. Title.
HN733.5.H78 2007
306.3'450951090511—dc22   2007006305